SOCIAL LEARNING AND IMITATION

SOCIAL LEARNING AND IMITATION

BY

NEAL E. MILLER

AND

JOHN DOLLARD

GREENWOOD PRESS, PUBLISHERS
WESTPORT, CONNECTICUT

Library of Congress Cataloging in Publication Data

Miller, Neal Elgar, 1909-
    Social learning and imitation.

    Reprint of the 1962 ed. published by Yale University
Press, New Haven.
    Bibliography: p.
    Includes index.
    1. Learning, Psychology. 2. Imitation. 3. Social
psychology. I. Dollard, John, 1900-   joint author.
II. Title.
LB1069.M5 1979   153.1'5   78-23728
ISBN 0-313-20714-3

Reprinted in 1979 by Greenwood Press, Inc.
51 Riverside Avenue, Westport, CT 06880

Printed in the United States of America

10 9 8 7 6 5 4 3 2 1

To
CLARK LEONARD HULL
AND
WILLIAM FIELDING OGBURN

FOREWORD

IMITATION has long been an important concept, as well in social theory as in social practice. In their endeavor to explain how societies are organized and held together, how cultures are transmitted from one generation to the next, social scientists have made wide use of the concept of imitation. As a key idea in theory and practice it has been the subject of much systematic discussion.

In this volume the authors have made a fresh attack upon the problem with a set of concepts which seem peculiarly relevant to it. If imitative tendencies are not instinctive they must be learned, the argument runs. This book offers a detailed discussion of how such learning takes place. The learning theory utilized for explanatory purposes is one which has been in the process of development at the Institute of Human Relations for a period of years under the general leadership of Professor Clark L. Hull. The authors have attempted to apply this theory to human data and in the course of such application to take a step toward development of a theory of *social* learning.

The research began with a study of concrete examples of imitative behavior as they appear in the lives of small children. It has therefore a firm empirical base in real life. These examples were collected from the observations of mothers who coöperated in gathering relevant data on their own children. Ten experiments, most of them on children, have been performed by the authors in order to test various implications of the hypothesis that imitative behavior is learned and that it can, likewise, be unlearned.

Like every scientific hypothesis this one is viewed as a beginning rather than as a terminus to effort in the field. The theory of imitation is an idea to be elaborated on, tested, and perhaps radically changed by further work. It is believed, nevertheless, to be a firm stride in the right direction and, further, an example of how certain complicated aspects of human relations may be analyzed and understood in terms of the principles and conditions of learning. This approach itself is likely to be one of the genuine contributions of the work. It proposes that those who work with the principles of learning (psychologists, social psychologists) cannot evolve a theory of social behavior without understanding the social order which sets the conditions for human learning. Conversely, technicians in the social sciences must consent to take some account of the principles governing that long learning experience which fits any individual for participation in the social order. From psychology, then, are derived the fundamental principles of learning, and from social science its prime conditions. Sooner or later the twain must meet.

The manner in which the work was done illustrates how research may be at once coördinated and coöperative. The authors have worked out between themselves a plan of coöperation which is not discussed in the volume but which is of interest for further work of this sort. Two important aspects of this plan may be mentioned. The first was that during the course of the research each author attempted to learn from the other the fundamentals of what he had to teach and to teach the other, in so far as possible, what the latter needed to know in order to assure a common basis of ideas and problems. The second item in the plan was a technique of freely using criticisms and disagreements as a means of eliciting rather than inhibiting further problem-solving responses.

While the volume is intended as a scientific report it may perhaps prove useful in connection with the teaching of social psychology and other social sciences.

MARK A. MAY, *Director,*
Institute of Human Relations.

July 1, 1941.

CONTENTS

FIGURES

PREFACE

IN this book we have attempted to apply training in two different fields—psychology and social science—to the solution of a common problem. It has seemed to us that each field has valuable contributions to offer to the other, and that both are essential to the eventual goal of an integrated science of behavior.

From the nature of this task it is our fate to write for a mixed audience. The problem of making the exposition rigorous enough for the technicians in the one field, and yet clear and informative enough for those in the other, has posed its special difficulties. Each of us has tried to change his mode of exposition (under duress from the other) to a style suited to nonspecialists. We hope that our most discriminating colleagues in each field will, as they read, tolerantly translate some of our paraphrases back into the technical terms in which each of us did his original thinking.

The book has been a coöperative enterprise in the fullest sense of the word. It was frequently hard to decide which of us had originated a particular conception, because it seemed so changed when reflected back by the other. We resolved not to attempt to decide the senior authorship of the book at the outset, but rather to assess the contributions made by each at the end of the research. If it were conventional and possible to do so, we would probably have decided to avoid the dilemma of senior authorship altogether, but inasmuch as we are constrained by custom to put one or the other name first, it was our mutual sense that they should be arranged as they appear on the cover.

We are continuously indebted to Professor Mark A. May for providing excellent conditions of work at the Institute of Human Relations. We are similarly under obligation to Professor George P. Murdock for aid in preparing the chapter on diffusion and for a most helpful reading of the manuscript as a whole. Professor B. Malinowski gave us a single but significant interview on the diffusion problem. Appreciation to colleagues at the Institute of Human Relations is difficult to allocate but strongly felt. No responsibility can attach to any of these for defects in the book as it appears. Mr. J. Allen Hickerson, Director of Training Schools at the State Teachers College in New Haven, and his colleagues gave very useful coöperation in making available for the experiments the necessary children from the New Haven schools. We are especially indebted to Mr. Fred Sheffield for helping to carry out Experiments 7, 8, and 9, and for drawing the figures which appear in the book, and to his wife, Mrs. Virginia Fairfax Sheffield, for aid in the same experiments and for reading the entire manuscript. Miss Alice M. White and Miss M. Eleanor Pierce were of invaluable assistance in the project, helping to prepare the manuscript for publication, and offering suggestions for content and style.

Acknowledgment is made to the following publishers from whose publications quotations are reproduced: D. Appleton-Century Company; Cambridge University Press; Columbia University Press; Thomas Y. Crowell Company; The Gorham Press; Harcourt, Brace and Company; Harper and Brothers; Henry Holt and Company; Houghton Mifflin Company; Alfred A. Knopf Company; J. B. Lippincott Company; Macmillan Company; McGraw-Hill Book Company; Methuen and Company; W. W. Norton Company; John W. Parker Company; Prentice-Hall Company; Charles Scribner's Sons; Simon and Schuster; University of Chicago Press; John Wiley and Sons; Williams and Norgate, Ltd. Acknowledgement for permission to quote is also extended to the editors and publishers of the following journals: *British Journal of Psychology, Journal of Genetic Psychology, Mind, International Institute of African Languages and Cultures* (Oxford University Press), *Pedagogical Seminary, Psychological Bulletin.*

N. E. M.
J. D.

SOCIAL LEARNING AND IMITATION

CHAPTER I

LEARNING: ITS CONDITIONS AND PRINCIPLES

HUMAN behavior is learned; precisely that behavior which is widely felt to characterize man as a rational being, or as a member of a particular nation or social class, is acquired rather than innate. To understand thoroughly any item of human behavior—either in the social group or in the individual life—one must know the psychological principles involved in its learning and the social conditions under which this learning took place. It is not enough to know either principles or conditions of learning; in order to predict behavior both must be known. The field of psychology describes learning principles, while the various social science disciplines describe the conditions.

Learning is a fact so familiar to human beings that it often does not receive the attention which it deserves. The difficult learning experiences of early childhood are forgotten by adults, and recalled to attention only by observing the blundering adaptations of children. Everyone at some time has tried to learn a skill and failed, without knowing why; or he has tried to teach and found others slow to understand. Such experiences drive home the fact that learning is not automatic. Where the principles are not understood so that the conditions can be correctly arranged, no learning takes place.

What, then, is learning theory? In its simplest form, it is the study of the circumstances under which a response and a cue stimulus become connected. After learning has been completed, response and cue are bound together in such a way that the appearance of the cue evokes the response. Everyone remembers learning to stop at a red light when driving an automobile. The cue pattern in this case is a simple one:

it consists of the red light, the street intersection, and perhaps the appearance of other cars moving across the highway. The response is equally simple: the right foot presses on the brake, the left foot on the clutch, and the car is brought to a halt. The cue of the red light has been associated with the response of pressing on pedals. Everyone remembers, similarly, that this response is not learned in one trial. The car must be slowly brought to a halt and stopped at the intersecting street. Errors have occurred, such as pressing too hard on the brake and stopping the car violently. Again, the distance to the intersecting street is badly gauged, and the car is stopped too soon; sometimes other cars are bumped in the process. In any case, after a series of trials, the connection between the light cue and the pressing response is established. The same technique of learning seems to operate in a great variety of situations. Under appropriate conditions the child learns to talk, to have good table manners, and to suppress the naughty words that he hears from his play group. Adults may learn to adapt to another person in the marriage relationship, to teach their children, and to grow old gracefully.

Learning takes place according to definite psychological principles. Practice does not always make perfect. The connection between a cue and a response can be strengthened only under certain conditions. The learner must be driven to make the response and rewarded for having responded in the presence of the cue. This may be expressed in a homely way by saying that in order to learn one must want something, notice something, do something, and get something. Stated more exactly, these factors are drive, cue, response, and reward. These elements in the learning process have been carefully explored, and further complexities have been discovered. Learning theory has become a firmly knit body of principles which are useful in describing human behavior.

Learning principles can, of course, operate only under specific material or social conditions. For human beings these conditions are those imposed by the society in which a particular individual lives. The analysis of social behavior seems to require a knowledge of learning principles, exactly as the analysis of any personality trait requires knowledge of the social conditions under which it was learned. In order to give point to this contention, the authors will present examples showing the need for learning principles in the analysis of characteristic social facts and, conversely, the necessity of a knowledge of learning conditions in the psychological sphere.

To take first a case from social science. The anthropological theory of diffusion provides the following facts: While the Indians of the eastern woodlands of North America were learning to use the gun which they took over from the whites, the whites in turn were learning a new style of warfare—they discovered the advantage of lying in ambush and shooting at the enemy from behind trees and rocks as the Indians did. While the gun was diffusing to the Indians, a military technique was diffusing to the whites. Is it a matter of chance that the whites did not adopt the bow and arrow and the Indians the close-order drill which was characteristic of the European armies? Seen from the standpoint of learning theory, it can hardly have been accidental. The Indians were heavily punished by the superior striking power of the gun, and to avoid this punishment they copied the use of the musket from the whites. The whites, on the other hand, suffered severely from the ambush techniques of the Indians. Each side, to escape punishment, learned a new set of responses.

To take a second example, the behavior of voters, or at least some voters, in a boss-ridden town has puzzled many observers. They often seem to act in defiance of their own best interests as widely conceived. They may be inordinately taxed to maintain service on a graft-inflated debt; they may be deprived of the best level of services which a city government can render; and they may be ruled and delivered by an arrogant machine.[1] The use of psychological principles may help to explain these apparently irrational loyalties. Many

[1] The following statements are based in part upon facts given in J. T. Salter, *Boss Rule* (1935), pp. 79–86.

voters in the lower social and income brackets have needs of
which the wider society seems to be unaware. These needs are
met by the political machine. Through the machine the voter
can satisfy some of his urgent wants without seeming to accept charity. The boss, for instance, has jobs to offer—not
always big jobs, but ones much appreciated by his constituents. The machine voter feels that he has some control over
these jobs and that they offer a less precarious form of security than open competition in the job market. This is a
primary reward for taking orders and voting the straight
ticket. The ward boss watches the rise of needs among his
constituents. If someone dies, he calls to express sympathy,
to aid in funeral arrangements, or he offers money to make
possible the conventional hospitality; the Christmas basket
and ton of coal are sent with his compliments. All of these rewards are immediate and therefore more effective than the
delayed consequences of good government. For other voters
still, the boss can tear up a parking ticket, overlook the in-
fraction of a fire law, or even induce authorities to ignore an
illegal business. It is clear, of course, that all the voters would
be better off in the long run if the city administration were
honestly and efficiently administered in the interest of the
whole community; but the boss's henchmen do not think in
terms of the long run. Their loyalty is won by the small but
promptly produced favors which they receive from the machine. Political attitudes in such a group will be as stable as
the rewards which reinforce them. If the machine loses its
power to deliver the coal or the protection, as the case may
be, it also loses its power to deliver the vote.

Examples indicating the usefulness of learning principles
in solving the problems of social scientists could be selected
from a variety of fields. What, for instance, are the mechanisms by which culture is transmitted from one generation to
the next? Since such transmission is not instinctive, it can
only be that social habits are taught to children by the adults
of the culture and learned by children from their elders. The
transmission of culture must follow the laws of learning. An
adequate understanding of the individual life in terms of ac-

quiring culture by learning is one of the important current
problems of social science.[2]

The stability of culture patterns, once they are acquired
by the individuals of a given generation, presents likewise an
interesting, though still obscure, problem. Are social habits,
once acquired through the learning of childhood, fixed and
immutable? Do they have a kind of gravitational property
which makes it difficult to change them, or do they respond to
one of the laws of habit which states that unrewarded habits
will disappear? If the habits of adults *are* constantly rewarded, what are the rewards in question? There are no de-
finitive answers to these questions at the present time, but
they seem bound to receive discussion in the future. On a
common-sense level, it seems likely that the satisfactions of
daily life maintain cultural habit. But rewards there must be
—or changes in the learning theory which seems to demand
them. In any case, the stability of culture patterns and habits is not to be taken for granted as a matter too obvious and
unimportant for close examination.

If social scientists find the knowledge of learning principles valuable in solving problems in their field, psychologists
will find it no less useful to emphasize the conditions under
which human learning takes place. These conditions for human beings are primarily social and cultural conditions. No
psychologist would venture to predict the behavior of a rat
without knowing on what arm of a T-maze the food or the
shock is placed. It is no easier to predict the behavior of a
human being without knowing the conditions of his "maze,"
i.e., the structure of his social environment. Culture, as conceived by social scientists, is a statement of the design of the
human maze, of the type of reward involved, and of what responses are to be rewarded. It is in this sense a recipe for
learning. This contention is easily accepted when widely vari-
ant societies are compared. But even within the same society,
the mazes which are run by two individuals may seem the
same but actually be quite different. In our own society, for

2 J. W. M. Whiting has studied this process in a primitive society (1941).

instance, a person at the top of the social hierarchy may look much like the same American as a person at the bottom of the hierarchy; but actually his life is differentiated from that of a lower-class person by a series of divergent customs and habits. No personality analysis of two such people can be accurate which does not take into account these cultural differences, that is, differences in the types of responses which have been rewarded.

The importance of knowing the conditions of learning can be illustrated from a common personality problem, i.e., that of aggressive individuals. Individual aggressiveness has often been supposed to be natural, or instinctive. In one group of aggressive persons, it is quite clear that social conditions have influenced the development of this personality trait. These are persons who have recently been socially mobile.[3] In the course of struggle for social advancement, these mobile individuals have found frequent occasion for aggressive responses. They have, for instance, competed in business with cut-throat severity, but have been rewarded by success. They have boldly copied the manners and habits of those above them in social position and, though often ridiculed, have often succeeded in achieving higher status. They have learned to strive, compete, and fight, where others have quietly accepted deprivations, and they have lived to see themselves superior. Since competitive and aggressive habits have been so highly and consistently rewarded, it is not surprising to find such persons displaying aggression in a great variety of situations. Seen in this context, the "pushiness" of the mobile person is not mysterious; it seems rather the inevitable result of the learning conditions of his life. The social structure of our society is so designed that it grants rewards to those who fight for them; in the course of so doing, it creates combative individuals. A psychologist understanding these conditions might well go on to make the following prediction: If the aggressive individual achieves status in a social group higher than his own, and if in the higher group his "pushiness" is no

[3] See W. L. Warner (1941), and Allison Davis and John Dollard (1940, p. 109).

longer rewarded but is, on the contrary, punished, such a trait will tend to drop out—although it may distinguish the recently mobile person during the time he is becoming adapted to the superior group.

The importance of social conditions can be further emphasized by considering the different ways in which people use alcoholic drinks at different levels in our society. There are definite social conventions which govern drinking in different social groups, although to state this is not to deny that there are also biological and psychological factors involved. If one did not know the social conditions, however, it would be easy to overestimate the importance of such factors. The matter can be exemplified, though in oversimplified form, from the data gathered on a small American town.[4] In the lower class, both men and women may drink, although the men seem to drink with much more freedom from criticism than do the women. There is little punishment for overindulgence and no urgency to "drink like a gentleman" among lower-class men. Getting drunk is not frowned upon. Lower-class individuals drink episodically—usually when they happen to have the money necessary to buy liquor. If these conditions were unknown, the drinking of a lower-class person might seem to be a very marked personality trait. Lower-middle-class individuals in the very same town drink little or not at all. They have religious scruples against it and are afraid that the habit of drinking would lead to their being confused with lower-class persons. Upper-middle-class people draw a distinction between men and women so far as drinking is concerned. The men drink quite freely, especially in their clubs, but they do not engage in mixed drinking with women. Upper-middle-class wives are expected to refuse alcohol when it

---

[4] The conception of a difference in custom regarding drinking habits was first suggested to one of the authors (Dollard) by Dr. Burleigh B. Gardner of the Western Electric Company of Chicago. See Davis, Gardner, and Gardner (1941, pp. 139–145, 147, 206). These findings were subsequently verified by Dollard. The statements above describe norms; within each class there are deviant individuals and, in some cases, deviant cliques. Psychological, and perhaps biological, differences appear regularly to exaggerate or minimize the behavior characteristic of each social class.

is offered. In the upper class, by contrast, both men and women drink, and there is no moral significance attached to drinking. There is, however, a code involved. While an upper-class individual is allowed to drink a good deal, he must "drink like a gentleman." He is punished with social scorn if he allows his drinking to lead to disorderly or aggressive behavior, such as is often characteristic of lower-class people.

If an individual moves from one of these social classes to another, he must change his habits with regard to the use of alcohol. If he moves into the lower-middle class from the lower class, he must learn to stop drinking or he will be thought vulgar. Lower-middle-class men who move into upper-middle class must learn to begin again, at least when they are with men. Upper-middle-class individuals who move into upper class must learn to become very liberal from the standpoint of their former upper-middle-class habits, or they will be thought stuffy. What is rewarded in one social class is punished in the other. It is clear that if a person from the town in question came into the hands of a psychologist in a clinic, it would be absolutely necessary for the latter to know the special social conditions with regard to drinking which were characteristic of the social class of the patient. Without a knowledge of these social conditions, a personality analysis of a given case of drinking would certainly be confused.

A further example from anthropological literature may serve to emphasize the importance of the social environment still more decisively. The Semang people of the Malay Peninsula[5] are known among anthropologists as excessively shy and timid. They are said never to respond to ill treatment with violence or treachery. In the face of hostility from others, they withdraw yet deeper into the jungle area which they inhabit. Is this a personality trait? Are these people naturally deficient in aggressive tendencies and constitutionally prone to flight? The question can be answered only by posing another: Have the conditions of life been such for the

---

[5] This discussion of the Semang is, as to fact, a paraphrase of that in G. P. Murdock (1934), pp. 95–104.

Semang that aggressive responses have been punished while escape responses have been rewarded? For some time past, the Semang have been in contact with a more powerful group, the Malays, who have regularly cheated them in trade, occasionally raided them for slaves, and slowly crowded them out of their lands. One may fairly surmise that in former times the Semang attempted resistance, but found it led only to severe punishment. Like a child who is punished first for a naughty act, and then for crying in protest at the punishment, their only resource was muteness and flight. Apparently, also, although aggressive responses were not rewarded, flight tendencies were successful and became stabilized. This stabilization took the form of culture patterns defining flight as the correct response to strangers. It is no longer necessary for each generation of Malays to punish each generation of Semang into learning escape behavior; this teaching is now done by the Semang with their own children. Conditions of learning which formerly taught the whole tribe to avoid contact with the dangerous Malays have now been absorbed into the culture, and form in turn conditions of learning for each Semang child.

In earliest life the conditions of learning and the principles of learning can be sharply and logically marked off one from the other. Social scientists are keenly aware of the rôle of primary drives, such as hunger, which are met by the distinctive conditions of learning characteristic of each society. Hunger, pain, and fatigue are clamorous and distinctive in the infant. The routines of feeding, the type of food offered, and the behavior of the nurse are carefully defined. As time passes in the life of the child, these crude drive tendencies become less visible—although they are never absent—and are replaced by various *social* motivations. These social motivations are variously called *secondary drives, acquired drives,* or *social attitudes.* Upon the primary drive of pain is built the (also painful) secondary drive of anxiety. Upon the crude hunger drive are built appetites for particular foods. All of these secondary drives are derived by the joint operation of psychological variables under the pressure of social conditions. It is these secondary drives which particularly interest the social scientist, because they form such a large and obvious part of social motivation. In an analogous though more complex manner, there arise also acquired drives toward gregariousness, social conformity, prestige seeking, desire for money, and, most important here, *imitativeness*. It is necessary to notice that once these social drives have been generated, they operate exactly as do the primary drives; but it is also crucial that they never lose their acquired, or dependent, character. A theory of social learning must give a full account of these social motivations, since they are so characteristic of the behavior of human beings.

The joint operation of psychological principles and social conditions will be exemplified by a detailed discussion of imitation. Imitation is a process by which "matched," or similar, acts are evoked in two people and connected to appropriate cues. It can occur only under conditions which are favorable to learning these acts. If matching, or doing the same as others do, is regularly rewarded, a secondary tendency to match may be developed, and the process of imitation becomes the derived drive of imitativeness.

The importance of the study of matched behavior is clearer when one considers the high rewards which attend joint social action. If all pull on the same rope, the cart moves. National unity of thought and action is important in a crisis. Individuals must be trained to pull harder on the rope when others pull and to act more decisively together when others act. Such joint action is often essential to the survival of a society.

Imitation is also important in maintaining social conformity and discipline. Individuals must be trained, in many situations, so that they will be comfortable when they are doing what others are doing and miserable when they are not. The culture patterns of a society have been achieved by many generations of trial-and-error behavior, and they constitute a tested way of life which has long proved its value. Individuals cannot be permitted to deviate too readily from it.

This desirable conformity to the social pattern is achieved, in part, by techniques of imitation which individuals acquire during the early years of life. It is important, therefore, to understand just how imitative behavior arises.

There seem to be two important types of action which go under the common name of *imitation*. In *matched-dependent* behavior, the leader is able to read the relevant environmental cues, but the follower is not; the latter must depend upon the leader for the signal as to what act is to be performed and where and when. The follower does not need to be keenly aware that his act is matched. This matched-dependent mechanism apparently plays a considerable rôle in the formation of crowds, and it will be found useful in the analysis of crowd behavior.

The second type of matched behavior is described here as *copying*. The copier must slowly bring his response to approximate that of a model and must know, when he has done so, that his act is an acceptable reproduction of the model act. Copying units are established early in the history of each individual, and appear to play a considerable rôle in all fundamental social learning. For instance, once the child has learned the fundamental phonemes of his speech, it is possible for him to copy any new word in the language. By copying, the correct word can be rapidly and efficiently elicited. Copying itself is, of course, learned only when the appropriate conditions of reward for learning it are present.

The method of this research is exemplified in the order of the chapters which follow. The authors first attempted to get some practice in applying learning theory to social behavior. Then, addressing the inquiry to the imitation problem, they selected and analyzed some examples of imitative behavior which were derived from a study of children. These examples were then discussed and dissected in the search for relevant variables. With a preliminary list of these variables, an attempt was made to manipulate them in experiments. From the experiments, there arose a more systematic statement of a theory of imitative behavior, derived under controlled con-

ditions. Once this theory had been tested, it was applied to
several problems of social behavior in order to determine its
usefulness. The evidence seems to show that imitative behavior follows the laws of learning and arises under the social
conditions which reward it.

CHAPTER II

FOUR FUNDAMENTALS OF LEARNING

CERTAIN simple, basic principles of learning are needed for a clear understanding of the essential processes involved in imitation and related forms of social behavior. Other principles are useful in explaining some of the less important details of imitative behavior, and probably all of the known facts about learning are relevant in some way or other to some aspect of the problem. In the interest of a sharp focus upon the fundamentals, however, only the most essential principles will be included in this discussion, which is not to be considered a complete survey of learning theory.

The field of human learning covers phenomena which range all the way from the simple, almost reflex, learning of a child to avoid a hot radiator to the complex processes of insight by which a scientist constructs a theory. Throughout the whole range, however, the same fundamental factors seem to be involved. In different examples of learning, the conditions are such as to bring the rôle of sometimes one, sometimes another, of these factors especially clearly into the spotlight. But even though the success or failure of the drama of learning may seem to depend now on one and again on another of these factors, all are essential to the final performance. These factors are: *drive, response, cue,* and *reward*.

In order to give a bird's-eye view of the manner in which these factors are interrelated, a concrete example of learning will be analyzed first; then each of the factors will be discussed separately.

A Simple Experiment

The fundamental principles of learning can be illustrated by a simple experiment which can easily be repeated by anyone who desires first-hand experience with the operation of the factors involved in learning. The subject is a girl six years old. It is known that she is hungry and wants candy. While she is out of the room, a small, flat piece of her favorite candy is hidden under the bottom edge of the center book on the lower shelf of a bookcase about four feet long. The books in the center of this row are all dark in color and about the same size. The other shelves contain a radio, some magazines, and a few more books.

The little girl is brought into the room; she is told there is a candy hidden under one of the books in the bookcase and asked if she wants to try to find it. After she answers, "Yes," she is directed to put each book back after looking under it and is told that if she finds the candy, she can keep it and eat it.

Immediately after receiving these instructions, the little girl eagerly starts to work. First, she looks under the few books on the top shelf. Then she turns around. After a brief pause, she starts taking out the books on the lower shelf, one by one. When she has removed eight of these books without finding the candy, she temporarily leaves the books and starts looking under the magazines on the top shelf. Then she returns to look again on the top shelf under several of the books that she has already picked up. After this, she turns toward the experimenter and asks, "Where is the candy?" He does not answer.

After a pause, she pulls out a few more books on the bottom shelf, stops, sits down, and looks at the books for about half a minute, turns away from the bookcase, looks under a book on a near-by table, then returns and pulls out more books.

Under the thirty-seventh book which she examines, she finds the piece of candy. Uttering an exclamation of delight, she picks it up and eats it. On this trial, it has taken her 210 seconds to find the candy.

She is sent out of the room, candy is hidden under the same book, and she is called back again for another trial. This time she goes directly to the lower shelf of books, taking out each book methodically. She does not stop to sit down, turn away, or ask the experimenter questions. Under the twelfth book she finds the candy. She has finished in 86 seconds.

On the third trial, she goes almost directly to the right place, finding the candy under the second book picked up. She has taken only 11 seconds.

On the following trial, the girl does not do so well. Either the previous spectacular success has been due partly to

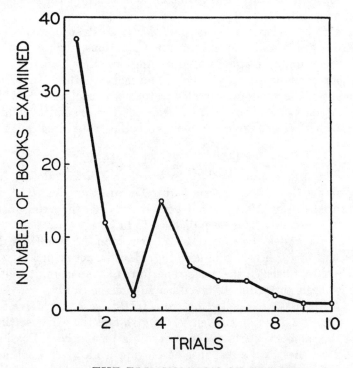

FIG. 1. THE ELIMINATION OF ERRORS

On the first trial the child looks under 36 wrong books and makes other incorrect responses not indicated on the graph before finding candy under the thirty-seventh book examined; errors are gradually eliminated until on the ninth and tenth trials the child makes only the one response of going directly to the correct book.

chance, or some uncontrolled factor has intervened.[1] This time the girl begins at the far end of the shelf and examines 15 books before finding the candy. She has required 86 seconds.

Thereafter, her scores improve progressively until, on the ninth trial, she picks up the correct book immediately and secures the candy in three seconds. On the tenth trial, she again goes directly to the correct book and gets the candy in two seconds.

Her behavior has changed markedly. Instead of requiring 210 seconds and stopping, asking questions, turning away, looking under magazines, searching in other parts of the room, picking up wrong books, and making other useless responses, she now goes directly to the right book and gets the candy in two seconds. She has learned. The dramatic manner in which her behavior has changed is illustrated in Figure 1.

Factors Involved in Learning

The first factor involved in learning is *drive*. Before beginning, the experimenters had to be sure that the little girl wanted candy. Had she not been motivated, the experiment would certainly have been doomed to failure.

Drive impels the subject to act or respond. *Response* is the second factor involved in learning. Had the act of picking up a book not been in the girl's repertoire of responses, it would have been impossible to teach her to find the candy.

Responses are elicited by *cues*. In this case, the drive for candy, the directions given to the girl, and the whole setting of the room are parts of the general pattern of cues. Possible specific cues to the response of picking up a given book are the sight of the color, size, and marking of the book and the position of that book in relation to the rest of the bookcase. Were there nothing distinctive about the correct book to serve as a cue, it would be impossible for the girl to learn to solve this problem.

[1] For example, the little girl might say to herself as a result of previous experience with hiding games, "He'll probably change the place now that I know it."

Since the girl's first natural response to the situation, looking under the top book on the upper shelf, does not bring her the candy, she is not rewarded. Since reward is essential to the maintenance of a habit, the unsuccessful response tends to be weakened and not to reappear. This gives other responses a chance to occur. The girl tries successively a number of different responses, asking questions, turning away, sitting down, and picking up other books. This is what is often called random behavior.

Finally, one of the responses is followed by seeing, seizing, and eating the candy. This is the *reward*. On subsequent trials a response that has been followed by reward will be more likely to recur. This increase in the probability of recurrence of a rewarded response may be expressed in shorthand fashion by saying that the reward has strengthened the connection between the cues and the rewarded response. Without some sort of a reward, the girl would never learn to go regularly to the correct book. The rewarding effect of the candy depends upon the presence of the drive and tends to produce a reduction in strength of this drive. After eating a large amount of candy, the girl would be satiated and stop looking for it.

The relationship among the fundamental factors may be grasped in a brief summary. The drive impels responses, which are usually also determined by cues from other stimuli not strong enough to act as drives but more specifically distinctive than the drive. If the first response is not rewarded by an event reducing the drive, this response tends to drop out and others to appear. The extinction of successive non-rewarded responses produces so-called random behavior. If some one response is followed by reward, the connection between the cue and this response is strengthened, so that the next time that the same drive and other cues are present, this response is more likely to occur. This strengthening of the cue-response connection is the essence of learning. The functions of each of the four factors will become clearer as they are described separately in more detail.

Drive

A drive is a strong stimulus which impels action. Any stimulus can become a drive if it is made strong enough. The stronger the stimulus, the more drive function it possesses. The faint murmur of distant music has but little primary drive function; the infernal blare of the neighbor's radio has considerably more.

While any stimulus may become strong enough to act as a drive, certain special classes of stimuli seem to be the primary basis for the greater proportion of motivation. These might be called the primary or innate drives. One of these is pain. Pain can reach stabbing heights of greater strength than probably any other single drive. The parching sensation of thirst, the pangs of extreme hunger, and the sore weight of fatigue are other examples of powerful innate drives. The bitter sting of cold and the insistent goading of sex are further examples.[2]

To people living in a society protected by a technology as efficient as ours, it is difficult to realize the full height to which these primary drives can mount. One of the basic aims of any social organization is to protect its members from the unpleasant force of severe motivation by providing satiation for drives before they mount to agonizing heights. Thus it is only when the social organization breaks down under ex-

---

[2] *Technical note:* Where subjective terms are used, they were adopted in order to express the main point in briefer phrases more meaningful to many readers and are not meant to have any refined technical or philosophical significance. Thus the specialist will understand that thirst can be defined objectively in terms of the effects of dehydration. The fact that animals can be trained to turn to the right when they have been deprived of water and to the left when they have been deprived of food (Leeper, 1935) is the objective basis for stating that thirst is a cue. The fact that a certain amount of dehydration increases the general level of activity is the objective basis for stating that thirst is a strong stimulus. This statement is further confirmed by the fact that the drinking, which reduces the increased level of activity, also has a rewarding effect. In further examples, it will be understood that hearing a sound of a given pitch means being stimulated by sound waves of a given frequency; feeling oneself run means stimulating certain proprioceptors in the course of making the responses involved in running; and trying a response means that the response is elicited.

treme conditions of war, famine, and revolution that the full strength of the primary drives is realized by the social scientist in his usually secure social circumstances.

The importance of the innate drives is further obscured by social inhibitions. In those cases in which our society allows a primary drive, for example the sex drive before marriage, to rise to considerable heights, a certain amount of negative sanction or social opprobrium generally attaches to frank statements about the drive and to vivid descriptions of its intensity. In some cases, the effects of this taboo upon speech spread even to thoughts, so that consciousness of the drive tends to be weakened and, in extreme cases, obliterated.

The conditions of society tend, besides obscuring the rôle of certain primary drives, to emphasize certain secondary or acquired drives. These secondary drives are acquired on the basis of the primary drives, represent elaborations of them, and serve as a façade behind which the functions of the underlying innate drives are hidden. Such experimental evidence as is available indicates that the acquired drives cannot remain indefinitely independent, but tend, like any habit, to become gradually weaker unless occasionally rewarded. A possible mechanism for the production and maintenance of acquired drive will be discussed briefly in the fourth chapter.

One of the strongest of the acquired drives is anxiety or fear. This drive mirrors pain, as it were, and is probably based primarily upon it. Various appetites are similarly based on other innate drives, such as hunger, thirst, and sex. Appetites can often summate with primary drives and provide a considerable portion of the motivation in circumstances under which the drive would otherwise be quite weak. Such acquired drives or appetites vary according to the social conditions under which they are learned and often impart a cultural coloring to the innate drives. Thus hunger may take the form of an appetite for particular foods; sex, that of an attraction to beautiful women; thirst, that of a desire for a specific type of drink. In short, acquired drives may assume the aspect of social needs.

Some of the stronger of the acquired drives or social needs

are not based on any single drive, but rather on a number of more primary drives. Indeed, it is probably from this fact that they derive their strength and persistence. Thus, the desire for money is the focus of many needs. During the course of his socialization, the individual learns that the possession of money is the means of gratifying many different needs and that the lack of money is a signal that he may have to bear the uncomfortable goading of many unsatisfied desires. Some of the drives upon which the desire for money is based are primary drives, such as hunger and cold. Others may be secondary, such as anxiety. Because of the number of different drives supporting the need for money, it is a rare occasion when the individual is without any primary motivation to summate with and activate his need for money. In fact, so omnipresent in our adult society is the desire for certain coins and bits of paper that it seems almost to operate as a primary drive. Yet it is obvious that this desire is not innate. Children have to be taught the value of money.

What may be called the desire for approval is established earlier than the craving for money. Like money, approval has been repeatedly associated with the gratification of many different primary drives, while disapproval has been repeatedly associated with the mounting of pain, hunger, and other forms of drive discomfort.

Such terms as pride, ambition, and rivalry point to another powerful core of acquired drives. These are probably related to the desire for approval, but are somewhat more generalized and have crystallized into the desire for institutionalized symbols of approval somewhat analogous in function to money. These trappings of prestige arouse responses of deference from others. They may, in fact, be more widely useful than money itself. In our society, for example, it seems to be easier to use the great prestige of a position at the top of the social hierarchy as an instrument to obtain money than it does to buy with money a position among the "best families."

Differences between one's own behavior and dress and those of one's associates can become cues arousing acquired motivation based on pain and other innate drives. Thus, under appropriate conditions, an acquired drive to match or imitate one's associates, particularly those enjoying superior prestige, can be established. The special conditions for establishing an acquired drive[4] to imitate will subsequently be described in detail.

The interlacing network of acquired drives appears to be based upon primary drives and rewards. It is one of the weaknesses of social science that neither the sociological condi- tions nor the psychological mechanisms for the acquisition of these drives have as yet been satisfactorily determined.

Without drives, either primary or acquired, the organism does not behave and hence does not learn. A dramatic example of the importance of drive may be drawn from the litera- ture of experimental psychology. It was once thought that old rats are more stupid than young rats. Certainly they learned more slowly in the laboratory experiments which had been conducted up to that time. Finally it occurred to an experimenter, Stone (1929a, p. 104), that mature animals kept underweight may not be starved as much as young grow- ing animals, even though the latter are allowed to gain. When he took especial care to see to it that both the old and the young rats were motivated by a maximal hunger drive, the apparent stupidity of the old rats disappeared.

Any teacher who has tried to teach unmotivated students is aware of the relationship between drive and learning. Com- pletely self-satisfied people are poor learners. Colonial gov- ernments have sometimes found it necessary to tax satisfied natives in order to create a need for money. Spurred by the prospect of interference with the satisfaction of their more primary drives, the natives would then learn the new work and continue to perform it for money.

Cue

The drive impels a person to respond. Cues determine when he will respond, where he will respond, and which re- sponse he will make.[3] Simple examples of stimuli which func-

---

[3] This way of describing cues was suggested to the authors in conversa- tion by Dr. John W. M. Whiting.

tion primarily as cues are the five o'clock whistle determining when the tired worker will stop, the restaurant sign determining where the hungry man will go, and the traffic light determining whether the driver will step on the brake or on the accelerator.

The relationship between the drive and cue functions of stimuli must be considered in more detail. Stimuli may vary in two respects: in strength and in kind. Thus sounds may differ in loudness and in pitch. Weak sounds have little innate drive value; the naïve child is not stirred to action by the onset of a cricket's chirp nor rewarded by its cessation. But weak sounds may be distinctive and have cue value; the individual can be trained to make one response to a weak sound of high pitch and a different response to a weak sound of low pitch. The more the two sounds differ in pitch, the easier it is to connect different responses to them; they are more *distinctive* as cues.

As sounds become louder, they increase in drive value. A noise of medium intensity may have a dynamogenic effect, causing the individual to be slightly more active and less likely to fall asleep. As sounds become extremely loud, they possess definite innate drive value and can arouse even the naïve infant to action. Furthermore, escape from an exceedingly loud noise acts as a reward. But loud sounds may vary in pitch and hence can serve as cues as well as drives. The individual can be trained to make one response to one loud sound and a different response to another.

Finally, different strengths of stimulation may themselves be distinctive and hence serve as cues. A child can learn to respond in one way to a word spoken softly and in a different way to the same word spoken loudly.

In general, stimuli may vary quantitatively and qualitatively; any stimulus may be thought of as having a certain drive value, depending on its strength, and a certain cue value, depending on its distinctiveness.

The occurrence of a specific response can be made to depend not upon any single stimulus alone, but upon a pattern of stimuli. A hurried driver speeding down the highway may respond differently to the combination of a sign indicating a reduced speed limit and a police car seen in the rear-vision mirror than he would to either the sign without the police car or the car without the sign.

Since drive and cue functions are two different aspects of the same thing, a stimulus, any given stimulus may possess, like the loud sound, an important amount of both functions. Thus a drive stimulus such as hunger may have a selective or cue function as well as its impelling or drive function. In fact, hunger is a part of the stimulus pattern involved in determining the response to the restaurant sign. An individual standing between a restaurant sign to the right and a hotel sign to the left will respond to the stimulus pattern of drive plus signs by turning to the right if he is hungry and to the left if he is tired.

Since many drives, such as hunger and fatigue, originate within the individual and are thus present wherever he goes, they are usually not specific enough, without support from more distinctive cue-stimuli, to elicit the correct responses. Hunger as the sole cue is not highly correlated with reward for the response of biting. Other cues must be present to indicate whether or not the thing bitten will be palatable.

The importance of cues in the learning process becomes apparent from an examination of cases in which learning fails through the absence of cues. The experiment already described of hiding candy under a certain book was repeated on a four-year-old child. When the candy was hidden under a distinctive red book in the middle of a row of black books, he learned to respond perfectly by the third trial. When the candy was hidden under a dark book in the middle of a long row of books of similar color, he learned during the first few trials to select books in that general region, but thereafter failed to show improvement during the next ten trials. If the cues are too obscure, as in this case, it is impossible to learn to make the correct response with precision.

Noticing a cue can in itself be a response which may be learned. This is called learning to pay attention.

Response

Drive impels the individual to respond to certain cues. Be
fore any given response to a specific cue can be rewarded and
learned, this response must occur. A good part of the trick of
animal training, clinical therapy, and school teaching is to
arrange the situation so that the learner will somehow make
the first correct response. A bashful boy at his first dance
cannot begin to learn either that girls will not bite him or
how to make the correct dance step until he begins responding by trying to dance.

The rôle of response in human learning is sometimes rather
difficult to observe, because of the fact that when the individual already has a good deal of social learning behind him,
verbal and other nonovert anticipatory responses may play
an important part in controlling his behavior. But cases of
verbal behavior are no exception to the rule. A person cannot
learn a new way of speaking or thinking until he has first
tried a new statement or thought. Much of the difficulty in
teaching arises in finding a situation which will produce
thoughts that can be rewarded.

The ease with which a response can be learned in a certain
situation depends upon the probability that the cues present
can be made to elicit that response. It is a case of "unto him
who hath shall be given." If the response occurs relatively
frequently, it is easy to reward that response and still further
increase its frequency of occurrence. If the response occurs
only rarely, it is difficult to find an occasion when it occurs
and can be rewarded. Thus, the initial tendency for a stimulus situation to evoke a response is an important factor in
learning. In-order to describe this factor, one may arrange
the responses in the order of their probability of occurrence
and call this the *initial hierarchy* of responses. The most
likely response to occur is called the dominant response in the
initial hierarchy; the response least likely to occur is called
the weakest response. The same situation may be described
in another way. It may be said that there is a strong connection between the stimulus and the dominant response and a

weak connection between the stimulus and the weakest response. The word "connection" is used to refer to a causal sequence, the details of which are practically unknown, rather than to specific neural strands.

Learning changes the order of the responses in the hierarchy. The rewarded response, though it may have been initially weak, now occupies the dominant position. The new hierarchy produced by learning may be called the *resultant hierarchy*. At the beginning of the experiment with the books, the response of selecting the correct book happened to be a late response in the initial hierarchy, coming after thirty-six responses of looking under other books and after other responses such as asking questions. At the end of the experiment, this response had become the first or dominant response in the resultant hierarchy.

Usually the order of responses in an initial hierarchy is the result of previous learning in similar situations. In those cases in which the order of the response is primarily determined, not by learning, but by hereditary factors, the initial hierarchy may be called an *innate hierarchy*. In the human infant, crying occupies a higher position in the innate hierarchy than does saying the word "No." Therefore it is much easier for an infant to learn to respond to the sight of a spoonful of medicine by crying than by saying "No."

Once having learned, the person responds in a new way. But if the correct response must always occur before it can be rewarded, what novelty is added by learning? The new feature is that the particular response rewarded now occurs regularly to a specific cue, whereas previously its occurrence at just that time and place may have been exceedingly infrequent. The connection between cue and response is the new product of learning. Often a number of different response units are connected to cues so that they all occur together, either simultaneously or successively. Thus a new pattern of responses is produced; the responses are old, but the combination is new. Once this new combination occurs frequently, variations in it may be points of departure for still further learning.

There are a number of different ways in which the response to be connected to a given cue as a new habit may first be elicited. The least efficient of these is the mechanism of random behavior. The drive elicits responses, one after another. As those high in the initial hierarchy are non-rewarded and extinguished, various weaker responses appear. These are new in the sense that they would not have been likely to occur before the stronger competing responses were extinguished. If one of these happens to be the desired response, it can be rewarded and the habit established.

After a person has learned to attach appropriate responses to specific words as cues, language can be of enormous assistance in eliciting the correct response early in the sequence. The problem confronting the little girl was vastly simplified by eliminating many irrelevant responses through the simple expedient of telling her that the candy was under a book in the bookcase.

Similarly, after a person has learned to attach appropriate responses to the cue of seeing another person perform an act, imitation can help the person to limit his range of trial and error. Provided he has learned the particular units essential to successful copying (a complex process which will be described in detail later), watching a demonstration of the correct response may enable the student to perform perfectly on the first trial. But if not all of the units and the techniques of combining them have been learned, the first trial may be halting and involve errors.

· One important function of culture, as Ford (1937; 1939) has pointed out, is that it represents a storehouse of solutions to recurrent problems. Various means of instruction are employed by the older members of society to get the younger members to perform just those responses which are most likely to be rewarded. ·

In psychological literature, insight and conditioning are often thought to be at the opposite poles, yet both are mechanisms which can cause the individual to perform the correct response on the first trial. As an example of conditioning, a child may thrust his hand against a hot radiator, be burned, and learn to withdraw it at the sight of the radiator. The question here is: How does the child come eventually to withdraw his hand from the radiator before he is burned? Obviously it is the primary or unconditioned stimulus of the burn which causes the child immediately to try withdrawal—the dominant response in his innate hierarchy of responses to this situation. This withdrawal is rewarded by escape from pain. Thus the first trial is a successful one; there are no errors. But at the same time that the child is withdrawing from pain, he is also withdrawing from the sight of the radiator and is rewarded for doing this. Thus a tendency is established for visual cues to elicit withdrawal before his hand touches the radiator. The important fact about conditioning, or associative learning, is that the correct response is dominant in the hierarchy of responses to the unconditioned stimulus. Therefore, that stimulus causes the subject to make the correct response on the first trial.

In cases involving insight or reasoning, a more complicated and less understood mechanism may achieve the same result. In a new situation, the function of reasoning or insight seems to be to produce a response which might otherwise not have been made. If this response is rewarded, it will be learned as the response to that situation. If the insight is not rewarded, it will be abandoned. The authors use all the insight at their command, facilitating their reasoning by the use of verbal and even mathematical symbols, in attempting to prepare demonstrations for their classes. If these demonstrations are successful, they are repeated year after year; if not, they tend to be abandoned. Insight, the conditioning technique, imitation, and verbal instruction are different ways of producing responses likely to be rewarded. Once produced, the responses are all subject to the same laws of trial-and-error learning, to rejection or selection on the basis of the effects of non-reward or reward.

If a response which would be rewarded does not occur, it is not learned. Radically new inventions are rare because the occurrence of the correct combination of responses is improbable. No one in the pre-Columbian New World ever

made a wheel, even though the Mayas built huge pyramids
and the Incas had paved roads. In all the rest of the world,
the wheel seems to have been invented only once. The history
of human society is teeming with the unborn spirits of useful
responses which for centuries did not occur, were therefore
not rewarded, and did not become cultural habits.

Reward

Drive impels the person to make responses to cues in the
stimulus situation. Whether these responses will be repeated
depends on whether or not they are rewarded. If the response
is non-rewarded, the tendency to repeat it to the same cues is
weakened. Pavlov (1927) has called this process *extinction;*
it will be discussed in more detail in the next chapter. In cases
of sophisticated human learning, the process of extinction is
facilitated by the learned habit of abandoning unsuccessful
responses quickly. Thus in the experiment, the little girl
went back to look under the same book only a few times and
only on the first trial. The failure to see candy became a cue
to abandon looking under that book.

As the dominant response is weakened by non-reward, the
next response in the hierarchy becomes dominant. As successive responses are eliminated by non-reward, the individual
exhibits variable or what has perhaps been misnamed *random
behavior*. It is this variability that may lead to the production of a response which will be rewarded.

If one of the so-called random responses is followed by an
event producing a reduction in the drive, the tendency to
make this response on subsequent exposure to the same cues
is increased. In other words, the connection is strengthened
between the stimulus pattern (drive and other cues) and the
response. Events producing such strengthening are called rewards. A more technical name for reward is *reinforcement*.
Relief from pain is a reward. Drinking water when thirsty,
eating food when hungry, and relaxing when tired are other
examples of primary, or innate, rewards.

If rewards are thought of as events producing a reduction
in the drive, that is, in strength of stimulus, the relationship

between satiation and reward becomes clear. Since it is impossible further to reduce the strength of a drive stimulus which is already zero, reward is impossible in the absence of drive. Thus, gulping food is no reward to a satiated animal and may even become painful so that regurgitation is rewarding.

If rewards produce reductions in drive, then too rapid repetition inevitably leads to satiation of the drive, with the result that the rewards lose their rewarding value until the drive reappears. In the absence of reward, the acts which have led to a previously rewarding event tend to be weakened through extinction. Such weakening is one of the factors which eventually cause responses appropriate to a given drive to cease in the absence of that drive. Did rewards not tend to weaken drives, there would be no mechanism for causing the individual to stop one line of satisfying behavior and turn to another.

Though it is convenient to think of rewards as events producing reductions in the strength of the drive stimulus, it is not necessary to be able to identify the drive which is reduced and the manner in which it is reduced in order to be able to determine empirically that certain events are rewards under certain circumstances and to make practical use of this information. Once it has been discovered that a given event, such as receiving praise from the mother, can be used as a reward to strengthen a given stimulus-response connection, e.g., the connection between the cue of a drippy feeling in the nose and the response of blowing the nose, it can be assumed that this same event can be used as a reward to strengthen other stimulus-response connections. Here the drive is probably some form of anxiety or desire to please the mother, but it is not absolutely essential to be able to identify the drive in order to discover that praise is a reward.

Any event known to strengthen stimulus-response connections may be called a reward. The term "reward" will be used hereinafter to refer to drive reduction, to events (such as eating when hungry) from which drive reduction may be reliably predicted, to the object (such as food) producing the drive reduction, and to other events empirically found to have the effect of strengthening cue-response connections. In the last instance, the definition is not circular so long as the fact that the event was found to strengthen one connection is used to predict that it will strengthen others.

The mention of praise brings up the topic of acquired rewards or, as they may sometimes be called, *secondary rewards*. Just as it is possible for previously neutral stimulus situations to acquire drive value, so also is it possible for previously neutral stimulus situations to acquire reward value. Relief from anxiety is an acquired reward. Receiving money, social approval, and higher status are other events with acquired reward value. Acquired rewards are enormously important in social life.

Experimental evidence indicates that the acquired reward value of an object or event is based upon more primary, innate rewards. This is confirmed by cross-cultural data. In different cultures, different objects and events have widely differing degrees of acquired reward value. In our society, metal and paper are used for money, among the Kwoma, shells. More interesting is the fact that in our society money is the route to many primary rewards and is exceedingly important as a secondary reward, while among the Kwoma money is primarily of use only to maintain friendly (i.e., non-aggressive) kinship relations and is less important as a secondary reward.[4] Experimental evidence indicates that the acquired reward value of an object or event tends to become weakened, like any other learned response, unless it is itself supported occasionally by some innate reward. An inflation provides conditions under which money loses value, but the dependence of some of the other acquired rewards upon more primary rewards is difficult to trace through the intricate fabric of our society. The mechanism of acquired rewards will be discussed in somewhat more detail later.

The same object may serve as an incentive with acquired drive value in one situation and as a reward in another. Food

[4] These data on the Kwoma were called to the attention of the authors by Dr. John W. M. Whiting. See his *Becoming a Kwoma* (1941).

at a tantalizing distance may serve as an incentive to more vigorous responses, and food in the mouth as a reward strengthening those responses. Similarly, being promised money is an incentive and receiving money, a reward. The incentive value of the object is based upon the more primary reward function. Food at a tantalizing distance loses its incentive value if one is never able to eat it, and the promise of money loses its incentive value if one is never paid. Common speech uses reward in a broad sense to include incentives; we shall attempt to use it in the narrower sense of its primary function of directly strengthening cue-response connections.

A connection strengthened by a reward functions automatically; seeing a child run out in front of the car will cause an experienced driver, riding as a passenger in the front seat, to press on the floorboard. The response has been rewarded by escape from anxiety when his own car has stopped in the past; when the passenger sees the child, he now presses his foot down without pausing to think: "I should stop the car, and this will do it." Indeed, as soon as he has time to think, he knows that the response is useless in this situation.

Often in human behavior, the causal sequence is more complex. A thirsty person in a strange house may turn on the water in the faucet to the right and find that it gets warmer instead of colder. Because of past experience with similar situations, he is likely to say to himself, "Oh, in this house the faucet on the left must be the cold water," at the same time turning on the water in the left-hand faucet. As the water gets colder, he may say to himself, "It's funny that the faucet on the left is the cold water." Soon the water is cold enough. He drinks it, and his series of acts is capped with a reward. The next time he comes into the same kitchen, he will have a greater tendency to reach to the left than before, although it may not be strong enough to overcome the strong habit of reaching to the right. While reaching to the right, he may suddenly react with one of the verbal responses which he made and was rewarded for in the previous situation. As soon as he says, "The faucet on the left is the cold water," this operates as both an incentive and a cue to elicit the response of reaching to the left. In this case a statement, or thought, about the reward (cold water) has been an important determinant of his behavior; stated in nontechnical terms, the man turns to the faucet on the left after realizing that it contains the cold water.[5]

The mechanism described above is common in adult human behavior. Since statements or thoughts about rewards frequently occur in the course of overt behavior, there may be a tendency to think that rewards function primarily in this way and to neglect the more fundamental automatic strengthening of a connection upon which even this mechanism is based. That the strengthening of connections really is more fundamental becomes obvious as soon as the question arises: How do the external cues happen to elicit the thought of the reward as an internal stimulus, and how is this internal stimulus connected with the overt response? Such connections seem to follow exactly the same laws as any others: they are strengthened by reward and extinguished by non-reward. The individual has had to learn as a child to respond appropriately, first when someone else tells him that the reward is to the left, and then when he tells himself that it is there. He has also had to learn to say to himself, in this particular situation, that the cold water is on the left. If the water had not appeared as a reward, he would not have been so likely to respond again with the same statement. Even in cases in which the individual is responding to the "hope of reward," this is founded on *past* reward. If cold water actually does appear, it makes the whole response series more probable the *next* time.

Without reward, people fail to learn. For example, a certain boy never learned much about playing a piano because his mother failed to understand the importance of praise and escape from anxiety as necessary rewards in this situation. She sat at his side during practice. As soon as he finally hit the right note, she would say, "Now, can't you get the fingering correct?" As soon as he got the fingering correct, she

[5] Such behavior may correctly be said to involve *expectancy*. Similar types of examples will be analyzed in more detail in Chapters IV and V.

would say, "Now, can't you play a little faster?" As soon as he played a little faster, she would say, "But the expression is very poor." Thus no response except that of walking away from the piano at the end of the session was followed by a complete escape from the anxiety-provoking criticism. The boy was never allowed to bask in the relaxing sense of achievement and reduced anxiety that comes with praise or the cessation of criticism. Under these conditions, the one response which was significantly rewarded, to wit, walking away from the piano, became more and more dominant in the situation. The boy failed to learn and, as soon as he was able, escaped practicing altogether.

Part of the seeming mental inferiority of lower-class children at school may be traced to lack of reward. In the first place, the teachers are not so likely to pay attention to them, praise them, and confer little signs of status, such as special tasks, as they are to reward middle-class children in these ways. In the second place, these children have never experienced, or seen at close hand in the lives of relatives, those advantages of better jobs which are the rewards for educational merit, and they consequently see less promise of attaining such positions. The teacher is less likely to reward them, and their own training has invested the types of event which the teacher controls with less acquired reward value.[6]

As long as an individual is being rewarded for what he is doing, he will learn these particular responses more thoroughly, but he may not learn anything new by trial and error.[7] This is partly because the further strengthening of the dominant responses makes the occurrence of any new responses less likely, and partly because its rewards, if ample, will keep the drive at a low level. Thus, in order to get the individual to try a new response which it is desired that he learn, it is often necessary to place him in a situation where his old responses will not be rewarded. Such a situation may be called a *learning dilemma*. In the absence of a dilemma,

---

[6] For a more detailed description of these conditions, see Davis and Dollard (1940), Chap. XIII.

[7] His behavior may change through other mechanisms, however, such as that of the *anticipatory response*. This will be described later.

new learning of the trial-and-error type does not occur. For example, a mother was worried because her child seemed to be retarded in learning to talk. Brief questioning revealed that she was adept at understanding the child's every want as expressed by its gestures. Having other successful means of responding, the child was not in a dilemma. He only learned his old habits of using gestures more thoroughly and consequently did not perform that type of random vocal behavior which would lead to speech. By gradually pretending to become more stupid at understanding gestures, the mother put the child in a dilemma and probably facilitated the learning of speech. At least, under these modified conditions, this child rapidly learned to talk.

The absence of a dilemma is one of the reasons why it is often difficult to teach successful people new things. Old, heavily rewarded habits must be interrupted before new learning can occur. When the accustomed rewards are withdrawn by unusual circumstances such as revolution, new responses may occur and, if rewarded, may be learned; Russian counts *can* learn to drive taxicabs and countesses to become cooks.

Examples of seemingly incidental learning may appear to contradict the assertion that drive and reward are essential conditions of learning. It seems probable, however, that such examples are merely instances of faulty analysis of obscure conditions of acquired drive and acquired reward. An individual whose life history is rather well known to the authors shows almost no incidental learning during many trips from New Haven to New York in the cars of various friends. That he is not mentally deficient is demonstrated by the fact that he shows a good deal of incidental learning when walking through strange forests. He has never been punished for failing to note directions while driving with intelligent friends. But, for failing to note directions carefully enough in the woods, he has on earlier occasions suffered the fatigue of plowing through dense underbrush and crossing steep gullies, has been scratched by thorns, stung by hornets, and gone hungry. Finding the blazes of a trail has been followed by a reduction in the strength of a number of innate drives. As a result of these primary experiences, he now finds that he is slightly anxious whenever disoriented in the woods and that the response of rehearsing landmarks produces a rewarding reduction in this anxiety. Thus, what might be superficially taken to be an exception actually illustrates the importance of motivation and reward in human learning.[8,9]

Summary

Four factors are essential to learning. These are: drive, cue, response, and reward. The drive stimulus impels responses which are usually channelized by cues from other stimuli not strong enough to act as drives but more specifically distinctive than the drive. If the first response is not rewarded, this creates a dilemma in which the extinction of successive non-rewarded responses leads to so-called random behavior. If some one response is followed by reward, the con-

[8] Various assumptions of the authors concerning motivation and reward may now be evaluated. It seems almost certain that drives and rewards play an important rôle in the performance of learned responses. This general assumption is an indispensable part of the present exposition of social learning and imitation. Two more specific hypotheses seem quite probable: namely, that drives and rewards are essential to the occurrence of any learning, and that all drive reduction acts as a reward. Finally, and least certainly established, is the hypothesis that reduction in the strength of stimulation is the only source of reward. Because these hypotheses seem to the authors to be the best ones available, an attempt is made to apply them consistently throughout the book. Changes in these hypotheses would alter certain elements throughout the systematic structure of the argument advanced in this book. Most of the practical conclusions are so well founded on empirical fact that major alterations in them seem unlikely. No assumptions are made concerning the mechanism producing the correlation between reward and strength of connection.

[9] *Technical note:* Electrical recording of the responses of afferent nerves indicates that the sudden onset of a new stimulus produces at first a strong burst of impulses from the sense organ which rapidly diminishes in strength till a plateau of stimulation is reached (Adrian [1928], pp. 67, 116). This diminution is called adaptation. According to the principles which have been outlined, such a reduction in strength of stimulation should, if marked enough (as might be the case following the sudden onset of a relatively strong stimulus), act as a reward to any responses associated with it. Careful experiments may reveal that such a mechanism accounts for certain cases of learning which might superficially appear to be exceptions to a rigorous drive-reduction theory of reward.

nection between the stimulus pattern and this response is strengthened, so that the next time that the same drive and other cues are present, this response is more likely to occur. Since rewards presumably produce their effect by reducing the strength of the drive stimulus, events cannot be rewarding in the absence of an appropriate drive. After the drive has been satiated by sufficient reward, the tendency to make the rewarded response is weakened so that other responses occur until the drive reappears.

CHAPTER III

SIGNIFICANT DETAILS OF THE LEARNING PROCESS

PRINCIPLES governing significant aspects of the learning process have been formulated as a result of many careful experimental studies. The most important of these principles will be described briefly. For ease in reference, each principle will first be defined and then illustrated before its function is discussed. Since adequate summaries are available elsewhere,[1] no attempt will be made to describe the evidence supporting each of these principles.

Extinction

Reward is essential to the learning of a habit; it is also essential to the maintenance of a habit. When a learned response is repeated without reward, the strength of the tendency to perform that response undergoes a progressive decrease. This decrement is called *experimental extinction*, or, more simply, extinction.

When the little girl, looking for candy, picked up a book and did not find any candy under it, her tendency to pick up the same book again was reduced. In this case, previous training having already established a general habit of not looking in the same place twice in this kind of a situation, one performance of a non-rewarded response usually eliminated it for the rest of that trial. In the absence of previous training, the process of extinction is often much slower. A fisherman who has been rewarded by catching many fish in a certain creek may come back to that creek many times, but if these visits are never again rewarded by securing fish (as a sub-

---

[1] See Hull (1934a; 1941*), Hilgard and Marquis (1940), and their references. For more rigorous theoretical formulations, see Hull (1929; 1930a; 1932; 1939a).

goal with acquired reward value), his visits will gradually become less frequent and less enthusiastic.

The process of extinction should not be confused with forgetting. Forgetting occurs during an interval in which a response is not practiced. Extinction occurs when a response is practiced without reward.

If non-rewarded performances did not weaken the tendency to repeat a habit, maladaptive habits would persist indefinitely. The apparent function of extinction is to eliminate responses which do not lead to reward, so that other responses can occur. Thus, when the little girl did not find candy under the first book, she ceased looking under that book and went on to pick up other books. Non-rewarded responses occur when the innate hierarchy is not adapted to the conditions of the specific environment, when the conditions in the environment change so that a previously rewarded response no longer is adequate, or when a response has previously been rewarded by chance. The effects of extinction tend to correct the results of these conditions.

The process of extinction is usually not immediate but extends over a number of trials. The number of trials required for the complete extinction of a response varies with certain conditions.

Stronger habits are more resistant to extinction than weaker habits. Other things equal, any factor which will produce a stronger habit will increase its resistance to extinction. One such factor is a greater number of rewarded training trials. Thus, a storekeeper is more likely to give up trying to sell a new line of goods if he fails to make sales to a series of customers near the beginning of his experience with these goods than he is if he has the same streak of bad luck after having made many successful sales. Two additional factors producing a stronger habit and hence a greater resistance to extinction are: a stronger drive during training and a greater amount of reward per trial during training.

The resistance to extinction is also influenced by the conditions of extinction. Fewer trials are required to cause the subject to abandon a given response when the drive during extinction is weaker, when there is more effort involved in the responses being extinguished, when the interval between extinction trials is shorter, and when the alternative responses competing with the extinguished response are stronger.

Finally, the rapidity with which a response is abandoned can be influenced by habits established during previous experiences with non-reward in similar situations. Thus, for the child in the experiment with the books, not finding candy under an object was a cue which, during the child's previous life history, had always been associated with non-reward for the response of looking again under the same object during the same trial. Under different circumstances, a fisherman who happens to cast many times in the same pool and then is rewarded by catching a fish on a cast which follows the cue of a previously unsuccessful cast, can learn to try many casts in the same pool.

Acquired drives and acquired rewards are as subject to extinction as is any other form of habit.[2] A little girl acquired a great desire to see a certain guest during a period when he happened to bring the girl presents on his visits to the family. After a number of visits on which the guest did not bring her presents, her desire to see him waned. Similarly, the delicious aroma of foods can lose its ability to whet the appetite of professional cooks; and promises, if not at least sometimes fulfilled, can lose their acquired reward value.

Although the process of extinction may be slowed down by certain factors, all habits that have to date been carefully investigated in the laboratory have been found to be subject to extinction. Thus, there is reason to believe that seeming exceptions to extinction, such as the examples of so-called functional autonomy cited by G. W. Allport (1937, pp. 190–212), are either cases in which the habit has become so strong that evidence of extinction is hard to notice during the number of non-rewarded repetitions observed, or cases in which the habit is actually being supported periodically by unrecognized conditions of drive and reward. It seems inadvisable

[2] This assertion is based on data to be published by N. E. Miller from a series of experiments on acquired motivation and acquired reward.

to depend on the eternal persistence without reward of crucial responses from one's employer or one's wife.

Many facts about the details of the process of extinction have been demonstrated by careful experiments; its causes are less well understood. In the course of the present investigation, an analysis, which will be described in detail in Appendix 1, was made of the factors which tend to cause a child to stop crying. This analysis suggests that extinction does not constitute a new principle, but is the result rather of conditions favoring the reward of responses which are incompatible with the response being extinguished.[3]

Crying loudly for a period of time produces strong stimulation from tenseness in the throat, soreness of the throat, and fatigue. The stopping of crying is followed by reduction in the strength of these stimuli. In this way the responses involved in stopping crying are rewarded. With these responses rewarded every time the infant stops, they will gain in dominance unless the effects of this reward are offset by greater rewards for the response of crying. Thus, unless crying is rewarded, the tendency to cry will be progressively weakened by competition with the tendency to stop crying.

In a similar manner, other responses involve an increase in stimulation from muscle tension and fatigue. Stopping these responses produces a reduction in the strength of this stimulation. Thus muscle strain and fatigue are drives constantly motivating the subject to stop the response he is making; escape from muscle strain and fatigue are ever present to reward stopping. Extinction occurs unless the effects of the drive of fatigue and consequent reward for stopping are overridden by the effects of other stronger drives and rewards. But fatigue, even though overridden by the effects of stronger drives and rewards, will continue to mount during a long series of trials. Thus the motivation to perform the re-

[3] Guthrie (1940) and Wendt (1936) have maintained that extinction may be a process of learning responses incompatible with the original response. But they have not suggested any way in which such incompatible responses could be rewarded.

sponse may be weakened somewhat by increasing competition with fatigue. Experimental evidence indicates that, exactly as would be expected on the basis of this hypothesis, a long series of trials, even though rewarded, may have a transitory effect resembling weak extinction. Pavlov has recognized this phenomenon, which is called "inhibition of reinforcement."[4]

As the strength of the stimulation associated with the response increases, extinction shades over by imperceptible degrees into punishment. As a person continues eating, eventually the hunger drive is reduced to zero. Beyond this point the drive can be reduced no further, and reinforcement ceases. For a while escape from fatigue lurks as a minor reward for stopping the effort involved in eating. Eventually, however, a much stronger drive and reward enter the scene. Stomach distention becomes painful. This pain is reduced by responses of reverse peristalsis, such as belching. The reduction of pain rewards these responses and strengthens their connection to the cue of a full stomach. But even incipient reverse peristalsis tends to be incompatible with the response of eating. Thus, the subject learns to stop eating.[5]

The stronger drive, and hence greater escape-reward, which may be secured through relatively strong punishments produces a more rapid and permanent abandonment of a response than do the weaker and more diffuse rewards presumably involved in extinction. More definite overt evidence of conflict is also usually observed.

[4] *Technical note:* In the case of glandular responses, such as salivation, the source of stimulation which is present when the response is made and reduced when the response is stopped is more difficult to discover. This, of course, does not mean that it is necessarily absent.

It may be that "escape from the stimulation of fatigue" is only one of the factors which may reward extinction. Another similar factor could be "escape from the stimulation produced by conflict." In the case of extinguishing a rat's habit of running down an alley for food by removing the food as a reward, the conflict would be between the responses of eating and those elicited by the sight of the empty food dish. See Miller and Stevenson (1936).

[5] The behavior of infants definitely indicates that the response of stopping eating when the stomach is full must be learned. These observations are confirmed by unpublished experimental results secured by students working with Miller.

In conclusion, mere repetition does not strengthen a habit. Instead, non-rewarded repetitions progressively weaken the strength of the tendency to perform a habit.[6] Usually the tendency to perform a habit does not disappear immediately. The number of trials required for extinction depends on the strength of the habit, on the particular conditions of extinction, and on past experience with non-rewarded trials. Extinction may be caused by the fact that escape from the stimulation of muscle tension and fatigue rewards stopping. Definite punishment can eliminate a habit more quickly than can mere non-reward. The fact of extinction emphasizes the importance of reward.

Spontaneous Recovery

The effects of extinction tend to disappear with the passage of time. After a series of unsuccessful expeditions, a fisherman may have abandoned the idea of making any further trips to a particular stream. As time goes on, his tendency to try that stream again gradually recovers from the effects of extinction, so that next month or next year he may take another chance. This tendency for an extinguished habit to reappear after an interval of time during which no non-rewarded trials occur is called *spontaneous recovery*.

The fact of recovery demonstrates that extinction does not destroy the old habit, but merely inhibits it. With the passage of time, the strength of the inhibiting factors produced during extinction is weakened more rapidly than the strength of the original tendency to perform the habit. In this man-

---

[6] This fact argues strongly against the position held by the old associationists which would seem to demand that every repetition of an association between a stimulus and response, whether rewarded or not rewarded, should strengthen that association. Guthrie (1935) attempts to escape this dilemma in a very ingenious application of the principles of association to the problems of motivation and reward. To date, his statements of assumptions and deductions of consequences have not been systematic enough for us to convince ourselves of either the soundness or unsoundness of his position. If Guthrie's principles should be adequate, they would not contradict the importance we have ascribed to rewards, but rather explain it in terms of more fundamental principles.

ner, a net gain is produced in the strength of the tendency to perform the habit.

Many carefully controlled experiments have demonstrated that a certain amount of spontaneous recovery is a regular characteristic of extinguished habits. After enough repeated extinctions, however, the habit may become so completely inhibited that it shows little tendency to reappear. Habits which have been disrupted by punishment are much less subject to recovery than habits which have been disrupted by extinction.

Spontaneous recovery follows as a natural deduction from the hypothesis that extinction is the product of stimulation from fatigue. According to this hypothesis, the performance of the response to be extinguished produces increased stimulation from fatigue. Stopping the response is followed by a rewarding reduction in this stimulation. Thus is built up a habit of responding to the fatigue and accompanying cues by stopping. With the passage of time, however, the fatigue will disappear as one of the cues eliciting the responses involved in stopping, and these will consequently be weakened. Released from competition with stopping, the extinguished response will be relatively strengthened, i.e., will recover. If stopping has been rewarded strongly and often enough, however, the other cues in the situation may elicit so strong a tendency to stop that recovery from extinction will not be complete.

Even if the hypothesis advanced above to explain extinction and recovery in terms of more basic principles should turn out to be incomplete or false, the facts of extinction and recovery remain and play important rôles in the learning process. The function of extinction is to force the subject to try new responses. If any of these responses are rewarded, they will be strengthened to the point where their competition may permanently eliminate the old habit. If none of these new responses is rewarded, however, their extinction plus the recovery of the old response will induce the subject to try the old response again. Recovery is adaptive in those situations in which the absence of reward is only temporary.

44 *Social Learning and Imitation*

Generalization

The effects of learning in one situation transfer to other situations; the less similar the situation, the less transfer occurs. Stated more exactly, reward for making a specific response to a given pattern of cues strengthens not only the tendency for that pattern of cues to elicit that response, but also the tendency for other similar patterns of cues to elicit the same response. The innate tendency for this to occur is called *innate stimulus generalization.*[7] The less similar the cue or pattern of cues, the less the generalization. This is referred to as a *gradient of generalization.*

No two situations are ever completely the same. In the experiment with the little girl, for example, the books were put back into the bookcase in slightly different patterns of unevenness on different trials, and the girl approached the bookcase from different angles. In many other types of learning situations, the variability of the correct cues is considerably greater than in this experiment. Therefore, if the response were completely specific to the pattern of cues associated with its reward, learning would be impossible, for the specific pattern of cues would never repeat itself in exact detail. If the cues eliciting the response were completely generalized, on the other hand, it would also be impossible to learn; the girl could never learn to select a specific book because she would have an equally strong tendency to pick up each of the other books. This dilemma is partially resolved by an innate gradient of generalization, so that there is a stronger tendency to respond to cues in proportion to their similarity to those present in preceding situations in which the response was rewarded. As a solution to this dilemma, the gradient of generalization is supplemented by the process of discrimination and by the mechanism of the acquired equivalence of cues. These will be discussed later.

Examples of generalization are common in everyday experience. A child bitten by one dog is afraid of other animals and more afraid of other dogs than of cats and horses. Na-

[7] Acquired, or secondary, generalization is discussed in Chapter V.

tives who have learned to escape punishment by concealing facts from white administrators or missionaries tend to transfer these habits to the anthropologists they meet in the field.

The phenomena of generalization have been studied in detail by Pavlov (1927), Bekhterev (1932), and a host of other subsequent experimenters. Generalization can occur either on the basis of the qualitative similarity of the cues involved, or on the basis of identical elements in the two situations. Perhaps ultimately these are reducible to the same thing.

The gradient of generalization refers to the qualitative differences or cue aspect of stimuli. The *distinctiveness* of a cue is measured by its dissimilarity from other cues in the same situation, so that little generalization occurs from the cue in question to other cues in the situation. Thus the distinctiveness of a cue varies with the other cues that are present. A red book in a row of black books is a more distinctive cue than is the same volume in a row of other red books, because less generalization occurs from red to black than from one shade of red to another.

Once a response has been rewarded in one situation, the function of generalization is to increase the probability that the response will be tried in other like situations. For example, after the response of stopping at a tourist cabin near one town has been rewarded by an exceptionally good, quiet, cheap night's rest, generalization will increase the probability that the individual will try stopping at similar tourist cabins near other towns. If a generalized response is rewarded in the new, but similar, situations, the tendency to perform that response in these situations will be further strengthened.

Discrimination

If a generalized response is not rewarded, the tendency to perform that response is weakened. By the reward of the response to one pattern of cues and the non-reward or punishment of the response to a somewhat different pattern of cues, a *discrimination* may gradually be established. The process of discrimination tends to correct maladaptive generalizations. It increases the specificity of the cue-response connection.

By being rewarded for stopping at tourist cabins in the
West and non-rewarded for stopping at tourist cabins in the
East, a person may gradually learn to discriminate between
the two situations on the basis of the geographical cue. But
the process of learning to discriminate is complicated by the
fact that the effects of extinction also generalize. Thus, after
being non-rewarded for stopping at a series of tourist cabins
in the East, our heroes of the highway may be reluctant to
stop at tourist cabins in the West.

The less different the cues in the two situations, the more
generalization will be expected to occur, and hence the more
difficult it will be to learn discrimination. If the cues are too
similar, so much of the effects of reward may generalize from
the rewarded cue to the non-rewarded one and so much of the
effects of extinction may generalize from the non-rewarded
cue to the rewarded one, that it will be impossible to learn a
discrimination.

Gradient in the Effects of Reward

Delayed rewards are less effective than immediate rewards.
In other words, if a number of different responses are made
to a cue and the last of these responses is followed by reward,
the connection to the last response will be strengthened the
most, and the connection to each of the preceding responses
will be strengthened by a progressively smaller amount. Similarly, if a series of responses is made to a series of cues, as
when a hungry boy takes off his hat in the hall, dashes
through the dining room into the kitchen, opens the icebox,
and takes a bite to eat, the connections more remote from the
reward are strengthened less than those closer to the reward.
In this series, the connection between the sight of the hall
closet and the respónse of hanging up the hat will be
strengthened less than the connection between the sight of the
icebox door and the response of opening it.

In the experiment performed on the little girl, it was necessary for her to make the response of approaching the bookcase as well as to make the response of selecting a specific
book. If the effects of reward were completely specific to the

final response performed, picking up the correct book, she would not learn to approach the bookcase and hence would not find the candy. On the other hand, if the effects of reward were completely general, the response of taking out the wrong book would be strengthened just as much as would the response of taking out the correct book, and learning would be impossible. This dilemma is resolved by the *gradient of reward*.[8] The connection between the cue of the sight of the bookcase at a distance and the response of going toward the bookcase is sufficiently strengthened by each reward to cause the little girl to run toward the bookcase faster and more eagerly on successive trials. But the response of picking out the correct book is strengthened more by the reward than are the earlier responses of picking out the wrong books. Thus the response of selecting the correct book eventually crowds out the responses of picking out the preceding wrong books, and the sequence of behavior is shortened. Since it is physically impossible for the girl to take a book from the bookcase before she arrives there, the responses of taking out a book do not crowd out those of running to the bookcase.

The gradient of reward accounts for an increase in tendency to respond, the nearer the goal is approached. Because cue-response connections near the reward are strengthened more than connections remote from the reward, a hungry man on his way to dinner has a tendency to quicken his pace in rounding the last corner on the way home.

The gradient of reward also explains why, after both a longer and a shorter route to the goal have been tried, the shorter route tends to be preferred. A thirsty child learns to secure water from drinking fountains in the park. Approach to a fountain seen nearby is usually followed more immediately by the rewarding goal response of drinking than is approach to a fountain seen at a distance. Thus during a series of trials in which both fountains are approached, the connection between the cue of seeing the near fountain and the response of approaching that fountain is the more firmly

[8] The gradient of reward is what Hull originally called the goal gradient (1932; 1934c).

established. The response with the stronger connections
crowds out the weaker connection; approaching the near
fountain becomes dominant in the hierarchy. Similarly, a
child will learn to approach that one of two equally distant
fountains where fewer people are waiting in line for a drink.

With human subjects who have had the proper social training, symbolic stimuli that have acquired a rewarding value
are often used to bridge the gap between the performance of
an act and the occurrence of an innate reward. Money or
even the thought of making money can be immediately associated with the performance of a task; after an interval, the
money can be immediately associated with some primary reward, such as eating. In this way, the decrement which would
be expected on the basis of the gradient of reward is markedly lessened. Similarly, a parent punishing a child is likely
to attempt to eliminate the effects of the time gap between
stealing and punishment by a verbal rehearsal of the circumstances of the crime. As would be expected, younger children
who have had less training in responding to symbolic stimuli
are less affected by such a procedure and hence more influenced by immediacy of reward. Similarly, lower-class individuals who have not been taught to save—that is, have had
less opportunity of having the presence of a bank balance immediately associated with primary rewards—are more influenced by immediacy of reward. But even in the cases in which
well-established habits of responding to symbolic stimuli help
to bridge the gap between the response to a cue and the reward of that response, the gradient of reward is not completely masked; more immediate rewards are regularly more
effective than more remote ones.

In summary, the effects of reward are not limited to the
particular cue-response sequence which is immediately associated with reward but also strengthen other cue-response
connections less immediately associated with reward. This
spread of the effects of reward has the function of strengthening the connections to responses comprising the first steps
of the sequence leading to reward. It can be greatly facilitated if certain stimuli involved in the sequence acquire a sub-

goal, or secondary rewarding value, by repeated association with the primary reward. Nevertheless, the effects of reward taper off in a gradient, so that the connections immediately associated with the reward are strengthened more than remoter connections. This gradient of reward has the function of tending to force the subject to choose the shortest of alternative paths to a goal and to eliminate unnecessary responses from a sequence.

Anticipatory Response

From the principle of the gradient of reward and from that of generalization, an additional principle can be deduced: namely, that responses near the point of reward tend wherever physically possible to occur before their original time in the response series, that is, to become anticipatory. When the little girl was looking for candy, the response of selecting the correct book moved forward in the series and crowded out the originally prior response of selecting the wrong book. Since the same cue, the bookcase within reach, elicits both responses, it was not necessary for generalization to occur. But the cues from the bookcase were fairly similar at different distances—when it was just beyond reach and when the girl was removing one of the books. Thus, the girl tended to start reaching before she actually arrived at the bookcase. This tendency for responses to occur before their original point in the rewarded series is an exceedingly important aspect of behavior.[9] Under many circumstances, it is responsible for the crowding out of useless acts in the response sequence; under other circumstances, it produces anticipatory errors. As will be noted in Chapters IV and V, anticipatory responses may produce stimuli playing an important rôle in acquired motivation and in reasoning and foresight. At present, the simpler dynamics of anticipatory response will be illustrated.

A child touches a hot radiator. The pain elicits an avoidance response, and the escape from pain rewards this re-

[9] The functional significance of anticipatory responses has been pointed out by Hull (1929; 1930b; 1931).

sponse. Since the sight and muscular feel of the hand approaching the radiator are similar in certain respects to the sight and muscular feel of the hand touching the radiator, the strongly rewarded response of withdrawal will be expected to generalize from the latter situation to the former. After one or more trials, the child will reach out his hand toward the radiator and then withdraw it before touching the radiator. The withdrawal response will become anticipatory; it will occur before that of actually touching the radiator. This is obviously adaptive, since it enables the child to avoid getting burned.

A person at a restaurant orders a delicious steak, sees it, and then eats it. The taste of the steak elicits and rewards salivation. On subsequent occasions, the sight of the steak or even its ordering may elicit salivation before the food has actually entered the mouth.

A person sees a green persimmon, picks it up, and bites into it. The astringent taste evokes the response of puckering the lips and spitting out the fruit. This response is rewarded by a decrease in the extreme bitterness of the taste. Upon subsequent occasions, puckering of the lips and incipient spitting responses are likely to have moved forward in the sequence so that they now occur to the cue of seeing a green persimmon instead of to the cue of tasting it.

In the foregoing examples, the anticipatory aspect of the learned responses was adaptive. The tendency for responses to move forward in a sequence, however, does not depend upon the subject's insight into the adaptive value of the mechanism. That the principle of anticipation functions in a more primitive way than this is indicated most clearly by examples in which it functions in a maladaptive manner.

A rifleman pulls the trigger of his gun and then hears a loud report which elicits blinking of the eyes and a startle response by the whole body. The end of the loud stimulus is closely associated with these responses and has a rewarding effect.[10] On subsequent occasions, the cues involved in press-

[10] This rewarding effect of the termination of the sound is clearer in cases where sounds of this loudness persist longer. Then the individual may try a

ing the trigger tend to elicit the blinking and the startle. These anticipatory responses are likely to occur before the gun is actually fired and to cause the bullet to swerve from its mark. This tendency is maladaptive, but, as all marksmen know, is so strong that it can be inhibited only with difficulty. In this example, it should be noticed that the cues which touch off the anticipatory response are proprioceptive ones which the subject receives as a part of the act of tensing his muscles to pull the trigger. Thus, the maladaptive startle can be eliminated readily if the subject squeezes the trigger so gradually that no specific cues precede the explosion in a regularly predictable manner. That such a practice has been found desirable is a tribute to the strength and the involuntariness of the tendency for responses to become anticipatory.

A small boy comes home at night hungry from play. He cleans his shoes on the doormat, comes in, passes the door of the dining room, where he can see food on the table, hangs his hat carefully on the hook, goes upstairs, straightens his tie, brushes his hair, washes his face and hands, comes downstairs to the dining room, sits down, waits for grace to be said, and then asks, "May I have some meat and potatoes, please?" Eating the food is the rewarding goal response to this long series of activities. On subsequent occasions, there will be a strong tendency for responses in this sequence to become anticipatory. He will tend to open the door without stopping to clean off his shoes, and to turn directly into the dining room without stopping to hang up his hat or to go through the remainder of the sequence. These acts will be likely to crowd out other preceding responses in the series because the connections to these acts have been strengthened relatively more by being nearer to the point of reward. If he secures food, the anticipatory responses will be still more strongly rewarded and will be more likely to occur on subsequent occasions. The response sequence will be short-circuited. In this way, the principle of anticipation often leads to the adaptive elimination of useless acts from a response sequence.

number of different responses and be more likely to repeat on subsequent occasions those which were more closely associated with the escape from the sound than those which were less closely associated with the escape.

If the response of turning directly into the dining room without stopping to remove the hat and clean up is not followed by food, however, it will tend to be extinguished as a response to cues at this inappropriate point in the series. A discrimination may eventually be established. Similarly, the acts of washing, brushing the hair, waiting quietly during grace, and saying "please" will tend to be abbreviated and crowded out by competition with anticipatory responses unless the latter are either punished or continuously extinguished. Those short-cuts which are physically and socially possible will be strengthened by more immediate rewards; others will be punished or extinguished. Thus behavior tends gradually to approximate the shortest, most efficient possible sequence.

Like all other discriminations, the type which results in the elimination of a non-rewarded anticipatory response from a sequence becomes easier as the cues to be discriminated become more distinctive. According to the principle of generalization, anticipatory responses are more likely to occur the more similar the cues in the different parts of the sequence. Thus, the boy is most likely to make an anticipatory entry when passing the dining room door if his hands happen to be relatively clean and his hair well brushed. If the cues are too similar, anticipatory errors will regularly be expected to intrude.

Anticipatory responses may play an important rôle in communication between people by providing significant stimuli to other persons. An infant not yet old enough to talk was accustomed to being lifted up into its mother's arms. Because often followed by innate rewards, being in the mother's arms had achieved an acquired reward value. As a part of the response of being picked up, the infant learned to stand up on his toes, spread his arms, arch his back in a characteristic way. Subsequently, when the child wanted to be picked up, this response moved forward in a series; the infant performed in an anticipatory manner as much as possible of his part of the sub-goal response. He stood on his toes, spread his arms, and threw his head and shoulders back. He could not, how-

ever, bend his knees, which would have been a part of the
next response, because this would have conflicted with the activity of standing. Since his parents rewarded this gesture by
picking him up, he used it more and more often.

All of the stages in the evolution of a gesture have been observed in pairs of albino rats. The hungry animals are placed
in a cage in which there is a single, small dish of powdered
food. The first rat discovers the food and commences to eat.
The second rat comes over, notices the food, braces himself,
and violently bats the first rat out of the way. To the strong
stimulus of receiving the blow, the first rat withdraws and is
rewarded for this withdrawal by escaping from the blow.
After a number of such episodes, the response of withdrawing becomes anticipatory so that it occurs at the sight of the
second animal's starting his blow. As this procedure is repeated, the second rat's response of returning to his food becomes more and more anticipatory, so that the sweep of his
paws in batting at the first animal is progressively shortened.
Eventually the whole process is reduced to a mere gesture.
The second rat raises his paw, the first retreats from the food,
and the second goes directly to the food without attempting
to strike a full blow. The tendency for the responses of both
rats to become anticipatory has caused a gesture to be substituted for a fight.

A similar type of communication by means of involuntary
anticipatory responses occurs when an athlete unwittingly
"telegraphs" his punches or points his play. The clever opponent learns to observe such gestures and respond appropriately. The rôle of anticipatory responses as a means of
communication is enormously elaborated by the conditions of
social life.

CHAPTER IV

A BASIS FOR ACQUIRED DRIVES AND ACQUIRED REWARDS

RESPONSES can not only produce stimuli to which others react, but can also produce stimuli to which the subject himself reacts. These stimuli function in exactly the same way as other stimuli; if they are strong, they have drive value; if they are distinctive, they have cue value. There is reason to believe that the drive value of self-induced stimuli is the basis of acquired drives, acquired rewards, and purposes, and that the cue value of these stimuli is the basis of foresight and reasoning. Language, which plays such an enormously important rôle in human behavior, is an elaborate system of responses producing stimuli which act as cues.

The principles discussed in preceding chapters are all backed by many careful experimental studies. Unfortunately, the dynamics of stimulus-producing responses is only beginning to be thoroughly investigated. Hence, the principles to be presented in this chapter and the following one will be more tentative and subject to revision than those previously explained. Because the problems to be dealt with are of extreme importance in understanding social behavior, it will be necessary to step boldly out into this less safely mapped territory, following what seem to be the best hypotheses that can be ventured at this time. It will be strange if further attempts to use and test these hypotheses do not demonstrate that they need correction on at least certain points. A general statement having been made as to the tentative nature of the material of the next two chapters, further qualifications will be omitted in the interest of a clearer and simpler exposition.

The stimuli which are produced by the subject's own responses have exactly the same properties as any other stimuli. Strong stimuli have drive value, and a reduction in their strength acts as a reward. To the extent that these stimuli are distinctive, they have cue value. The same stimulus may be both strong and distinctive and hence may act as both drive and cue. The drive functions of strong response-produced stimuli and the reward functions of a reduction in the strength of these stimuli will be discussed in this chapter, and the cue function of distinctive response-produced stimuli will be discussed in the next chapter.

In an explanation of the mechanism of extinction, use has already been made of the stimulation from the fatigue and muscle tension which responses may produce. Stimuli from fatigue may have a drive value; escape from such stimulation may have a reward value. Thus there is a motivation to stop arduous work and a reward for relaxation.

It is probable that all responses produce fatigue, which upon occasion can become an intense stimulus. Specific responses can produce other forms of strong stimulation. In some very simple examples, the responses are overt and directly observable. Pinching oneself or biting one's tongue or cheek are examples of such responses which can produce stimuli strong enough to have painful drive value. The drive-producing effects of these particular responses are ordinarily not of great social significance, although some of them are occasionally used by an earnest student desiring to keep awake at a dull lecture.

Extreme tensing of the whole body may produce stimuli strong enough to have drive value; relaxing may eliminate these stimuli and have reward value. Most of the responses which are the basis of socially significant acquired drives and acquired rewards are internal responses not so readily subject to direct observation. Reverse peristalsis is one such response. It produces strong stimuli which are at least an important component of the drive or emotion of disgust. The history of nausea as an acquired drive based on reverse peristalsis may be analyzed in detail. The original stimulus might be the sight of a boat, plus persistent middle-ear stimulation produced by the rocking of a boat, plus a full stomach. The effects of the rocking on the middle ear and the full stomach produce a variety of strong sensations which act as a primary drive. Successful regurgitation reduces the strength of these stimuli and rewards the response of reverse peristalsis. After a number of severe experiences, the response may be strongly connected with all of the cues in the pattern. Thus, by generalization, even the stimuli of getting aboard a ship in a calm harbor may evoke a tendency toward reverse peristalsis.

The stimulation of being on the deck of a ship in the calm of a harbor is weak and thus has almost no drive value by itself. Since it is distinctive, however, it does have cue value. After the subject's experience with stormy weather, the pattern of cues presented by the ship acquires the tendency to elicit a response, reverse peristalsis, which produces a strong stimulation, nausea. The subject has learned to feel very uncomfortable in the presence of cues which were previously neutral.

This acquired drive is learned, but it may also serve as the basis for further learning. The subject is driven to restlessness whenever aboard a ship. If he walks down the gangplank and away from the ship, most of the cues eliciting the response of reverse peristalsis disappear, and so the response and the strong stimulation which it produces tend to cease. This rewards the subject for walking away from the ship. Thus he may learn a new habit: avoiding ships even in calm harbors.

Through a similar process of learning, the sight of food which has previously made one sick can acquire drive value so that the subject may learn to avoid places where he is confronted with this food. Escape from the strong stimuli produced by reverse peristalsis is the reward in such learning.

In the above discussion, the drive value of the stimuli produced by reverse peristalsis has been emphasized. Like other strong stimuli, however, response-produced stimuli can act not only as drives but also as cues. Thus, the feeling of nausea may be not only the drive which impels a person to take a walk in the cool air, but also the cue which elicits the response of walking rather than eating.

That appetite can be acquired and can increase the drive value of weak hunger is definitely established. It might be suggested that the hunger cramps themselves are responses subject to learning and hence probable sources of acquired appetite. Unfortunately, Carlson's (1919, p. 151) data fail to confirm the hypothesis that hunger cramps are subject to learning.[1] Thus it cannot yet be said that we know what responses produce the stimuli involved in various appetites for food. That appetites can be acquired and can serve as drives motivating further learning, and that the acquisition and extinction of appetites follows the same laws as other habits, appear to be established.[2]

If a subject with his appetite whetted turns away from the delicious aroma of food, he may escape a certain amount of increased stimulation produced by the responses elicited by the aroma, but the hunger persists. If he turns toward the food and eats it, he allays both the appetite and the hunger. Thus, although disgust and appetite are both acquired drives, the subject will learn to get disgusting food out of his sight and appetizing food into his mouth.

The rôle of response-produced stimuli in producing acquirable[3] drives may further be illustrated by the analysis of

[1] That hunger cramps are a derived source of hunger rather than a primary source is suggested, however, by the fact that dogs with a vitamin B deficiency may stop eating several days before the hunger cramps cease and, if injected with vitamin B, will resume eating several days before the hunger cramps resume (Cowgill, *et al.*, 1926; Rose, *et al.*, 1929–30). A definite answer to the question of what rôle hunger cramps play in producing the hunger drive and whether they may be subject to learning when tests are conducted under circumstances different from those used by Carlson cannot be given at present.

[2] For a preliminary report of experiments on acquired drives see Miller (1941a).

[3] Since the fact that responses such as reverse peristalsis produce strong stimulation is a function of the structure of the body, the mechanism of the drive itself is *innate;* it is the capacity of a previously neutral cue to set this mechanism into motion which is acquired. Thus these drives might be referred to more accurately (but less gracefully) as acquirable instead of acquired drives. Acquirable drives can be connected to cues according to the principles of learning; primary drives cannot.

an example involving anxiety. A child is led to the dentist's for the first time. On his way in, the stimuli in the outer office and in the inner office are relatively weak and function merely as cues with little drive value. After he gets settled on the chair and the dentist starts drilling, the child suddenly receives a jab of pain. This strong primary drive elicits a number of responses, some of which might serve directly to get the child out of the dentist's chair. Others function indirectly by preparing the body for greater action and by producing strong stimulation which can function as an acquirable drive, namely, that commonly called fear or anxiety. In the pattern of fear responses, the child's hair tends to stand on end, perspiration to ooze out of the skin, muscles to tense, the heart to beat faster, adrenalin to be poured into the blood, and vessels in the stomach to constrict, forcing out the blood. These responses produce a complex of strong stimuli. The child feels goose pimples on his skin, feels tenseness in the skeletal muscles, has a strong, stirred-up, taut feeling in the pit of his stomach. These strong fear stimuli summate with the pain to further motivate the child to get out of the chair.

When eventually the dentist stops drilling for a moment and the pain is markedly reduced, all responses occurring at this time are rewarded. This means that the next time the child is hurt, he will be more likely to wince, to cry, or to make whatever overt response was occurring at the time when the pain was relieved. Similarly, the child will be more likely to react with the internal responses producing the anxiety stimulus. At the moment, these responses of crying and anxiety will be weakened because of the disappearance of pain as a drive and cue. But the next time he is brought into the same situation, the child will be more likely to cry and be afraid.[4]

----

[4] This process is complicated by the fact that the act of relaxing the anxiety responses is coincident with the end of the anxiety stimulus and hence rewarded by the cessation of anxiety. This relaxation may eventually move forward in the series and become an anticipatory response to cues indicating that the end of pain is near, thus reducing anxiety at this point. In this manner a sophisticated subject can come to experience much less anxiety at the prospect of short than long duration of pain. For a more detailed discussion of a similar sequence see Appendix 1.

By the process of generalization, the cues associated with pain become capable of eliciting not only crying and wincing but also the other responses producing the anxiety stimulus. Anxiety occurs as an anticipatory response.

The anxiety reactions learned as responses to the cues arising in the dentist's office may produce stimuli strong enough to motivate further learning. The child may be thrown into trial-and-error behavior in the dentist's office even when not being hurt. If one of his responses succeeds in removing him from the dentist's office, this response will remove the cues eliciting the anxiety-producing responses and hence will be rewarded by a reduction in the strength of the anxiety stimulus. The child may thus learn to avoid everything associated with the dentist's office.

In order to simplify the discussion, only peripheral stimulus-producing responses have been considered in this analysis. The child learns to respond to the sight of a dentist's chair with a slight bristling of the hair on his back which gives him the feeling of goose pimples. In the case of fear, physiological evidence seems to indicate that an important part of the response-produced stimulation[5] may originate not in the periphery but within the central nervous system. The child may also learn to respond to the sight of the dentist's chair with a reaction of the thalamus, which sends strong impulses back up to stimulate another part of the brain, the

[5] *Technical note:* It is obvious that "response," as here used, is not restricted to the conventional usage, in which a response is defined as a muscular contraction or a glandular secretion. It is also obvious that "stimulation" is not restricted to the conventional usage, in which a stimulus is defined as an energy change activating receptors. According to the present usage, a response is any activity within the individual which can become functionally connected with an antecedent event through learning; a stimulus is any event to which a response can be so connected. This definition is not circular for cases in which the events referred to have been empirically identified. Thus "sitting up" in dogs is known to be a response because it can be functionally connected by reward with the antecedent command, "Sit up!"; the command is thereby known to be a stimulus. Stimulus *A* may be used to determine that *1, 2, 3,* and *4* are responses; response *1* may be used to determine that *a, b, c, d* are stimuli. Then a prediction may be made that the connections *b-2, c-3, d-4*, etc., are learnable.

cortex.[6] As long as the thalamic response is learned according
to the same principles of learning as other habits and produces impulses which travel back to sensory areas, the fact
that it is central rather than peripheral is of anatomical
rather than psychological importance. The relevant point is
that a danger cue which is a weak stimulus has acquired the
ability to elicit responses which produce strong stimuli. These
stimuli act as an acquired drive, anxiety, and a reduction in
them has a rewarding effect.

Any cue that acquires the ability to elicit the anxiety or
fear responses and hence to produce the anxiety stimuli acquires drive value. Conversely, any cue that acquires the ability to stop the fear responses and hence to reduce the fear
stimuli acquires reward value for the frightened individual.
According to the conditions of past experience, cues for
heightened anxiety may be a large adversary, a terrified
friend, being cornered, the failure of avoidance responses to
produce the usual results, and other forms of helplessness.
Stimuli with anxiety-reducing value may include seeing
powerful friends appear, feeling one's finger on the trigger
of a gun, feeling oneself run very fast, and stimuli from
other forms of action which in the past have been associated
with escape.[7]

6 In the case of a peripheral response, the supposed anatomical path is
from eye to cortex (where learned connections have been made) to skin,
where the response of a muscle stimulates a sense organ, which sends impulses back to a sensory area of the cortex. In the case of a central response, the supposed pathway is from eye to cortex (where learned connections have been made) to thalamus, where nerve cells are stimulated, which
send impulses back up to a sensory area of the cortex. For a more detailed
description of the physiological mechanism referred to, see Bard (1934),
Cannon (1929), and their references. Note that the thalamus is supposedly
stimulated in this case by being released from inhibition.

7 According to this hypothesis, it is the past association of various forms
of action with the rewarding internal relaxation of successful escape that
gives many forms of action most of their anxiety-relieving ability. In Pavlovian terms, the stimuli produced by action serve as conditioned inhibitors to
the anxiety responses. In some cases, very vigorous action may produce relief by also distracting attention from the danger cues. This view contrasts
sharply with Mowrer's (1941) hypothesis that anxiety is a discrepancy between preparation for action and action and hence is automatically dissi-
pated by the occurrence of the act prepared for. The authors agree, how-

The stimuli produced by the anxiety responses can serve not only as drives but also as cues. After the individual has learned to escape from many different painful and anxious situations by stopping and withdrawing, the anxiety stimulus may become a cue for stopping and reversing whatever response is in progress. After this has been learned, any cues arousing anxiety would be expected to tend to elicit stopping and retreating, even though the subject had not had a chance to stop or retreat in the original painful situation responsible for connecting the anxiety to those cues. Punishment often functions indirectly in this way. Anxiety is attached to the punished act, either directly or through symbolic rehearsal of the act while punishment is being administered. Later this anxiety serves as a cue to elicit stopping the act. After the act is abandoned, reduction in anxiety serves as a reward.

Anxiety is one of the innate responses to pain. The physiological reactions producing the sensation of anxiety can easily be learned as responses to new situations, while those producing the original pain cannot. Therefore the anxiety is referred to as an acquirable drive and the pain as a primary drive.

Anger is another of the acquirable drives. Evidence from newborn children and from the behavior of decorticate animals seems to indicate that an already patterned response of anger and potential aggression exists as one of the learnable responses in the innate hierarchy. One part of this reaction consists of very vigorous external responses, such as the pattern of threshing, striking, and clawing exhibited in a severe temper tantrum. Another part of this pattern consists of various internal responses which prepare the body physiologically for vigorous action and also produce strong internal stimulation exciting the body to vigorous action. Physiological studies (Bard, 1934; Cannon, 1929) indicate that a considerable number of the peripheral stimulus-producing responses involved in anger are similar to those in fear. It is thought (though the evidence is not completely conclusive)

ever, with Mowrer's main contention that a reduction in anxiety serves as a reward.

that the differences between anger and fear are the result of differences in the central, or thalamic, responses supposedly involved. Whatever their ultimate locus, the responses producing the sensations of anger seem to be subject to the laws of learning.

Since anger appears to be an acquirable drive, the pattern

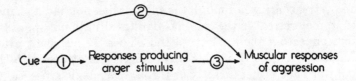

FIG. 2. DIFFERENT POINTS AT WHICH THE PATTERN OF ANGER AND AGGRESSION IS SUBJECT TO MODIFICATION BY LEARNING

(1) The responses producing the anger stimulus can be connected to different cues; (2) different muscular responses of aggression can be connected to different cues; (3) different muscular responses of aggression can be connected to the anger stimulus.

of anger and aggression is subject to modification at several points, as represented diagrammatically in Figure 2. The first of these is the connection between various cues and the responses producing the anger stimulus; the individual learns in which situations to become angry. The second is the connection between these same cues and the overt responses of aggression; the individual learns which responses of aggression to make in various situations. The innate pattern of threshing and striking already referred to seems to determine the likelihood of occurrence of certain responses in initial trial-and-error situations. With further learning, various responses can be eliminated from the innate pattern (including even the internal responses producing the sensation of anger), or other responses such as swearing can be inserted into the pattern. The third of these points subject to modification is the connection between the response-produced stimulus of anger and the overt responses of aggression. Through learning, anger becomes connected to those responses which are most rewarded, in the same way that external stimuli ordinarily become connected to rewarded responses. Actually, the final aggression usually is a response to a pattern involving cues from the external situation and both cues and motivation from the strong internal stimulus of anger.

Reward is the selective agent in the learning which produces the adult habits of aggression. It seems probable that a more detailed analysis of social conditions will indicate that one of the circumstances in which the responses involved in the anger pattern are likely to be rewarded is that in which habits motivated by a drive and leading to a reward are blocked by the intervention of another individual. Under these circumstances, responses of aggression are likely to cause the other individual to get out of the way and thus allow the reward to be secured.[8] Another condition in which the more vigorous activity motivated by the response-produced anger stimulus is likely to be rewarded is that in which a motivated response usually leading to reward is prevented by some sort of a physical obstacle, such as a sticking door.[9] Both of these conditions will be recognized as the type of situation usually referred to as a frustration. According to this analysis, whether or not aggression will be high in the hierarchy of responses to frustration or *any other pattern of cues* will depend upon whether past conditions have been such as to reward aggression as a response to the cues in question or ones similar to them.[10]

[8] Whiting has adopted this hypothesis, testing it in his analysis of data on the socialization of the Kwoma (1941). He finds that an additional important condition for the reward of responses of aggression among children is that the opponent be younger than the aggressor; he also finds that, as would be expected under these circumstances, children are likely to respond to interference by younger children with aggression and by older children with avoidance or fear.

[9] It can readily be seen that aggression will not be as likely to be rewarded unless some habit capable of achieving the reward is already present and unless a drive to be reduced is also present.

[10] In a previous book, *Frustration and Aggression* (Dollard, *et al.*, 1939),

A reduction in anger can serve as a reward in the same way as can a reduction in anxiety or any other acquirable drive. Thus any situation capable of eliciting a relaxation of the responses producing the anger stimuli acquires a rewarding capacity. It seems probable that individuals learn to relax after completing a successful act of aggression, because relaxation before completing successful aggression is not rewarded whereas relaxation afterward is. Thus the performance of certain acts of aggression (as indicated by the cues of seeing and feeling oneself perform these acts) may acquire a rewarding capacity to reduce the strength of the anger stimulus. Furthermore, acts of aggression may acquire additional reward value by association with the more primary rewards secured by the aggression. Such a process might account for the cathartic effects of expressing certain forms of aggression.[11]

The drive value of response-produced stimuli is functional in enabling the organism to make more vigorous responses. A person can exert a stronger grip on an object if he stimulates himself by gritting his teeth and tensing the rest of the muscles in his body. Upon awaking from a deep sleep, a person is at a disadvantage because he lacks the stimulation from a certain background of muscle tonicity. This tonicity can be built up more rapidly if he pinches or slaps himself or supplies some other sort of stimulation. The advantages of anger and fear in eliciting strong responses have already been mentioned.

As has been pointed out, any cue that acquires the capacity to inhibit or relax a response which produces strong stimulation becomes able to serve as an acquired reward. From this formulation it follows that acquired rewards can be ef-

no stand was taken on the issue of whether the frustration-aggression relationship was innate or acquired. The hypothesis put forward here is that the position aggression will occupy in the initial hierarchy of responses to any situation is largely a product of learning. It is a refinement of the original frustration-aggression hypothesis. See also Miller (1941b).

11 In cases where aggression is punished, this tension-reducing effect can, of course, be more than balanced by increased anxiety. Catharsis seems to be most effective in the presence of certain "safety signals."

fective only in the presence of response-produced drives,[12] just as innate rewards can only be effective in the presence of innate drives.

By acting as an acquired reward, the sudden appearance of an external stimulus, even one of moderate strength, may result in a net decrease in the total amount of stimulation. For example, a frightened person lost in the dark may suddenly see a bright light, which has become to him a cue to the relaxed behavior characteristic of food and safety. The light may produce a moderate increase in the amount of stimulation reaching him through his eyes, but a marked decrease in the amount of stimulation from anxiety responses.

Because acquired drive value and acquired reward value are each attached to cues by learning, it is possible to learn the discrimination of responding differently to rather similar patterns of cues. The same stimulus object may acquire in slightly different contexts the capacity to serve as either an incentive or a reward. Thus, the near prospect of money at a tantalizing distance has an acquired drive value; money in the hand has an acquired reward value. To an infant, the sudden appearance of the mother with the bottle has an acquired reward value; but if the bottle is not given to the child, its near, but not near enough, presence eventually elicits responses producing anger or other stimuli of drive strength. In general, drive value is attached to those situations in which intense activity is rewarded, and acquired reward value to those in which subjects have learned that they can afford to relax.[13]

One way in which acquired drives differ from innate drives

[12] Unless it should be found that certain learnable responses are capable of reducing the strength of stimulation from primary drives.

[13] *Technical note:* According to the present hypothesis, it should be impossible for the same pattern of cues simultaneously to have both acquired reward and acquired drive value, though they might function in these two ways in rapid succession. Cases in which the same stimulus seems to act as a reward and simultaneously to elicit more vigorous responses might on analysis prove to be instances in which the total amount of stimulation was decreased, but the connections to the *specific* response being observed were strengthened by the acquired reward. For example, food near at hand may

is that they are much more difficult to define and specify exactly. This is just what should be expected from the mechanism proposed. Drive value is acquired by attaching to weak cues responses producing strong stimuli. But it is possible to attach different stimulus-producing responses to the same cue. Thus both fear and anger may be aroused in the same situation. To make the problem still more complicated, slightly different proportions of two or more stimulus-producing responses may be attached to different cues. Thus one situation may make a person very angry and slightly anxious, whereas another may make him slightly angry and very anxious. Furthermore, different individuals may learn to respond to the same cue with different mixtures of stimulus-producing responses. One individual may be angry, disgusted, and afraid while another is only afraid. In this way acquired drives would be expected to blend with each other in a baffling series of combinations, varying with the complex social conditions responsible for their acquisition.

be found to decrease total tenseness while strengthening the excitatory potential to grasping and chewing responses.

As an alternative to the present hypothesis, it might be assumed that there are two different kinds of stimulation, one of the type commonly called unpleasant and another of the type commonly called pleasant, and that either a *reduction* in the strength of the former or an *increase* in the strength of the latter acts as a reward. Then cues would acquire reward value either by becoming able to elicit responses producing a reduction in the strength of unpleasant stimulation or by becoming able to elicit responses producing increased pleasant stimulation. As long as such responses (or perhaps pleasure itself) were subject to the laws of learning, most of the basic structure of the foregoing exposition would remain the same.

If some stimuli are inherently pleasant and rewarding, however, it is difficult to see why responses producing these stimuli should ever stop short of extreme fatigue or other shifts introducing unpleasant stimulation. It would also probably be necessary to posit some special mechanism to account for the dependence of the pleasant aura of many stimuli upon periodic association with incidents of marked drive reduction. For these reasons, an attempt has been made to carry through consistently on the more parsimonious hypothesis that all rewards (commonly experienced as pleasures) involve some reduction in the total strength of stimulation. This hypothesis is much less firmly established than the principle that rewards are essential to learning or that drive reduction acts as a reward. Another possible hypothesis would be that a reduction in the strength of any stimulus serves as a reward whether or not it is balanced by a concurrent increase in the strength of some other stimulus.

In the same way, the rewards which reduce, or are the goals of, acquired drive can vary from situation to situation, from individual to individual, and from culture to culture.[14] Thus a child may learn to reduce his anxiety about breaking a dish by crying and seeming penitent when his parents are present, and by picking up and hiding the broken pieces when no one has seen the accident. In different societies, different symbols of status are evolved by associating the conventional stimuli of the culture with reduction of primary drive.

Another way in which acquired drives and rewards differ from innate drives and rewards is that acquired drives and rewards are much more changeable.[15] If an individual achieves an acquired reward, instead of being satiated, he is likely soon to try with increased vigor for a more ambitious goal. The instructor who has finally been promoted to an assistant professorship may not settle down, but rather strive with increased vigor to move the next step up the academic ladder. This is not strange. As soon as he receives his first promotion, he is rewarded by an increase in salary, which in turn means better food and many other primary and acquired rewards. Having been rewarded for striving to move up in the academic hierarchy, it is not surprising that he should continue to so strive. The prospect of a second promotion elicits stronger stimulus-producing responses and becomes an increased incentive. Each achievement on the way to a promotion acquires a greater capacity to elicit temporary anticipatory relaxations which act as rewards for the achievement of sub-goals.

[14] Some acquirable drives, such as disgust and anxiety, are named with some reference to the stimulus-producing responses responsible for them; others, such as vanity, avarice, and desire to be with people (gregariousness), are named for the situations arousing them or the goals satisfying them. In these latter cases, the internal components may differ from person to person. One person's avarice may be motivated by fear, another's by appetite for good food.

[15] The writers are grateful to Professor E. W. Bakke of the Yale Department of Economics for pointing out in a discussion of the Institute's Monday Night Seminar the differences between the motivations he has observed in his research (1940, pp. 3–103) and the primary drives used in animal experiments.

In a similar manner, if the responses producing an acquired drive are never rewarded, they gradually become extinguished. The worker who is never rewarded by increased wages for the extra efforts he makes in attempting to improve his condition is rewarded by escape from fatigue every time he lowers his ambitions and relaxes his efforts. Eventually his goal becomes simply holding his job. The way a person responds with acquired motivation is determined by the reward which society administers. In general, our society, particularly through age-grading and promotions in the public schools, rewards the progressive adoption of higher levels of aspiration and punishes resting on one's laurels, so that remaining too long at the same level of performance or status acquires the capacity to elicit anxiety which can only be removed by some action indicative of progress.

A more minute analysis of the structure of our society, which sets the conditions of learning, should make possible better prediction from learning principles as to the ways in which acquired drives and rewards function.

CHAPTER V

HIGHER MENTAL PROCESSES

Innate Bases for Adjustment

THE higher mental processes are based on elaborations of the simpler innate or instinctive modes of adjustment. The function of the higher mental processes can be brought out more clearly after a brief résumé of the simpler mechanisms. One of the important innate functions is primary drive. The innate mechanism for drive is provided by various nerve endings and receptors so arranged that strong stimulation is produced when the body is injured, starved, cold, etc.[1]

Drives move the individual to respond. But even in the naïve individual, not all responses have an equal probability of occurrence. For each primary drive, there is an innately determined preferential order, which we have called the *innate hierarchy*. In many instances, such as the flexion reflex which produces withdrawal from painful stimuli, the dominant response in the hierarchy is likely to avoid the strong stimulus. Similarly, but less certainly, the crying of a hungry infant is likely to bring the adult with food to terminate hunger. Different strong stimuli have an innate tendency to elicit different responses. Stepping on a thorn with the left foot elicits withdrawal of the left foot and extension of the right, and stepping on a thorn with the right foot elicits withdrawal of the right foot and extension of the left. Thus the strong drive stimuli also have distinctiveness or cue value. In certain lower animals, the innate hierarchy of responses to a given situation may include one elaborate, patterned response which

---

[1] Though drives are often correlated with needs, it should be clearly noted that not every situation in which the body suffers from a need produces strong stimulation which acts as a drive. The body may need more oxygen but die of carbon monoxide poisoning without any stimulation being produced which is certain to rouse the individual to action.

is definitely dominant over all others. Such responses are called instincts. The particular instinctive response which occurs usually depends not only on the drive stimulus which is present, but also on other weak but distinctive stimuli which act as cues.

As many writers have pointed out, fixed instincts may fail to be adequate for adjustment to a changing environment. In most animals, and particularly in man, the innate hierarchy is subject to modification by learning. The basis for learning is, of course, the innately rewarding value of an escape from strong stimulation, which strengthens the connections to the responses most closely associated with that escape. For learning to occur, the response in the innate hierarchy must be dominant by a narrow enough margin so that its extinction, if not rewarded, will allow the occurrence of other responses.[2]

Even where most final adjustments are the product of learning, the innate hierarchy still plays an important rôle in determining which responses are most likely to occur to certain stimuli and which responses will not be tried at all and hence not learned. When the arrangement of responses in an innate hierarchy consists of combinations which are quite likely, with slight modification, to be rewarded, it may vastly simplify the process of learning. For example, as the infant matures, highly coördinated step and balancing reflexes appear as innate responses to various forms of proprioceptive stimulation. These innately coördinated stepping and balancing patterns form a nucleus of responses which with relatively little modification can be remade into a great variety of habits ranging all the way from walking to running back a punt through a field of opponents for a touchdown. Locomotor habits are learned with infinitely more ease than they would be if the innate hierarchy were not already heavily weighted in favor of response patterns likely to be rewarded.

Learning enables the individual to perfect and modify ad-

---

[2] It seems that in addition to the factor of sheer strength of response, some types of connections, such as those involved in spinal reflexes, are much less subject to modification by reward than others.

justments based on the innate hierarchy. In man, these modifications may be very great. Cultural activities in particular —those distinctive of a nation, a community, a class, a sect, or other social groups—are characteristically learned.

Learning enables the individual to acquire better adjustments to situations in which he has had experience. But what of new situations? It would be inefficient for the individual to have to fall back upon his innate hierarchy in every new situation. The simplest solution to this problem is provided by the mechanism of *innate generalization*, whereby responses rewarded in one situation tend to transfer to other similar situations. The course of innate generalization is determined by sensory structures which make certain cues seem similar and others different. But just as it is impossible for an innate hierarchy to be adapted to changing conditions, so is it impossible for an innate basis of generalization or transfer of training to produce perfect adaptation to new conditions. Two situations which at one time should, for the best interests of the organism, be reacted to similarly may change so that they should be reacted to differently at another time.

Acquired Cue Value

One of the adjustments to this dilemma seems to be the capacity of the individual to learn to pay attention to certain relevant aspects of the complex of cues and to base his generalization primarily upon these aspects. Thus a lieutenant may learn to pay attention to the spread eagle on a colonel's shoulder and salute anybody wearing this, irrespective of his physique, style of uniform, or other innately more distinctive cues. To a certain extent, paying attention is a matter of learning to respond by directing the sense organs so that they will be exposed to the relevant cues. Responses of looking at other cues are extinguished; responses of looking at the silver eagle on the shoulder are rewarded; a discrimination is established. To the naïve civilian, the eagle appears in the context of a fat face with a ruddy complexion, or of a lean face with a sallow complexion, and in many other stimulus configurations. The eagle is at first not significant in

these contexts, because the other cues are innately more striking, and because civilian training has rewarded noticing faces
and their expressions, rather than shoulders and their in-
signia. If the lieutenant stops to look first at the shape of the
face, the facial expression, and other aspects of a new officer
whom he meets, he may be reprimanded for not behaving appropriately, e.g., saluting. He learns to escape from the anxiety induced by punishment by looking first at the eagle on
the shoulder and then responding appropriately to it. After
the lieutenant has learned, upon meeting any new man in
uniform, to look first of all at the shoulders, where the insig-
nia are worn, rather than at the face, the eagle will be seen
more distinctly than other cues not looked at. Thus the eagle
will be more likely to be the basis for either new learning or
generalization than the other cues.

In some cases, paying attention may involve more central
factors. These have not been investigated in detail, but Lashley's (1941*) results seem to indicate that these factors, even
if central, are subject to modification by learning, and hence
in the present system may be functionally classified as responses. Learning to respond to similar classes of cues in different contexts (circularity, triangularity, twoness) is called
abstraction and plays an important rôle in the higher mental
processes.[3] Not much is known about the intimate details of
the processes involved in abstraction. It is known, however,
that it can be facilitated by teaching the individual to respond in the same way to a large number of different cue
patterns all containing the crucial element (Hull, 1920).
The response is always rewarded whenever the crucial element is present and never when this element is absent. Thus
the response becomes more and more strongly connected to
the relevant cue and extinguished as a response to other cues.

Once the individual has learned in a variety of situations
to make a given response to the cue relevant to the category

---

[3] It seems likely that one of the factors which makes the mental processes
of man so much "higher" than those of animals is a greater capacity to respond selectively to more subtle aspects of the environment as cues. This
problem is far beyond the scope of the present investigation.

in question, this response may facilitate further reactions to the category abstracted by producing an additional cue common to the different situations. A lieutenant learns to salute every time he sees the eagle on a colonel's shoulder. As he salutes, he stimulates proprioceptors within his own body and feels himself saluting. Thus the act of saluting produces an additional cue which is common to the situation of meeting any colonel, tall or short, fat or thin. Further responses, such as saying, "Yes, Sir," with proper respect, may be attached to the cues produced by just having saluted, as well as to the cue of the eagle. First the lieutenant looks at the shoulder, making the eagle more distinctly visible as an external cue; then he salutes, providing himself with internal cues which are likewise common to all situations involving meeting a colonel. These and other acquired cue-selecting and cue-producing responses form a basis for the lieutenant's concept of a superior officer.

It can be seen that the mechanism of acquired cue value parallels that of acquired reward value. Just as it is possible through learning to connect to a weak stimulus a response which produces a strong stimulus and thus gives the weak stimulus an acquired drive value, so is it also possible to connect to a relatively obscure stimulus a response which produces a distinctive stimulus and thus gives the obscure stimulus an acquired cue value.[4]

Counting is an important cue-producing response. A person who has not learned to count can respond to oneness, two-

[4] One form of response-produced cues seems to blend very closely with the stimulus pattern which elicits it. This is the factor which is added to the bare external stimulation and is called perception. That it is the result of response-produced stimulation is suggested by the fact that it is delayed, more influenced by past experience, and more variable than the immediate effects of external stimuli. Closely related to perception is imagery, which can, to a certain extent, mirror the effects of previous cues in the absence of these cues. Although imagery and perception have not been carefully studied from this point of view, it seems probable that they follow the same laws of learning as do other responses, even though the responses producing these cues may possibly occur within the organizing centers of the brain. (See p. 59, n. 5.) That perceptions are modifiable by learning is indicated by the common observation that members of a strange race tend to look alike until one has learned to respond differently to them.

ness, or even fiveness, but he cannot learn to respond with perfectly accurate discriminations to large numbers of objects. A person who has learned the response sequence involved in counting can learn to discriminate perfectly between small differences in large numbers. Without counting, the grocer cannot tell whether or not he has exactly three dozen oranges; with counting, he can discriminate perfectly. It will be remembered that in an illustrative experiment mentioned in Chapter II, the younger child was unable to learn to find candy under the correct one of a long row of similar black books. Had he been able to count, his responses to these similar books would have given him a quite distinctive cue, the thirteenth book, which could have been the basis for learning exactly where to find the candy.

A cue which would otherwise not be distinctive can acquire greater distinctiveness in two ways: the individual may learn to direct his sense organs toward that cue, or he may learn to react to that obscure cue with a response, such as counting, which produces a more distinctive cue.[5] As the innate distinctiveness of a cue (or pattern of cues) is enhanced, further learned responses are more likely to be attached to that cue, and it is more likely to operate significantly in the transfer of training from one situation in which it is present to others in which it is also present.

Acquired Equivalence of Cues

It is sometimes desirable for the individual to be able to learn to generalize from one situation to another despite the fact that these situations have no external cues in common. For example, the various enemies surrounding a tribe may not be distinguished by any single physical cue in common; that is, an enemy may be just as similar to members of the tribe as he is to other enemies. Nevertheless, it may be desirable for a member of a tribe to learn to generalize a given response, say avoidance, to all enemies.

[5] Both of these mechanisms are relevant to the process of *copying* as analyzed in Chapter X.

Such generalization can be mediated by response-produced cues. In this example, however, there is no common external cue to which a common response may be connected, like the eagles on the shoulders of colonels. A common response must be connected to each individual enemy; and once such a response is acquired through a number of separate learning situations, cues produced by this common response can serve as the common stimuli necessary for generalization. The tribesman may learn at different times to respond to each of a number of different people with the same word, "enemy."[6] This verbal response produces a cue which is common to all these enemies. Once this response is learned, the cue which it produces may mediate the transfer of other responses. The tribesman may transfer his various responses of retreating, threatening, fighting, etc., learned as reactions to one enemy, to any other person whom he also calls an enemy.

The details of the mechanism for this transfer may be illustrated briefly. A man is rewarded by social praise for hurling a particularly colorful taunt at some enemy in a minor squabble which does not come to actual blows. This taunt becomes strengthened as a response to the cue of seeing that enemy. Just previously, however, the man has perhaps said aloud or to himself, "He is an enemy." Thus the responses involved in making the taunt are attached not only to the cue of the sight of the particular enemy, but also to the cue of hearing or feeling himself say the word "enemy." On a subsequent occasion, an individual who looks quite different, but whom the man has also learned to call an enemy, appears. The cue of hearing or feeling himself call the other person an enemy produces the verbal cue to which the response of hurling a taunt has been attached. Thus the man generalizes the rewarded epithet from one enemy to another. Friends are not

---

[6] Many children learn to respond to all people with fear, except those whom they have learned to call *friends*. The word "friend" serves as a cue to mediate generalizations in a manner similar to that illustrated in this example. In most cases, both mechanisms probably work at once, so that an enemy is either anyone whom the person has been taught to call "enemy" or anyone whom he has not been taught to call "friend."

so likely to be taunted in this way because they do not elicit the cue-producing response of saying the word "enemy."[7]

Generalizations based upon response-produced cues are more modifiable than those based upon innate similarities. If the man learns to stop calling an individual an enemy and to start calling him a friend, the whole pattern of responses elicited by the word "enemy" will cease to generalize from other enemies to this individual, and a whole new mode of behavior, consisting of responses which have been rewarded in the presence of other people called friends, will tend to appear. It is obvious that this modifiability of response-mediated generalization makes it superior to innate generalization as a means of adjustment to a changing environment.

Response-mediated generalizations play an important rôle in social behavior, where many of the most important categories are culturally rather than innately determined. To begin with a humble example, the Roman numeral *III*, the Arabic numeral *3*, and the written word *three* are innately quite distinctive as cues. But training in our society has attached the same cue-producing responses to each of these patterns of stimulation. The most obvious of these cue-producing responses is the verbal one; but there are a host of other responses, such as holding up three fingers, which tend to occur in minimal form, supply additional cues common to these three stimuli, and mediate generalization from any one to the others.

Murdock (1941*) has demonstrated the rôle of kinship terms in the generalization of the incest taboo. National names, class names, local names, and occupational names, together with many other responses which cluster around each of these verbal designations, provide responses which supply cues affording a basis for partial stimulus equivalence between persons to whom the same responses have been learned. Stereotypes (Lippmann, 1930, pp. 88–94) function in this way. A name, e.g., Negro, mediates the transfer of a whole pattern of responses to any individual called by that name.

---

[7] For a more technical discussion of such acquired, or *secondary generalization*, see Hull (1939b).

Lippmann has stressed the point that responses are often maladaptive when so generalized. As long as behavior is cued to the word "Negro," or other parts of the stereotype, discriminations are not made on the basis of personality patterns and social class.

That response-produced cues actually do play the crucial rôle which has been ascribed to them is demonstrated by carefully controlled experiments. Birge (1941) has shown that if young children are taught to call two very different stimulus objects by the same name, other responses (such as reaching for the objects) are more likely to generalize from one to the other than when the two objects have been given different names. She has also shown that such generalization is much more likely to occur when the children say the name aloud, so that it is certain that the cue-producing response is actually present, than when they do not say the name aloud.

The mechanisms involved in facilitating the generalization of responses from one situation to another have been emphasized. One of these is learning to discriminate, single out, and pay attention to obscure cues present as relevant similarities in the external stimulus situation. Another of these mechanisms is learning to react with a response producing a cue which gives two otherwise different situations a degree of acquired similarity. The examples used to illustrate these types of generalization have been simple. It is probable, however, that the generalization of responses to relevant cues, either externally present or response-produced, plays an important rôle in much more complicated and less understood situations—even in the highest forms of intellectual activities.

According to the traditional story, Newton was started on his application of the principle of gravity to celestial mechanics by generalizing a response from a falling apple to the moon. An apple and the moon are different in many respects, but are similar in that both are bodies possessing mass. Newton presumably responded on the basis of this similarity. The response generalized was a verbal one, "pulled toward the earth." Newton is reputed to have said to himself in effect, "If an apple is pulled toward the earth, the moon should be pulled toward the earth."[8] When more is understood about the detailed mechanisms of such generalization and the innate capacities which make it possible, a step will be taken toward the better understanding of one of the crucial factors involved in higher mental processes.

Foresight

Sometimes the responses of an individual do not seem to be connected to cues immediately present in the environment, but rather to his knowledge of what is likely to happen next. Such behavior is commonly called *foresightful*. A simple example from an animal experiment may serve as an illustration.

The purpose of the experiment (Miller, 1935) was to see whether animals would combine two separately learned habits in a foresightful manner. In the first stage of the experiment, hungry rats were started at the beginning of a short alley and learned to run the length of the alley, to go through a curtain, and to enter a box where they found a special device consisting of a narrow angular passageway in which, by turning sharply to the right, they got food.

In the second stage, the special device was removed from the box at the end of the alley and taken to another part of the room. Here the animals were placed directly in front of the device and allowed to enter. As soon as they had turned their heads sharply to the right and started to eat, they were given an electric shock. This elicited anxiety and retreat which were rewarded by escape from shock.

In the third stage of the experiment, the animals were placed at the start of the alley. This was to determine whether the two separately learned habits would be combined so that the animals would no longer run down the alley. A curtain at

---

[8] It will be recognized that similar types of generalization have played important parts in the construction of other scientific theories. According to Einstein (1938, p. 286), "It has often happened in physics that an essential advance was achieved by carrying out a consistent analogy between apparently unrelated phenomena."

the far end prevented them from seeing the special angular
device which, for purposes of additional control, was absent
on this trial. The animals started to run down the alley and
then stopped.

A control test (in which animals were shocked in a device
that had not been associated with the alley) indicated that
this tendency for the animals to stop was not produced by
emotional upset, primary stimulus generalization, or other
such factors. The two habits may thus be said to have been
combined in a foresightful manner. The animals had learned
that running down the alley led to the special angular device.
At another time, without running down the alley, they had
learned to avoid the shock in this device. Combining these
two separately learned habits, they now refused to go down
the alley. How was this foresightful behavior produced?

In the first stage of the experiment the animals learned to
run through the alley and into the special device with the
narrow angular passageway containing food. Because of the
gradient of reward, the last response before eating—turning
sharply to the right—was strengthened the most. This response tended to become anticipatory so that the rats started
to turn to the right soon after being put into the alley and
were observed to run down the right-hand side of the alley.
According to the present theoretical analysis, learning that
the alley led to the reward device consisted of learning to respond to cues in the alley with anticipatory responses such as
turning to the right. Later when the animals were placed directly in front of the reward device in another part of the
room, they turned to the right and felt themselves turning
immediately before receiving the shock. Thus the responses
of anxiety and retreat became connected to the cue produced
by the response of turning to the right. When the animals
were placed at the start of the alley, the external cues present
there elicited similar responses of turning to the right producing internal cues similar to those associated with the
shock. Thus anxiety and retreat were generalized from the
special device to the alley. That the anticipatory cue-producing response actually played an important rôle in mediating

this generalization is indicated by the fact that a previous experimenter (Tolman, 1933), who had not taken pains to see that such a response was present, had failed to secure foresightful behavior.

In human beings some foresight seems to be mediated by nonverbal anticipatory responses similar to those present in the rat. It is often difficult for the individual to explain in words the basis of such foresight. Where the mediating response is a verbal one, it is more easily described. A human subject in an experiment similar to that on the rat might report: "On my way down the alley, I started to say to myself how good the food would taste in the reward device; then I remembered the shock, a cold shudder ran down my spine, and I stopped."

Language

Cue-producing responses play an important part in the higher mental processes. In all societies, children are taught a special set of such responses—the language current in the group. Learning a language supplies the child with an enormous arsenal of cue-producing responses and with habits of using those responses in ways which have been found socially valuable.

Words by themselves usually are weak stimuli, serving as cues rather than drives, except on those rare occasions when someone shouts or sings very loudly. During the educational process, the individual learns to make many fine discriminations between words as cues. The sound of a word, though a weak stimulus, may acquire drive value in the same way that any other cue may acquire drive value. The individual may learn to react to the weak stimulus of a softly spoken insult with a response of anger producing a stimulus strong enough to have considerable drive value. Threatening words may become cues eliciting strong anxiety, and words of praise, at first relatively neutral, may, by association with primary rewards, acquire strong reward value.

Because of the extreme importance of language as a product of social learning which, in turn, influences the course of subsequent social learning, some of the significant steps in the process of learning to speak will be briefly sketched.

A child's first vocal behavior is crying. This response is high in the innate hierarchy of responses to any exceedingly strong stimulus, such as cold, hunger, or pain. Its dominance may be further increased by learning. Crying is frequently rewarded by the appearance of an adult who covers the cold child with a warm blanket, feeds the hungry child, or removes a stabbing pin. Perhaps as a result of these rewards, a child's later vocalization seems often to have a shrill character like fragmented parts of the crying behavior. If the crying and speaking situations are similar enough so that the effects of these rewards for crying generalize to the vocalizations involved in speaking, it might be expected that children who have been cared for every time they cry would learn to speak more readily than those who have not. Whether these two situations actually are similar enough so that sufficient generalization occurs to have any practical effect is an unsolved problem.

At the same time that the child is practicing his own crying responses, he is learning to respond to the voices of others. Adults who are feeding, fondling, and otherwise caring for infants usually talk to them; thus certain tones of the human voice acquire a reward value and may later be used to soothe the fretful child. It seems possible that this acquired reward value of the sounds in the language generalizes to sounds which the child makes while he is babbling and helps to reinforce his babbling behavior.[9]

In general, a child's first contact with the more formal

[9] It would be interesting to compare the babbling behavior of different children after an attempt had been made to give different phonemes a special acquired reward value. One child would be talked to with a certain phoneme while being fed and with a different but equally pronounceable phoneme while being dressed or having some other routine performed which seems to annoy him. A second child would be talked to with the first phoneme while being dressed and the second while being fed. Each child would be talked to with both phonemes for an equal length of time. The babbling behavior of the two children would then be compared. The prediction would be that the child would learn to babble with the phoneme which had been given an acquired reward value more than with the other.

aspects of language is in learning to use words spoken by other people as cues for his responses. A sharp "No!" is followed by punishment, which can only be escaped by stopping or retreating. Eventually, stopping becomes anticipatory and occurs to the word "No" spoken sharply, without the punishment. At the same time, "No" is acquiring an anxiety-arousing value, so that any response which brings an escape from a torrent of "Noes" is rewarded. Exactly which verbal cues a child will learn to respond to and how he will learn to respond to them depends, of course, upon his learning capacity at the particular age and upon what his parents try hardest to teach him.

At the same time that the child is being rewarded for making more responses to words as cues, he is gradually learning another aspect of language, namely, how to make the response of uttering words.[10] If a cooky is out of reach, the response pattern of pointing at it with the body and eyes and reaching for it with the hand is often rewarded by inducing some older person to give the child the cooky. If this gesture is accompanied by a sound, it is more likely to be rewarded. If the sound seems to be some appropriate word, such as "Look-at," reward is still more likely. Eventually, the more effortful parts of the gesture drop out, and the verbal response, which is least effortful and most consistently rewarded, becomes anticipatory and persists. The mechanism of reward gradually differentiates language from its original matrix of other, more clumsy, overt responses. The child learns to talk because society makes that relatively effortless response supremely worthwhile.

The child is given meticulous training in connecting words to objects and connecting acts to words. He is also given careful training in connecting words to other words, in combining words into sequences of stimulus-producing responses. The child must learn to combine words according to the rules of grammar; he is corrected thousands of times for grammatical mistakes. Unfortunately, no one has made a thor-

---

10 As will be shown in Chapter XIII, imitation plays an important rôle in this process.

ough learning analysis of the system of habits involved in combining words into grammatically correct sentences. It must be highly complex since it involves abilities which are not possessed by animals or feeble-minded persons. Precisely what these abilities are is not well understood.

The habits involved in grammar are habits which govern the manner in which other learned responses, words, and phrases are combined. Thus they might be called higher-order habits. But the habits of grammar are not the only higher-order habits which the child learns. By combining words and sentences into unsuccessful requests and into successful requests, into inadequate instructions and into adequate instructions, into poor descriptions and into good descriptions, into unsuccessful arguments and into successful arguments, into wrong explanations and into correct explanations, the child receives punishment for certain combinations of words and reward for others.

The child is given careful training in responding to the spoken word as a cue; he is taught to follow directions. He is also given meticulous training in producing the appropriate word as a response. The child first learns to respond with a different word to each of many simple stimulus situations; then he is taught to combine words into larger patterns paralleling complex relationships and sequences of events in the environment. In this way, he accumulates a store of different stimulus-producing responses which he can use later in guiding his own behavior.

The child receives a certain amount of social reward for carrying out this final step of using language to guide his own behavior. He is praised if he comes near the glass bookcase, says, "No, no," and then retreats. In being taught to keep his promises, he is also rewarded specifically for using his own words as cues to guide his own responses.

Since speaking is a type of activity which can occur without interfering with most other responses, it is easy for speech to move forward in the sequence of acts and become an anticipatory response. Thus speaking comes to play an important rôle in thinking and reasoning. But a series of spoken words, like any other series of acts, tends to become shortened as anticipatory responses crowd out any dispensable units. Thus the individual quickly learns to think in terms of abbreviated speech; the gross responses of making sounds, useless in thinking though necessary in talking, are omitted. This process is facilitated by a certain amount of punishment for thinking all one's thoughts aloud. Whether or not the responses in the adult are in terms of actual slight speech movements or are in terms of learned neural connections which function as stimulus-producing responses is as yet an unsettled research problem.

Reasoning

Although reasoning is very important in social behavior, many of the details of the dynamics of reasoning are not yet well understood. This much seems clear: The function of reasoning is to shorten the process of overt trial and error by causing the individual to avoid responses which would be likely to be errors or to make early in the sequence responses likely to be rewarded. Without reasoning, the responses likely to be rewarded might only occur much later, if at all. If these responses actually are rewarded, they are learned; if not, they tend to become extinguished.

Cue-producing responses are important in the process of reasoning. In the response-mediated generalizations which have already been discussed, two separately acquired habits were combined to produce the generalized response. In one of the examples, a tribesman learned the habit of calling two people enemies. He also learned the habit of taunting one of these people. As a result of a combination of these two separately learned habits, he taunted the other person. Such a combination of two separate items of experience (putting two and two together) is one of the characteristics of simple reasoning.

Most examples of reasoning, however, seem to involve longer sequences of cue-producing responses. Sometimes these progress smoothly with one response rapidly cuing the next; sometimes one sequence after another is abandoned, so that the process resembles overt trial and error.

Since primary rewards and punishments are usually not administered during the episodes of trial and error involved in reasoning, the responses must be selected or rejected by the acquired reward value or acquired anxiety value of the cues which they produce. If a response produces a cue which has been associated with reward, that response and the responses leading to it are strengthened, tend to persist or recur, and thus to become cues for still further responses. If, on the other hand, a response produces a cue to which anxiety-producing responses have been connected, that response and the others leading to it tend to be weakened and not to be cues to further behavior. The individual learns to cease making responses which produce cues arousing anxiety; stopping such responses is rewarded by reduction in anxiety.[11]

In some cases, the cue-producing responses employed in reasoning may be abbreviations of the gross responses which have actually been employed in carrying out the act contemplated. This seems to have been the case with the rat which tended to turn right in the experiment on foresight. With human beings, the sequences of cue-producing responses employed in reasoning have often been learned by the individual as a part of his culture. These may be responses of language or of mathematics. In reasoning out the design of an apparatus, an experimenter may find it desirable to draw diagrams. One part of the diagram becomes a cue which determines the way he will design the rest of the apparatus. After he has made a satisfactory diagram, he will use it as a cue to guide the further responses of building the apparatus. If the apparatus fails, he is likely to abandon it; if it brings him fame and fortune, he may go on designing similar gadgets for the rest of his life.

---

[11] Similarly, response sequences are weakened if they produce cues which have been associated with non-reward. In Pavlovian terminology (1927), such cues might be called *conditioned inhibitors*. According to our hypothesis, escape from fatigue is the primary reward teaching the subject to halt responses producing such cues.

Some of the dynamics of reasoning may be illustrated in slightly more detail by the analysis of a simple example. An instructor who was working on a paper to read before a research seminar knew that it was conventional to spend approximately an hour reading a paper at that seminar and wondered how many typewritten pages he should write. Having been embarrassed in the past for appearing before seminars with papers that were either too long or too short, he was motivated to write a paper of approximately the correct length.

His initial response in this dilemma was one which had often been rewarded in other similar dilemmas. He said to himself, "I'll ask Professor Smith."[12] This response, performed either subvocally or centrally (the exact locus is of anatomical rather than functional importance), produced a stimulus pattern which was a cue to a number of further responses. At first, these responses produced a temporary relaxing sense of reassurance, which seemed to reward and strengthen the response of saying to himself, "I'll ask Professor Smith." But in the past experience of this instructor, permanent relaxation after thinking of an idea had never been rewarded. He had learned that one cannot afford to tarry too long at a sub-goal. In such situations he had been rewarded for tensing again to spur himself to greater action. The additional drive produced by this tension, together with the cue of saying to himself, "I'll ask Professor Smith," resulted in a slight tendency to get up out of his chair and go downstairs. As soon as he raised his head, however, he became aware of cues indicating the lateness of the hour. Previously, in the presence of such cues, he had tried to look for people in similar situations and had discovered that persons of professional status, including this professor, were rarely to be found in their offices at night. As a result of these experiences, the responses of pulling at locked doors and saying to himself, "He is not in," had become anticipatory to the cue of lateness of the hour. Instead of continuing downstairs,

---

[12] This verbal response seemed to come up as automatically as any simple motor habit.

therefore, he tended to stop, almost before starting, and to say, "He is not in."

The occurrence of these responses, however, produced cues which had been connected with further responses. He had frequently been rewarded by getting information from homes over the telephone when he had found that people were not in their offices. He said to himself, "I'll telephone him." The cue produced by this response immediately touched off a twinge of anxiety. Punishment had long since taught him not to telephone people too late at night. The anxiety was a cue and a drive to terminate this response sequence.

With these responses stopped, the cue of the work on his desk again caused him to say to himself, "How many pages for the paper?" This response produced cues which elicited first the association of a paper for the meetings of the American Psychological Association. Then he said to himself, "An A.P.A. paper is fifteen minutes, and six pages." To these cues were attached in this context strong anticipatory responses originating from experiences of ultimate success with other similar problems; a triumphant instant of anxiety reduction was followed by additional motivation to continue.

Up to this point, symbolic trial and error had played the chief rôle in determining the manner in which his internal stimulus-producing responses followed each other. First, the response occurred which was highest in his initial hierarchy of responses to the momentary context of cues. When this response produced cues with acquired reward value, it persisted and served as a cue to still further responses. When, on the other hand, it produced cues with acquired anxiety value or cues to which inhibition had been attached by extinction, it was abandoned and the next dominant response in the hierarchy occurred.

As soon as the succession of stimulus-producing responses had led to the arithmetical formulation of the problem, the subject reached a point where past learning provided not only each of the responses which formed a unit of reasoning, but also the manner in which to combine the responses rapidly in order to cue himself for the final response suitable to problem solution. His arithmetic teacher had taught him all the units of adding, multiplying, and dividing and how to combine them appropriately in various types of problem situations. He therefore said to himself, "If I read six pages in a quarter of an hour, then I will read four times six, or twenty-four pages, in one hour." This became the cue to counting the pages already written and saying to himself, "Five more pages will make it the right length." This last verbal response reduced his anxiety over the danger of possible embarrassment and served as a cue to guide his further writing.

At the end of the seminar, his colleagues congratulated him on his paper. While he was being rewarded, he said to himself, "I am glad I figured out a paper of the right length," and rapidly rehearsed some of the responses which had been successful links in the process. This rehearsal probably strengthened the acquired reward value of the cues produced by these responses.

The function of reasoning in the example analyzed was to cause the instructor to write a paper of appropriate length. Had he proceeded by sheer trial and error unaided by reasoning, he might have been punished for reading a good many papers far too long or too short before finally being rewarded for reading one of the right length. Since the reasoning produced a paper of exactly the right length, he learned the appropriate response in a single trial.

As a result of the acquired reward of solving this problem and the final reward of reading a paper of the correct length, the instructor also learned something about the technique of solving such problems. The connection between the various segments of cue-producing responses involved in the reasoning were strengthened. Should he forget how many pages to read in an hour, it would be easier for him to solve the same problem in the same way a second time. Since most of the units of the reasoning are applicable to other similar problems, it would be easier for him to solve these also. He could, for example, quickly tell how many pages to read in thirty minutes or in two hours.

By being rewarded for using cue-producing responses, the instructor tended to learn to initiate the symbolic process, to stop and think rather than ask somebody else or give up. The dominance of symbolic responses relative to various forms of direct action was probably increased in the resultant hierarchy. In this particular example, such an effect is difficult to demonstrate conclusively. In other instances, it is clear that the habit of stopping overt action and taking time to think can be learned. A tenderfoot is taught[13] that when he is lost in the woods, he must not immediately dash off in some direction that might take him still farther away from the trail, but must sit down, rehearse his last actions, and canvass all possible plans of action before initiating any of them. A person who has acquired this habit is almost certain to behave more adaptively than one who strikes off immediately and without thought.

The tendency to use cue-producing responses in a dilemma can be strengthened by rewards; it can also be weakened by extinction or punishment. Thus, in some people, so much anxiety has been attached to the cue-producing responses involved in mathematics that they never try this mode of problem solution. Often, if such people can be encouraged to try learning mathematics again, they become able to solve problems which have previously been impossible for them. Sometimes it seems that people fail to show the intelligence of which they are capable because they are afraid to express original, unconventional ideas either to others or to themselves. In solving difficult problems, it is advisable not to discard a bad idea too soon; if the sequence of cue-producing responses is allowed to progress further, some element in the obviously impractical idea may supply the cue to further responses leading to an adaptive solution.[14]

[13] This instruction is usually verbal: The individual is presented with cues arousing anxiety as an acquired drive and rewarded for rehearsing in words what to do when lost. Because the process of socialization has already connected overt responses to these words, they can sometimes lead to the desired behavior.

[14] It may be ventured that one of the capacities which make for better reasoning is the ability to respond with many different cue-producing re-

The final step in the reasoning process is to respond overtly in some instrumental way to the last cue-producing response. As a result of his experience, the instructor was rewarded not only for figuring out the proper length for his paper, but also for letting this be the cue to write a paper of that length.

Reactions to response-produced cues are not always dominant over competing responses. Sometimes people who have not been rewarded for translating certain types of ideas into action may dismiss them as too theoretical. At the depth of the recent economic depression, one of the authors figured out that if conditions got much worse, so that stocks went appreciably lower, the whole financial structure would be disrupted so much that no form of investment would be profitable. He therefore reasoned that one could not lose, but only gain, by buying stocks. The reasoning seemed perfectly sound to him. It was a good idea, but he did not act on it. Others who acted on similar ideas made considerable money; he did not. As might be expected from the foregoing analysis, the reasoning process is a rather tenuous chain which may be readily broken at any link. Often reasoned responses to a drive or an environmental cue are overridden by more direct, unreasoned responses.[15]

sponses at once so that further responses may be elicited on the basis of a pattern of cues representing many different units of experience. For reasoning to occur at all, according to the present analysis, the individual must respond to some cue with a response producing a further cue and also must respond to that cue-producing response while it is still present. Thus the hypothesis demands that the reasoning individual be able to respond to at least two different cues at once with two different responses.

[15] For a more rigorous discussion of some of these same problems, with special reference to animal experiments, see a series of articles by Hull (1930b; 1931; 1934b; 1935).

CHAPTER VI

A PATTERN CASE OF IMITATION

IMITATIVE behavior has attracted the attention of humanists and social psychologists for centuries. The small child sits in father's chair, scuttles around in his carpet slippers, or wants her hair done up like mother's. "Copy-cat" is a well-known reproach to the socially aspiring. Explanations of imitative behavior have varied from time to time, but each serious attempt has leaned heavily upon a particular psychological theory. The analysis proposed here is no exception. It rests upon a psychology which may be called, in brief, a reinforcement theory of social learning. It derives from the work of Pavlov (1927), Thorndike (1911; 1914; 1940), and Watson (1919), although it should not be confused with the detailed position of any one of these writers. Its best current statement and synthesis have been made by Hull (1941*). The basic position has already been outlined. The present object is to see its relevance in a restatement of the nature of imitative behavior.

Common speech has already directed attention to imitative acts. Language, being a folk creation, would not be expected to provide a very exact discrimination of the forms of action which it lumps under the general term "imitation." It is, indeed, this inclusiveness of common speech which poses the scientific problem and demands that the scientist make further and more exact distinctions. The authors have decided to use three phrases to indicate the sub-mechanisms which seem to account for all or most of the cases for which the term "imitation" is ordinarily used. These mechanisms are: *same* behavior; *matched-dependent* behavior; and *copying*. The authors agree with Faris (1937) that no single sub-mechanism will adequately account for all cases of imitation, but disagree with him in that they hold that the three sub-mechanisms, derived from a single general learning theory, suffice to account for all cases.

Same behavior does not require the detailed analysis which will be given to the other two types of imitation. The characteristic fact is that two people perform the same act in response to independent stimulation by the same cue, each having learned by himself to make the response. Two persons, for instance, may take the same bus because each reads the card indicating its destination. Similarly, the crowd at a football game resolves itself into an ordered unit, each group of individuals presenting their tickets at the proper gate, each independently discriminating the letters above the proper doors and making similar adaptive responses. *Same* behavior may be learned with or without imitative aids.

Copying also will be mentioned only briefly at this point. In the characteristic case, one person learns to model his behavior on that of another. It is crucial that the copier know when his behavior is the same; the essential learning in copying centers around this knowledge. The copier must have criteria for the sameness and difference of the acts he performs. He must be aware that his copy falls within the band of tolerance as a match for the model act. Training to copy often begins with an external critic who rewards similarity and punishes dissimilarity; in the end the copier must be able to respond independently to the cues of sameness and difference.

The third mechanism, that of matched-dependent behavior, will be discussed in detail in the present chapter. It is extremely important in social life. It tends to occur whenever one person is older, shrewder, or more skilled than another. Younger people match behavior with, and are dependent upon, older people. Stupid children must, perforce, follow their more intelligent associates. Householders prepare for an ice storm when their scientists (meteorologists) give the sign. Social climbers must follow their status superiors through an intricate routine of watching and imitating. Learners of a foreign language must learn the appropriate situations in which to use certain words by following those who already speak the foreign tongue. The study of socialization in children offers innumerable examples where children match behavior with their elders and are dependent on them for cues as to when to do so. It will be useful and perhaps interesting to discuss one full-bodied example of such dependence matching as it was recorded by a gifted child observer. Such examples force us to fit theory to the actualities of social life. Since imaginary examples often lead to imaginary solutions, the authors have insisted that every example presented have an actual location in space and time and that they be able to give names and circumstances in further elaboration if necessary.

The following case is instructive just because the imitative behavior was maladaptive. Two boys—Jim, aged six, and Bobby, aged three—were playing a game with their father in the living room of their house. The father explained that he would hide two pieces of candy while the children were out of the room. When he gave the signal, they were to return and look for the sweets. When each child found his piece of candy, he could eat it. The father put one piece of candy under a pillow on the davenport and the other beside the radio cabinet. The older child came into the room, followed by his younger brother. The older boy, Jim, looked in the fireplace. The younger brother, Bobby, followed and looked there also. Jim looked inside the piano bench; so also did Bobby. Then Jim looked under the pillow on the davenport and found his piece of candy. Thereupon he stopped looking. Bobby was now helpless. He went again and looked under the pillow where his older brother had found his candy, but of course had no success. Finally, Bobby's candy was produced and given to him.

On a succeeding trial of the same game, exactly the same thing happened. The younger child would look only in the places already examined by his older brother. He could not respond to place cues by looking for himself.

This behavior, comical when it occurred, is nevertheless worthy of attention. It could not have been acquired in previous situations of the identical kind since this occasion was the first when the game was played. Perhaps it was acquired in other but, in some respects, similar situations. A search of the life histories of the children proved that the latter was the correct surmise. The younger child had been rewarded for matching behavior with the older in a large number of situations which had cue elements in common with that of the game. It appears, therefore, that the tendency to match had generalized in this case from other similar cues to the cues of the new game. Out of the many rewarded examples of dependence matching discovered as the "background" for the game, one is selected for exposition. It is not advanced as proof of our theory. Such proof can come only from the better controlled conditions and the more exact communication of the experiments to be subsequently reported. The example, however, is intimately related to the structure of the experiments which follow. It shows, pattern perfect, the crucial elements in one type of imitative behavior.

A Case of Matched-Dependent Behavior

The same two children, each a year younger, were playing in their bedroom, which was adjacent to the family kitchen. The kitchen opened upon a back stairway. It was six o'clock in the evening, the hour when father usually returned home, bearing candy for the two children. While playing in the bedroom, Jim heard a footfall on the stairs; it was the familiar sound of father's return. The younger child, however, had not identified this critical cue. Jim ran to the kitchen to be on hand when father came in the back door. Bobby happened on this occasion to be running in the direction of the kitchen and behind Jim. On many other occasions, probably many hundreds, he had not happened to run when Jim did. He had, for instance, remained sitting, continued playing with his toys, run to the window instead of the door, and the like; but on this occasion, he was running behind his brother. Upon reaching the kitchen, Jim got his candy and Bobby his.

On subsequent nights with similar conditions, the younger child ran more frequently at the mere sight of his older brother running. When he ran, he received candy. Eventually, the behavior, under pressure of continued reward, became highly stabilized, and the younger child would run when the older ran, not only in this situation but in many others where time and place stimuli were different. He had learned in this one respect to *imitate* his older brother, but he had not learned to run at the sound of his father's footfall.

Apparently, learning in this and other similar situations, in which responding imitatively was rewarded, generalized to the game and was the source of the maladaptive imitation observed there. Since imitation was not rewarded in the game, we should expect a discrimination eventually to be established; the younger child should learn not to imitate in such a situation.

Analysis of the Behavior of the Imitator Child

Bobby's behavior can be analyzed in the form of a learning paradigm, as follows:

Imitator

Drive ----------- Appetite for candy

Cue ------------- Leg-twinkle of brother

Response ------- Running

Reward -------- Eating candy

Analysis of Leader's Behavior

The leader's problem is slightly different; his behavior parses out as follows:

Leader

Drive ---------- Appetite for candy

Cue ------------ Father's footfall

Response -------- Running

Reward --------- Eating candy

The leader in this case is reacting to the stable environmental cue provided by culture, i.e., the father's footfall on the stair, but otherwise his problem is identical with that of the imitator, or follower. Jim had obviously completed his learning of the connection between footfall and the running response before Bobby had commenced his. It might be added that it is not essential in every analysis of this type of imitation to know all of the factors operating to determine the leader's act. It is enough actually to be sure that he is following a cue which the imitator cannot discriminate.

Complete Paradigm of Matched-Dependent Behavior

The relationship between the acts of leader and imitator can be put together into one diagram as follows:

	Leader	Imitator
Drive	Appetite for candy	Appetite for candy
Cue	Father's footfall	Leg-twinkle of leader
Response	Running ===== dependent ----> matched ----	Running
Reward	Eating candy	Eating candy

It will be noted above that the responses are *matched*, thus fulfilling one important condition of imitative behavior. It is further clear that the response of the imitator is elicited by cues from the act of the leader. His behavior is therefore *dependent* on that of the leader. Simple, or simple-minded, as an analysis so detailed of an incident so humble may seem, it represents, nevertheless, a large class of cases of social behavior which is called imitative. Such cases are frequently encountered when the history of the act is not known, and therefore the observer cannot be certain that the imitative act was learned. Every case ought at least to be examined to see whether the variables called for by the learning hypothesis are not in fact present.

In order to emphasize the crucial rôle of learning princi-

ples in the behavior of the imitator child above, one can look
at the elements of the paradigm from another standpoint. If
Bobby had had no drive—that is, if he had not been hungry
for candy—it would have been impossible for reinforcement
to occur, and the connection between the response and the cue
of the leg-twinkle would not have been fixed. If he had been
unable to perceive his brother's cue—if, say, he had been
blind—it would have been impossible for the learning to occur. If he had been unable to make the response of running—
if, for instance, he had been kept in the room by a barrier
which only his brother could leap—it would have been impossible to learn the imitative response. If he had not been rewarded on the occasions when he did follow his brother, he
could not have learned to imitate. This example should indicate, therefore, that imitative acts of this type follow the laws
of learning. What is crucial about them is that the cue from
the leader's behavior is often more stable than other cues provided by the environment. If the leader child is, for instance,
responding to the cue of the hands of a clock, he can make his
response more regularly and discriminatingly than can the
imitator child, who must depend on the cue of the leader's action. If, for example, the leader is gone for the day, the imitator child will be unable to make his response at all.

In social life, individuals are constantly being placed in
situations analogous to the one above. The young, the stupid,
the subordinate, and the unskilled must depend on the older,
the brighter, the superordinate, and the skilled to read cues
which they cannot themselves discriminate. They can respond
only in the wake of those better instructed. Society, as will be
shown, is so organized that the situation diagrammed above
occurs over and over again. Imitative responses are not confined to childhood. They can and do appear at any time along
the life line where the situation calls for them. They can be
outgrown and abandoned when the need for them disappears;
or they can be a permanent feature of the life of every individual, as in the case of dependence upon the skill of the political leader, the scientist, or the expert craftsman.

CHAPTER VII

THE LEARNING AND THE GENERALIZATION OF IMITATION: EXPERIMENTS ON ANIMALS

AN analysis of an observed example of imitative behavior has led to the conclusion that certain conditions of social life reward the learning of imitation. An attempt will be made to verify experimentally the deduction that imitation will actually be learned whenever these conditions are present. In a subsequent chapter the structure of society will be examined in more detail to see just how regularly these conditions are met.

Certain difficulties lie in the way of an experimental study of the learning of imitation. Older human subjects are very sophisticated, having already learned a great deal about imitating as a result of their past experience under the conditions of socialization. Infants young enough to be relatively naïve have such a limited response capacity that it is difficult to work with them. Moreover, it is difficult to secure opportunities for subjecting young infants with malice aforethought to those drastic conditions of controlled primary drive and reward which are essential to a successful experiment.

In order to circumvent these difficulties, it was decided to perform one series of experiments on older children and one series on albino rats. The advantage of working with older children is, of course, that they are conveniently available in school and that their responses and acquired motivations are subject to a relatively high degree of verbal control. The disadvantage is that they have already had experience with imitation, so that the problem becomes not how the first tendencies to imitate are learned but how tendencies already present may be progressively altered by additional experience.

Fortunately, work with animals affords an opportunity

for investigating the very topics which cannot be investigated with older children. It enables one to determine how the principles operate in an organism that is relatively naïve and has not already had considerable experience with social conditions rewarding imitation in some situations and non-imitation in others. Furthermore, a more rigid control may be exerted over the primary drives of animals than over those of children. If imitation can be learned by a lower animal like the rat, the mechanism involved is presumably one of such a fundamental nature that it can operate independently of language and might be expected to occur early in the life history of a human being.

Whenever experimental work is done with animals, the question arises whether or not the results will be relevant to human behavior. In the present case, the problem to be investigated arose from an analysis of a real example of human behavior. Thus it is certain that the problem under investigation is relevant to human behavior. Furthermore, the analysis of the example of human behavior had indicated exactly what conditions should be necessary before imitation can be learned. These conditions have been summarized in the paradigm presented in the preceding chapter. The crucial question thus becomes: Can these particular conditions be met in an experiment on albino rats?

A knowledge of the capacities of rats indicates that they are suitable subjects. They can be motivated by hunger, thirst, and other drives. When driven, they can perform a variety of responses. Rats can be rewarded by substances such as food and water which reduce their drives. Rats can learn; rewards have the effect of strengthening the tendency to perform the responses preceding the reward. In learning, the responses of rats can be connected to cues from the external environment. And, finally, rats can be taught to discriminate between different distinctive cues. Since rats have these capacities, which according to the present analysis are the capacities essential for the acquisition of the human tendency to imitate, the theory demands that under the proper conditions they can be taught simple forms of imitation.

Experiment 1. Learning To Imitate

Because the experiments on albino rats start nearer the base line of "no previous training to imitate," they will be described first. The purpose of the first experiment was to verify the deduction that, given the conditions specified by our analysis, imitation will be learned.

The first of these conditions for the learning of imitation is that a motivated leader be present who has already learned to respond correctly to a relatively difficult cue in the environment and whose correct response affords the potential imitator an easy relevant cue. In the example analyzed, this condition was met by the fact that the older child, Jim, wanted candy and had already learned to respond to the relatively difficult cue of hearing the father's footstep at about six o'clock in the evening by running pell-mell to the back door. In making this response, he stimulated the younger child, Bobby, with a cue that was more distinctive than the footstep.

A knowledge of the capacities of albino rats suggested that the color (black or white) of a small card seen at a distance would be a suitable environmental cue to serve the same function for a leader rat that the footstep did for Jim. It is known that albino rats can use such a color difference as a cue, but that this is a somewhat difficult discrimination for them to learn.

The correct response which the leader rat was taught to perform to this cue was that of turning in the direction of the black card and running to it. Hungry animals were started on the stem of the simple elevated T-maze illustrated in Figure 3, ran down to the choice point, turned in the direction of the black card, ran down to the end of the arm, and secured food. The black card was placed at the end of the arm containing food; a white card at the end of the other arm. On successive trials, the position of the black card and food was shifted from right to left in a random order. After the leaders had learned this discrimination, their response of turning at the choice point and running down the correct arm of the

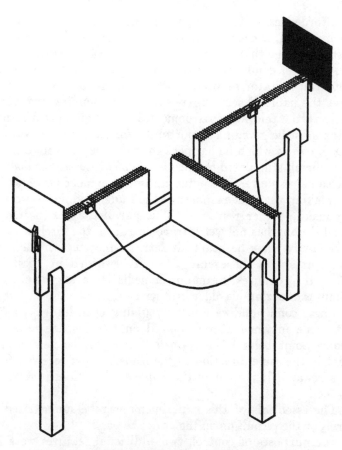

FIG. 3. APPARATUS FOR LEARNING OF
IMITATION BY RATS

The imitator (or non-imitator) is started behind the leader on
the short arm of the apparatus. The leader has been trained to
discriminate between the two cards, one black and one white, at
opposite ends of the long arm of the apparatus. Food for the
leader is placed in the sunken cup at the base of the correct
card. Food for the imitator (or non-imitator) is concealed by
a hinged lid which is pulled up by a string if the animal makes
a correct choice.

T afforded naïve followers, which were then placed directly behind them, a near and moving stimulus which was a more distinctive cue than the remote and stationary cards.

A further condition for the learning of imitation is that a potential imitator be present who is motivated but does not have the habit of securing reward by responding independently to the relevant environmental cue. This potential imitator must be given an opportunity for random behavior, in the course of which he happens to make the correct response while being stimulated by the visual cue of the leader making the same response. The potential imitator must be rewarded for making the same response as the leader and non-rewarded for making other responses. This parallels the situation in which Bobby has not yet learned to run to the kitchen to secure candy when he hears his father's footstep on the back stairs at six in the evening, but is rewarded by receiving candy if he chances to run out immediately after the obvious stimulus of seeing his older brother run.

These conditions were met by giving each hungry, naïve rat trials in which it was placed on the T-maze near the choice point behind the trained leader. If the new animal went in the same direction as the leader, it too received food as a reward; if it went in the opposite direction, it received no food.

The essentials of this experiment may be summarized in terms of the paradigm on the opposite page.

For purposes of control, two additional features were introduced into the design of the experiment. A second group of followers was rewarded for non-imitating, i.e., for turning in the opposite direction from the leader. This group will be called the non-imitators. After both the imitators and non-imitators had learned to respond correctly, a test was run to determine whether they had learned to respond to the cue produced by the response of the leader or whether they had learned to respond only to the environmental cue of the cards. First, the cards were removed from the apparatus. Then two new groups of leaders were introduced, one trained to turn consistently to the right and the other to turn consistently to the left. Imitators and non-imitators were given trials behind these new leaders. Each animal was given a series of trials in which right-turning and left-turning leaders were alternated in an unpredictable manner. Since the cards were absent, any following or non-following on these

	Leader	Imitator
Drive	Hunger	Hunger
Cue	Color of card	Leader running and turning
Response	Turning toward card	— — matched — — Following leader
Reward	Food	Food

(Cue/Response connected by: – – dependent – – ↗)

test trials would have to be on the basis of cues provided by the responses of the leaders.

Now that the general rationale of the experiment has been discussed, specific details of the apparatus and procedure may be described. Readers not interested in such technical details may skip directly to the results, page 109.

Apparatus

The diagram of the apparatus is presented in Figure 3. It is a modified, elevated T-maze, of convenient table height, 34 inches. The stem of the T from the start to the choice point is a path, 18 inches long and 1⅛ inches wide, formed by a strip of quarter-inch wire mesh, rigidly supported from underneath by the edge of a board. The narrowness of this elevated path serves to prevent the imitators and non-imitators from passing the leaders. Between the choice point and each of the arms of the T is a gap 4¾ inches wide. This gap serves a double purpose. It tends to slow down the leader at the choice point so that the follower is directly behind him, and it prevents the follower from cutting corners and passing the leader at the choice point.

Each of the arms of the T is a mesh path similar to the stem of the T. Eight and one-half inches down each path from the gap is a sunken food cup covered flush by a hinge; the leader can run directly over this cup to the end of the arm, and then, if the follower has made the correct choice, the cup may be opened to reward him by pulling a string attached to the hinge. Sixteen and a half inches from the gap is the food cup for the leader. Immediately beyond this, at the end of the T, is the holder into which the proper cue card is clipped. The cue cards are 10 inches wide and 8 inches high, clipped to the end of the T, their edge flush with the back of the leader's food cup. The card at one end of the T is black; that at the other is white.

Subjects

The subjects were thirty-two male albino rats of Wistar strain. Eight of these, used as the leaders, were trained to discriminate between the cards. For purposes of control these animals were divided into two groups, four trained to go to the black card and four trained to go to the white card. These animals were approximately five months old; all others, approximately three months old. Eight more rats, four trained to turn to the right and four to turn to the left, were used as leaders in the control test at the end of the experiment. Sixteen animals were trained as followers, or dependent subjects. These animals were divided into two main groups, eight rewarded for imitation and eight for non-imitation. Each of these groups was further divided into two subgroups; four animals were given their trials behind leaders trained to go to the black card, and four behind leaders trained to go to the white card.

Procedure

The first step was to train the leaders to respond to the cue of the proper card. For purposes of control, half of the leaders were trained to secure food on the arm of the T containing a black card and the other half were trained to secure food on the arm of the T containing a white card. On successive trials, the position of the cards, right or left, was changed in an unpredictable manner.[1]

After the leaders had thoroughly learned this discrimination, they were given practice trials, during which they were followed by animals used in exploratory work and not included in the data of the main experiment. This was necessary because sometimes the presence of a follower shoving from behind would disrupt the behavior of the leader and cause him to make a wrong choice. After the leaders had made twenty errorless trials in succession followed by another rat, they were considered to be ready for the main experiment.

In order to adapt the rats to be used as followers to run on narrow pathways and step across gaps, they were given a series of preliminary trials. The first day of preliminary training was performed on a straight, elevated path, with a gap but without choice points, which was of the same width and construction as the paths of the T-maze. This path was 10 inches long from start to gap. The gap was 4 inches wide, and beyond it was a path 6 inches long, ending in a food cup.

On the first trial, the animals, motivated by a twenty-four-hour hunger drive, were placed on the apparatus with their fore feet on the food-cup side of the gap and their hind feet on the other side. Their natural reaction was to step across, and they soon discovered the food. On the next trial, they

[1] As the particular rats used as leaders had been employed in a previous experiment involving somewhat similar discriminations, this training was really relearning. From the point of view of the problem at hand (the way in which the followers learn imitation), the manner in which the leaders have learned their response is irrelevant. The essential point is that they have learned regularly to perform a definite response to the proper cue.

were placed on the edge of the gap, and on the remaining trials at the start of the path.

The next day, the potential followers were given preliminary training on a somewhat longer runway with a somewhat larger gap. The distance from the start of the gap to the runway was 20 inches, the gap was 4¾ inches wide, and the food cup was 6 inches beyond the gap. On the third day of preliminary training, the animals were run on a path which was exactly the same as the one used on the preceding day except that the gap was 5½ inches wide.

After this preliminary procedure had trained the animals to be adept at running on narrow, elevated paths and stepping across gaps even longer than those to be encountered on the T-maze, they were ready for their first trials behind leaders in the main experiment. On the first trial, the hungry leader and the hungry follower were placed simultaneously on the start of the maze with the follower just behind the leader. The leader ran down and turned in the correct direction rather promptly. He was allowed to stay at the food cup until the follower had stepped across the gap onto one of the arms of the T. The experimenter recorded the direction in which the follower first stepped with all four feet across the gap. This response, whether in the same direction as the leader or in the opposite direction, occurring before the rats had received any specific training on the apparatus, was a test of the initial tendency for the rats to imitate or to non-imitate.

On this trial, those rats in the imitator group that turned in the same direction as the leader were rewarded by food in the little food cup built into the maze in the center of the arm directly behind the leader. Food in this cup was covered by a hinge while the leader ran past it and was uncovered by the experimenter immediately before the follower reached this point. The hinge covering the food was operated from a distance by a string so that the anticipatory responses of the experimenter would give no cues to the animal. If the animals in this group turned away from the leader, they would not find any food and were picked up by the experimenter and placed back on the elevated perches on which they were kept between trials.

The procedure of rewarding the group to be trained not to imitate was exactly the opposite. If they turned in the same direction as the leader, the food cup was not uncovered, and they did not receive food. If they turned in the other direction, the food cup was uncovered, and they did receive food.

The animals that made errors were given successive runs behind leaders turning in the same direction until they finally made a correct response. Each trial was a series of such runs terminated by the first correct response. Each animal was given seven trials a day.

The details of the procedure are summarized in Table I. It can be seen that the procedure used on the imitator and non-

TABLE I

PROCEDURE TO COUNTERBALANCE THE VARIABLES INVOLVED IN EXPERIMENT 1

R = cue cards placed so that leader will turn to right
L = cue cards placed so that leader will turn to left

Group I. *Dependent subjects rewarded for turning in same direction as leaders*

A. Leader goes to black card

Trial	1	2	3	4	5	6	7
Rat 1	R	L	L	R	R	L	L
3	L	R	R	L	L	R	R
5	R	R	L	L	R	R	L
7	L	L	R	R	L	L	R

B. Leader goes to white card

Trial	1	2	3	4	5	6	7
Rat 10	R	L	L	R	R	L	L
12	L	R	R	L	L	R	R
14	R	R	L	L	R	R	L
16	L	L	R	R	L	L	R

Group II. *Dependent subjects rewarded for turning in opposite direction from leaders*

A. Leader goes to black card

Trial	1	2	3	4	5	6	7
Rat 2	R	L	L	R	R	L	L
4	L	R	R	L	L	R	R
6	R	R	L	L	R	R	L
8	L	L	R	R	L	L	R

B. Leader goes to white card

Trial	1	2	3	4	5	6	7
Rat 9	R	L	L	R	R	L	L
11	L	R	R	L	L	R	R
13	R	R	L	L	R	R	L
15	L	L	R	R	L	L	R

imitator group was exactly the same in every respect except that the rats in the imitator group were rewarded when they turned in the same direction as the leader, while those in the non-imitator group were rewarded when they turned in the opposite direction from the leader. Within each group, all the other variables involved in the experimental procedure were balanced. On the first trial, half of the leaders turned toward black cards, and half toward white cards. For both of these groups of leaders, half of the turns were to the right and half to the left. On the second trial, half of the animals were placed behind leaders turning in the same direction as in the first trial; the other half were placed behind leaders turning in the opposite direction. On the following trials, alternations and non-alternations of direction succeeded each other in a pattern known to be unpredictable to rats.

On the following days, the same general procedure was repeated until each animal had received seven trials a day for twelve days, a total of eighty-four trials. On successive days, the order of turns was alternated so that an animal that had begun by turning to the left on one day would begin by turning to the right on the next.

Despite these precautions to vary the direction of turn, some of the animals, as is quite common in any form of discrimination experiment, showed a tendency to develop position habits; that is, they turned consistently to the right or the left irrespective of the direction of the leader's turn. These turns were, of course, rewarded by chance a certain per cent of the time. In order to facilitate the unlearning of these habits, the conditions of non-reward were strengthened by the addition of mild punishment. A rat persistently dashing in the wrong direction without stopping to expose himself to the cue would be snapped on the nose as soon as he stepped on the wrong arm of the T. The slight conflict introduced by this mild punishment was found to be sufficient to break up the position habit and to aid discrimination. The animals in the imitator group were given this mild punishment when they turned in a direction opposite to that taken by the leader; those in the non-imitator group were given this mild punishment when they turned in the same direction as the leader.

After the rats had received twelve days' training and appeared to have learned, they were given control tests to determine that the conditions of the experiment had actually taught them to use the leader's response as a cue. In order to make sure that the imitators and non-imitators were not merely responding to the cards, they were given test trials on which the cards were absent from the end of the T. For use on these test trials, a new squad of leaders was trained, some always to turn to the right, others always to turn to the left. By selecting leaders trained to turn in the proper direction, each follower could be given test trials in which the correct turns were sometimes to the right and sometimes to the left in an unpredictable sequence. The sequence employed for each animal was exactly the same as that used for its first day of training at the beginning of the experiment. On the second day of the control test, each animal received seven more trials. On each of these trials, the direction of the rewarded turn was opposite to that of the corresponding trial in the preceding day's sequence.[2]

Results

The results are presented in Figure 4. On the first trial of the experiment, there was no tendency for the animals in either group either to imitate by turning in the same direction as the leader, or to non-imitate by turning in the direction opposite to the leader.[3] On successive trials, the animals rewarded for imitating gradually learned to turn in the same

[2] From the point of view of experimental expediency alone, it would have been better to give the animals all of their training under the conditions of this control test. The other procedure was adopted in order to make clearer the parallel with the social conditions previously analyzed. The conditions of the control test are roughly analogous to those social situations in which the correct cues are completely inaccessible to the potential imitators—in other words, the extreme case of an obscure cue.

[3] That there is no definite tendency to imitate or to non-imitate is clear; but that the two groups both happen to come out exactly at the 50 per cent level is, of course, a matter of exceptional luck.

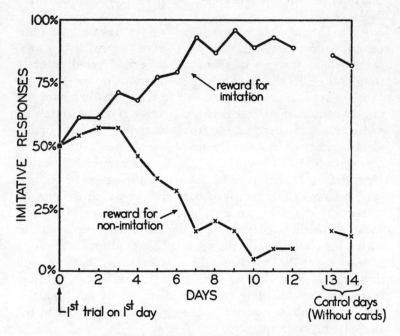

FIG. 4. CURVES SHOWING THE LEARNING OF
IMITATION AND NON-IMITATION
BY RATS

Eight animals were rewarded for turning in the same direction
as the leader, eight for turning in the opposite direction. The
learning of the first group to imitate is represented by the rise
in the upper curve; the learning of the second group to non-
imitate, by the fall in the lower curve. The initial tendency exhibited on the first trial of the first day is shown by the starting
point on each curve (which happens to be exactly at chance expectation for each group). This double point represents eight
measures for each group. All other points represent fifty-six
measures, seven trials on each of eight animals.

direction as the leader, and those rewarded for non-imitation, to turn in the opposite direction.[4]

The statistical treatment of the results shows that the differences produced are reliable. The results may be analyzed in a number of different ways. On the first day, there was no reliable difference between the two groups. On the twelfth day of training, the difference was of a magnitude to be expected by chance less than one time in a thousand.[5] Thus, the different conditions of reward produced a reliable difference between the two groups.

Taken separately, the learning occurring in each group is reliable. For the imitators, the difference between the first and twelfth day would be expected less than two times in one hundred by chance; for the non-imitators, the difference between the first and twelfth day would be expected less than one time in a thousand by chance.

That this learning resulted in behavior dependent upon cues produced by the leader's responses is indicated by the results of the control tests, in which the cards were removed from the ends of the T so that the response of the leader was the only cue present. On these tests, the difference between the two groups was of a magnitude to be expected by chance less than one time in a thousand. Thus, the theoretical analysis which demanded that appropriate conditions should lead

[4] The non-imitator group seems to show an initial tendency to learn a very slight amount of imitation at first before learning definitely to go in the opposite direction. These results may have been due to (a) chance, (b) some previous, very slight tendency to imitate which does not show up at first but only appears after the animals are running more vigorously for food, or (c) generalization from the fact that these animals had to run down the stem of the T behind the leaders in order to get to the choice point.

[5] The reliabilities presented in this experiment were calculated in the following manner. Each animal was given a daily imitation score which consisted of the number of times its first response on a trial was in the same direction as that of the leader. Since there were seven trials a day, these scores ranged from 0, representing perfect non-imitation, to 7, representing perfect imitation. For each group, daily scores of the animals were averaged. Then the standard error of each mean was calculated and the reliability of the difference determined according to Student's method which corrects for the errors otherwise introduced by the use of small samples (Yule and Kendall, 1937, p. 442, and Appendix, Table 5).

to the learning of matched-dependent and non-matched-dependent behavior is confirmed.

Experiment 2. Generalization to Leaders of Different Color

An examination of a case of human imitation showed that conditions were present from which, according to the principles of learning, one would expect imitation to be learned. The preceding experiment has just demonstrated that imitation actually is learned when animals are subjected to similar conditions. As a part of the analysis of the human example, it was assumed on the basis of learning principles that imitation learned in one situation would generalize to other similar situations. A series of experiments was designed to test this assumption.

One of the ways in which the stimulus situation involved in imitation may change is that the subject may learn to imitate one leader and subsequently be confronted for the first time with a different leader. The purpose of this experiment was to investigate the extent to which imitation would generalize from a leader of one kind to a different kind of leader. A certain amount of generalization was already involved in the control test, in which the cards were removed from the ends of the T, since new albino rats were used as leaders in this experiment. These leaders, however, were highly similar to the leaders used in the original learning. In the present experiment, the appearance of the leader was varied more radically by substituting black rats for the original white ones.

First, one group of black rats was trained to go always to the right for food, and another group of black rats was trained to go always to the left. Then, with the cards absent from the ends of the apparatus, the followers were given seven trials on each of two days behind the black rats as leaders. The trials to the right and to the left were alternated in the same balanced manner as in the preceding control test behind white rats.

The results are presented in Figure 5. On the first day's tests, the animals previously trained to imitate white leaders

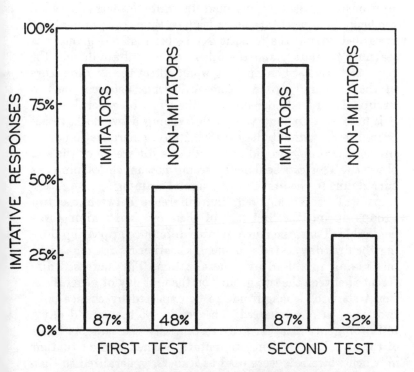

FIG. 5. GENERALIZATION OF IMITATIVE RE-
SPONSES FROM WHITE LEADERS TO
BLACK LEADERS

The animals in one group were originally trained to imitate
white rats used as leaders, those in the other group to non-imitate white rats. On the generalization test, a black rat, trained
as a leader, was substituted for the white rat. Each column in
the figure represents fifty-six measures, seven tests on each of
eight rats. The first test was conducted one day, the second test
the next.

showed a tendency to imitate black leaders, and the animals previously trained to non-imitate white leaders showed a tendency to non-imitate black leaders. Since each animal was rewarded during the tests, it is possible that one group was learning to imitate and the other to non-imitate during the seven test trials. Such learning would affect the average score of the tests and produce some difference between the two groups. In order to demonstrate the effect of generalization, it is necessary to show that such learning as would have occurred, even without the benefit of any generalization from previous training, would not produce a difference of the size observed. This can be done by seeing how much learning occurred during the first day of original training.

As will be remembered, the difference between the two groups during the first day of their original training was negligible. Thus, the much greater difference appearing during the first day of tests for generalization represents a definite saving produced by generalization. The increased difference between the two groups on the first day of generalization tests is of a magnitude to be expected by chance only two times in one hundred. The results of the second day's tests for generalization are substantially the same as those of the first. The tendency to imitate, learned in the situation in which white rats were used as leaders, generalized so that it immediately appeared in the new situation in which black rats were used as leaders.

Experiment 3. Generalization from One Drive to Another

The purpose of this experiment was to determine whether or not after animals had learned to imitate with one drive, hunger, as a stimulus they would generalize to another drive, thirst. In order to make this test, the animals were allowed to eat all of the dry food that they would, but were deprived of water for twenty-four hours. Then they were placed on the apparatus behind the same white leaders used for the no-card test and were run in exactly the same way, except that instead of finding food in the food dish on the correct side they found water in this dish. Since food was completely absent

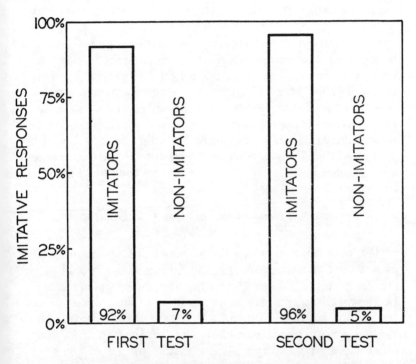

FIG. 6. GENERALIZATION OF IMITATIVE RE-
SPONSES FROM ONE DRIVE TO ANOTHER

In the original training, the animals were motivated by hunger
and rewarded with food. One group was trained to imitate, the
other to non-imitate. In these tests for drive generalization,
they were motivated by thirst and rewarded with water. Each
column in the figure represents fifty-six measures, the first turns
of seven trials on each of eight rats. The first test was conducted one day, the second test the next.

from the food dishes, these trials were not only tests for drive generalization, but were also controls on the exceedingly unlikely possibility that the animals in the preceding tests may have been guided by the smell of the food.

The results of these tests are presented in Figure 6. It can be seen that both groups definitely generalize the tendency to imitate or non-imitate from the original situation, in which they were motivated by hunger, to the new situation, in which they were motivated by thirst. The difference between the imitators and non-imitators was small during the first day of their original training; it was great during the tests for drive generalization. The increase in the size of the difference is of a magnitude to be expected by chance less than one time in a thousand.

Experiment 4. Generalization from One Environment to Another

The purpose of this experiment was to determine whether or not the habits of imitating and non-imitating would generalize from the T-maze to another apparatus similar in certain respects but quite different in others. This new apparatus is illustrated in Figure 7. It consisted of a central elevated starting platform isolated by an air gap from four other elevated platforms symmetrically placed at the four sides of the starting platform. The apparatus was designed so that rats placed on the central platform could step across the gap to any one of the four surrounding platforms. This apparatus presented a situation which was different from that employed in the original experiment, but in which imitating and non-imitating responses somewhat similar to those which the subjects had already learned could be made and recorded.

Before the test trials, hungry leaders were placed upon the central platform and trained to step promptly across the gap onto one of the surrounding four platforms to secure food. In the test trials, the general procedure was to place the two animals, leader and follower, on the central platform simultaneously in such a way that the follower was subjected to cues from the leader, but was not otherwise biased to go either in the same direction or in the opposite direction. This was accomplished by placing the leader diagonally across the central platform in the position indicated on the diagram,

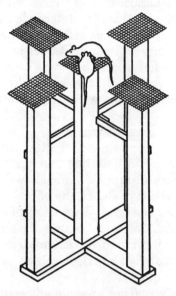

FIG. 7. APPARATUS FOR TESTING THE GEN-
ERALIZATION OF IMITATION TO A
NEW SITUATION

Half of the test animals had been trained to imitate and the other half to non-imitate on the modified T-maze illustrated in Figure 3. In this new situation, the test animal was placed on the center platform directly facing the middle of the side of the leader's body. Leaders were trained to step off immediately to one of the surrounding four platforms. Food for the leader was placed at the far end of each of these platforms. If the follower went to the same platform as the leader, he was fed behind the leader with a spoon; if he went to a different platform, he was picked up before he reached the food. Generalization was meas- ured by different rates of learning of the two groups different in previous training.

and at the same time placing a follower on the platform at right angles to the leader with his nose almost touching the center of the leader's side so that the two animals roughly formed a T. In order to make absolutely certain that the manner in which the experimenter placed the animals on the central platform did not bias the follower's choice in one direction or the other, an outside individual was called in who arranged the imitators and non-imitators in a random order on the elevated perches where they were kept between trials, so that the experimenters did not know which animals were imitators and which animals were non-imitators until after the experiment.

Each animal was given seven trials, in order to secure a better measure of its performance. So that all conditions except previous training in imitation and non-imitation would be constant for both groups, all animals were rewarded for imitating during these trials. If the effects of the previous training generalized enough to have an appreciable influence in this new situation, one would expect the animals that had previously been imitators to learn imitation more quickly, and the animals that had previously been non-imitators to learn imitation less quickly.

The reward for imitating was administered in the following way. Food for the leader was put at the end of each of the surrounding platforms. If the follower stepped on the same platform as the leader, he was immediately rewarded by being given food with a spoon. If the follower stepped onto a different platform, he was quickly picked up before he could reach the food at the end of that platform.

In order to counterbalance any effects of general orientation in the room, different animals were started on the first trial in different positions; that is, the leader-follower T-configuration was placed across different diagonals of the starting platform. On successive trials, the starting position of each animal was shifted. As has already been pointed out, the experimenters were unaware of which animals were imitators and which non-imitators, and hence could not unconsciously have given the two groups different correct cues.

Responses were scored as imitative if the follower stepped completely across the gap with all four feet onto the platform to which the leader had gone. Responses were scored as non-imitative if the follower stepped completely onto any other platform.

If chance alone were all that was operating, one would expect that the animals would on the average go to the same one of the four platforms as the leader 25 per cent of the time. On the seven test trials, the group that had previously been rewarded for imitating went to the same platform as the leader an average of 39 per cent of the time, or somewhat more than chance expectation. The group that had been previously rewarded for non-imitating went to the same platform on the average of 18 per cent of the time, or somewhat less than chance expectation. The difference between the two groups is of a magnitude to be expected approximately nine times in a hundred by chance.[6] Thus, though the difference is in the direction that would be expected if generalization had occurred, it is not a highly reliable difference.

Summary and Discussion

In this series of experiments, albino rats that had been living together in a conventional type of wire cage were first tested to see if they had any initial tendency to perform a very simple type of imitative response. The response selected was that of turning in the same direction as a leader at the junction of a T-maze. It was found that animals raised under these conditions had no marked initial tendency either to imitate by going in the same direction as the leader or to non-imitate by going in the opposite direction. Then the animals were divided into two groups. One group was rewarded for going in the same direction as a leader; the other group was rewarded for going in the opposite direction. Under these

[6] Not calculated as the reliability of difference between percentages, but calculated as the reliability of the difference between means of the scores for each rat according to the same procedure used for the other reliabilities previously cited. See page 111.

conditions, it was found that the two groups gradually learned to imitate and to non-imitate, respectively.

In order to make the situation more parallel to many of the social situations in which imitation would be expected to be learned, the responses of the leaders were guided by black and white cards which they had learned to use as cues. Control tests, in which the cards were removed and leaders were used that had been trained to make either right or left turns, indicated that under the conditions of the experiment the animals learned to use the response of the leader as their cue.

After this simple type of imitation had been learned in one situation, tests indicated that it generalized, that is, appeared without additional training in other similar situations. The two groups trained to imitate and non-imitate white leaders showed a highly reliable tendency, respectively, to imitate and non-imitate black leaders. After the two groups had learned to imitate and non-imitate when motivated by hunger, they showed a highly reliable tendency to imitate and non-imitate when motivated by thirst. After learning to imitate and non-imitate on the long, narrow runway of the T-maze, they showed a tendency, which, however, was not statistically reliable, to imitate and non-imitate in stepping off a small, square starting platform onto one of four adjacent square platforms.

That animals can learn the response of imitating (or nonimitating) under appropriate conditions of drive, cue, and reward, and that this response learned in one situation generalizes to other similar situations, confirms the theoretical analysis made in the preceding chapter. The next step is to determine experimentally whether or not such learning also occurs in human subjects, then to proceed further with an analysis of the extent to which the conditions under which one would expect imitation to be learned are actually present in our society.

Before this analysis, however, the relevance of this work to further animal experimentation may be briefly examined. Previous experiments (referred to in more detail in Appendix 2 on the history of imitation) have tested animals to see whether or not they start imitating when first introduced into a test situation. The experimenters have not, however, deliberately set up specific conditions in which the animal could be observed to learn to imitate. Relatively often, different experimenters have secured contradictory results. If one assumes that imitation is wholly an instinctive matter, such contradictory results are somewhat puzzling. If one assumes that imitation can be learned, it might be expected that experimenters would secure different results provided that the past environment of some animals had happened to reward imitation, while that of others had not.

More consistent results are to be expected when experimenters are more careful to test separately for the following different **factors:**

1. An innate, or instinctive, tendency to imitate the response in question;
2. An innate capacity to learn to imitate the response in question;
3. Environmental conditions which have rewarded the animal for learning to imitate under conditions similar enough to the experimental set-up so that generalization can occur.

In the present experiment, the second and third of these factors were found to be of crucial importance. Since the life history of the animals was not rigorously controlled from birth, one cannot certainly conclude whether or not innate tendencies to imitate had ever been present. The remote possibility that they had been present but had been overridden before the start of the experiment by uncontrolled rewards for non-imitating cannot entirely be ruled out. Though the evidence against instinct is not conclusive, the evidence for the influence of learning is overwhelming. In the presence of such definite evidence that even an animal as lowly as the rat can learn to imitate, the burden of further proof would seem to rest with anyone wishing to claim that any specific act of imitation is not learned.

CHAPTER VIII

THE LEARNING OF IMITATION: EXPERIMENTS ON CHILDREN

THE preceding experiments have indicated that as simple an organism as the rat can learn to imitate in one situation and will generalize this learning to other situations. Since the animals started out with no marked initial tendency either to imitate or not to imitate, the process of this learning could be followed clearly through a complete learning curve beginning with the chance behavior of an apparently naïve organism and ending with the finally perfected habit of imitative behavior. Animals were employed as subjects because of the greater probability that they would be initially naïve and the greater ease of controlling their basic drives.

Since the primary purpose of this investigation was to throw light on human behavior, additional experiments were performed on children. The purpose of these experiments is to demonstrate that, under the conditions demanded by the theory, imitation will be learned and, once learned, will generalize to new situations. Since the children were not naïve, having had a long history of training in social behavior, it was not to be expected that they would start out without any initial tendency either to imitate or to non-imitate. Thus the learning demanded by the theory could only be demonstrated by further-modifications in whatever initial tendency was present at the beginning of the experiment.

The procedure used in these experiments was similar in principle to that used in the animal experiments. First an independent subject, or leader, was given a cue enabling him to determine in which of two boxes candy was to be found. This cue was given by the experimenter, who pointed to the box which contained the candy before the dependent subject, or follower, was brought into the room. He was allowed to watch the leader make his choice and was then permitted to make a choice himself. Half of the dependent subjects were rewarded only if they went to the box that the leader went to, and the other half were rewarded only if they went to the box the leader did not go to. After the dependent subjects had reached a criterion of learning, they were given one set of test trials in the same situation to measure the direct effects of learning and another set of test trials in a different situation to measure the generalized effects of learning.

Experiment 5. Learning of Imitation by Children

The general set-up of the experimental situation is illustrated diagrammatically in Figure 8. In a room with an opaque door, two boxes were placed on chairs of convenient height ten feet apart. The starting position for the subjects was designated by a chalk mark on the floor ten feet from each of the boxes, so that the boxes and the starting position formed the corners of an equilateral triangle placed symmetrically in the center of the room. Each box was covered by a hinged lid, the projecting front of which formed a convenient handle for raising the lid. The boxes were deep enough so that it was impossible for the dependent subject to see what a box contained when the leader opened it. The rewards, placed in the correct boxes, were small gumdrops, one per trial for each child.

The subjects were forty-two first-grade children.[1] Twenty of them, selected at random, were placed in the imitative group, and twenty in the non-imitative group. Two subjects were used at different times as leaders.

The procedure was, first, to train the leader always to go to the box to which the experimenter had pointed, to stand in such a position as to shield the box from the dependent subject while opening it, and not to talk or give the dependent

[1] The authors are grateful to Mr. J. Allen Hickerson, Director of Training Schools at the State Teachers College in New Haven, to Miss Katherine A. Brennan, Principal of the Scranton School, and to the teachers in that school, for their coöperation in making an experimental room available and furnishing subjects for this experiment.

subject any uncontrolled cues during the experiment. The leader was told explicitly what to do, and was rewarded for correct behavior by candy[2] and punished for incorrect behavior by gentle admonitions.

After the preliminary training of the leader, the rewards

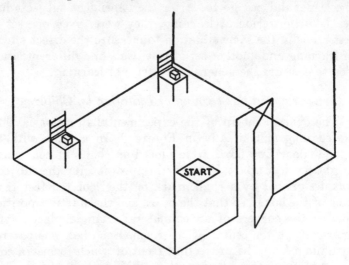

FIG. 8. THE SITUATION EMPLOYED TO TEACH
CHILDREN TO IMITATE

The door leading into the room was opaque, so that between trials the subjects could not see the experimenter put candy into the boxes and tell the leader which box to choose. If the subject was being trained to imitate, two pieces of candy were put into the same box; if the subject was being trained to non-imitate, one was put into each box. The starting position and the two chairs formed the corners of a ten-foot equilateral triangle. The boxes had hinged lids and were deep enough so that the subject at the starting position could not see whether the box the leader opened contained any more candy.

2 The leaders were told they could either eat the candy immediately or save it in a special paper bag given to them for that purpose. After the first several trials, the leaders usually saved the candy. Thus the acquired reward of gaining possession of the candy was immediately operative in a greater proportion of trials than was the innate reward of hunger reduction.

were placed in the appropriate boxes. If the dependent subject was to be trained to imitate, both pieces of candy were placed in the same box. If the dependent subject was to be trained to non-imitate, one piece of candy was placed in each box.

Next the experimenter gave the cue to the leader by pointing to the box to which he was to go. Then the dependent subject was brought into the room. The leader and the dependent subject were told to stand at the starting position. On the first trial, the experimenter gave the following directions: "Here are two boxes, there and there. Here is a piece of candy. You are to find the candy. He gets the first turn. Then you get a turn. If you don't find it the first time, you will get another turn."

After these directions, the leader was given his turn and the dependent subject his turn. If the dependent subject went to the wrong box, he was not allowed to correct his error immediately. He was sent out of the room and then given another turn, in which the candy was hidden exactly as before and the leader went to the same box. Turns were given under the same conditions until the subject went to the correct box and secured his reward. Thus each trial consisted of one or more turns, always ending in a correct response. On all trials after the first one, the experimenter merely lined up the two subjects at the starting point and then gave the leader his turn and the dependent subject his turn.

Position habits were ruled out by appropriate controls. On the first trial for half of the subjects in each group, the leader went to the right-hand box; for the other half of the subjects, the leader went to the left-hand box. On subsequent trials, the direction to which the leader went was alternated in an unpredictable manner.[3] For the imitative group, of course, the reward was always placed in the box to which the leader went, and for the non-imitative group, always in the opposite box. Since the dependent subjects could not see the cue given to the leader, and since the candy was hidden in the

---

[3] L R R L L R L for half of the subjects in each group, and R L L R R L R for the other half.

boxes and its position shifted from trial to trial, the response made by the leader was the only reliable cue to the dependent subject.

The subjects were given learning trials until their first response was correct on two successive trials. After they had reached this criterion, they were given two additional trials to test whether or not they had really learned.

Before the results are presented, the procedure may be summarized briefly in terms of the paradigm for the conditions of imitation. For the independent subject, or leader, the drives were the primary drive of hunger and the acquired drives of appetite for candy and desire for approval. The cue was seeing the experimenter point to the correct box.[4] The response was turning in the proper direction, going to the correct box, opening the lid, and taking the candy. The reward was getting and eventually eating the candy, and securing approval from the experimenter.

For the dependent subject, the drives were the primary drive of hunger and the acquired drives of appetite for candy and desire to secure approval by performing a correct response. The cue was seeing the leader go to a certain box. The response for the imitative group was turning toward the same box the leader had just gone to, walking to that box, lifting up the lid, and getting candy. For the non-imitative group, it was going to the opposite box. The use of language in the form of directions limited the random behavior of the subjects to the choice of one of two boxes. This simplified the problem by greatly increasing the likelihood that the correct response would quickly be made. The reward was finding the candy, involving the innate reward of eating candy when hungry and the acquired reward of securing approval from an authoritative adult by making a correct response.

The results are presented graphically in Figure 9. On the first turn of the first trial, 20 per cent of the imitators and 25 per cent of the non-imitators went to the same box as the

---

4 Since the dependent subject was not present when this cue was given, it represents the limiting case in which the environmental cue is not merely difficult, but impossible, for the dependent subject.

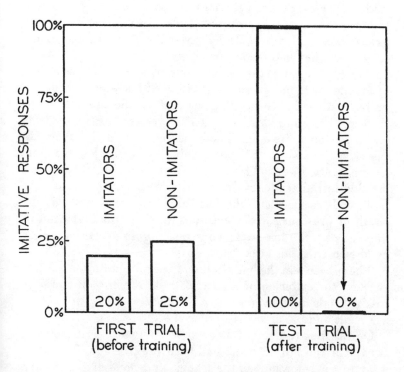

FIG. 9. THE LEARNING OF IMITATION
BY CHILDREN

Each column represents twenty measures, one test on each of twenty children. The choices on the first trial were made without any previous training in this situation. They indicate that the initial tendency of children in both groups to imitate was less than the 50 per cent to be expected by chance. The children in one group were rewarded for going to the same box as the leader, the children in the other group for going to the opposite box. After a criterion of two successive correct turns had been reached, test trials were given. These indicate that one group learned to imitate and the other to non-imitate.

leader. The difference between the two groups is well within the range of chance expectation. Since the subjects in the two groups were not differentially rewarded until the end of the turn after they had made this choice, the two groups may be combined to indicate the initial dominance in the test situation of a tendency to imitate in competition with a tendency to non-imitate. Initially, then, 22.5 per cent of the subjects chose the same box as the leader, and 77.5 per cent of the subjects chose the opposite box. These percentages differ from 50 per cent by an amount to be expected by chance less than one time in a thousand.[5] Thus, in the test situation, there was a reliable initial tendency for the dependent subjects to non-imitate. It seems plausible that this initial tendency was the result of previous social conditions in which the first child to find an object took it, leaving nothing to reward another child who tried imitation.[6]

The subjects in the imitation and the non-imitation groups reached the criterion of a correct first response on two successive trials in an average of 3.1 trials and 1.7 errors and of 2.4 trials and 0.4 errors, respectively.

On the first test trial following learning to a criterion, all twenty of the subjects who had been rewarded for imitating went to the same box as the leader, and none of the twenty subjects who had been rewarded for non-imitating went to the same box as the leader.[7] The different conditions of re-

---

[5] Calculated by the formula: Standard Error of percentage $= \sqrt{\dfrac{pq}{n}}$.

[6] It will be remembered that this is precisely what occurred in the first example analyzed in Chapter VI. Candy for the two children had been hidden in different parts of the room. Jim, aged six, took the lead in looking for the candy followed by Bobby, aged three, who looked in exactly the same places, and of course was non-rewarded. It was deduced that if similar games had continued to be played, Bobby would have learned the discrimination of non-imitating in this kind of a hiding-and-finding situation. The fact that the majority of the six-year-old children observed in this experiment started with an initial tendency of non-imitation in a hiding-and-finding situation suggests that the conditions under which Bobby was observed are common in our society and that, as was deduced, children will learn in these conditions to discriminate the hiding-and-finding situation as one in which not to imitate.

[7] The results on the second test trial were substantially the same.

ward had produced different responses in the two groups. Starting out approximately the same, one group learned to imitate, the other group to non-imitate. For both groups, the difference between the behavior on the very first trial of the experiment and that on the test trials after learning is of a magnitude to be expected by chance less than one time in a thousand.

Experiment 6. Generalization of Imitation

In the preceding experiment, two groups of subjects had learned to imitate and non-imitate, respectively. The purpose of the next experiment was to determine whether or not these habits would generalize, so that tendencies to imitate and non-imitate would appear when the children in the two groups encountered a somewhat different situation for the first time.

The new situation consisted of four boxes placed on chairs, arranged on the corners of an imaginary ten-foot square. In the center of this square was marked a starting position. All of the boxes were alike. For purposes of reference, they may arbitrarily be referred to by position as boxes *1, 2, 3,* and *4.*

While the dependent subject was out of the room, the experimenter gave the leader his cue by pointing to one of the boxes. As a control for position habits, or other constant errors, the leader was directed to a different box for different subjects. Thus, for the first subject in the imitator group and for the first subject in the non-imitator group, the leader went to box *1.* For the second subject in each group, he went to box *2,* etc. Since there were forty subjects in all, the leader went to each box ten times.

After the cue had been given to the leader, rewards were placed in the boxes. For the imitator group, two pieces of candy were put into the leader's box; for the non-imitator group, one piece of candy was put into each box. The candy was, of course, concealed by the lid of the box.[8]

---

[8] Since these rewards were seen by the dependent subjects only *after* the performance of the response recorded in this test, they could not possibly have influenced the results of the test. They were introduced in order to

After the rewards had been placed and the leader given his cue, the dependent subject was brought into the room. Both subjects were told to stand at the starting position marked on the floor in the center of the ten-foot square formed by the boxes. The following instructions were given: "Here are four boxes. You are to find the candy. He is to have the first turn. Then you get a turn." After these in-

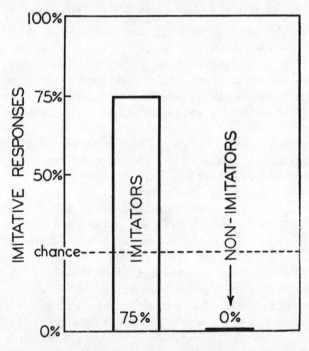

FIG. 10. THE GENERALIZATION OF IMITATION
TO A NEW SITUATION BY CHILDREN

After being trained to imitate or non-imitate in the situation represented in Figure 8, the subjects were tested in a new situation, in which they had to choose among four boxes arranged on the corners of an imaginary square. Each column represents twenty measures, one test on each of twenty children.

maintain the imitation and non-imitation of the subjects so that they could be used in an additional experiment to be reported in Chapter XIII.

structions, the subjects were always both faced toward the same side of the square. The leader was given his turn; the dependent subject was left free to watch. Then the dependent subject was given his turn. Each dependent subject was given only one turn.

The results are presented in Figure 10. Because there were four boxes, the chance expectation would be that 25 per cent of the subjects would choose the same box as the leader. Actually 75 per cent of the subjects who had been trained to imitate in the other situation chose the same box as the leader. None of the subjects who had been trained not to imitate chose the same box as the leader. There is less than one chance in a thousand that the score of the imitator group could have been produced by chance, and only one in a hundred that the score of the non-imitator group could have been produced by chance. Thus the test furnishes reliable evidence that both the tendency to imitate and the tendency to non-imitate generalize extensively enough to appear on the first trial in the new situation.

To summarize, the results of the experiments on children agree with those of the experiments on animals. They confirm the deductions from learning principles by demonstrating that imitation of a given response will be learned if rewarded and that, when learned in one situation, it will generalize to new, somewhat similar situations.

CHAPTER IX

VARYING CASES OF MATCHED-DEPENDENT
BEHAVIOR

IN the experiments on children described in the preceding
chapter, one set of responses, namely walking and box
opening, was selected for intensive study. These responses
exemplify the learning and unlearning of matched-dependent behavior under controlled conditions, although they are
not, of course, the only ones to which imitation theory applies. The cases in this chapter, drawn again from real life,
will show how various are the types of responses and stimuli
which may be linked by the matched-dependent mechanism.[1]
They also show the varied social circumstances under which
imitative behavior can occur.

The cases which follow were selected to illustrate rather
than prove our hypotheses concerning imitative behavior.
Proof that the factors alleged, and only these factors, were
operative would require closer observation than was possible
and perhaps experimental control. The cases cannot properly be called hypothetical because a part of the history of the
learning of the imitative act was present in each case; still,
the data are by no means complete and the analysis is therefore far from satisfactory. There is a further risk in the
analysis of such real examples. To some, the discussion may
seem in whole or part oversimplified; others may feel that the
analysis is overelaborated and pedantic. These risks have
been incurred to show how complex may be the analysis of
even trifling bits of human behavior and to give a concrete
hint as to how imitation theory may be applied to actual examples of behavior.

In the first case, the imitative cue raises a secondary appetitive drive which determines the goal rather than the means

[1] Our factual material is selected from the observations and records of a
number of mothers on their small children.

of reaching it. In the second, it is a secondary reward (parental attention) which fixes the connection between cue and response. The third case shows that part of the value of a cue may be that of indicating the feasibility of a particular response at the time in question. A final example reveals the rôle of the secondary drive of rivalry in imitative action.[2]

In the first example, which follows, it will be noted that the hunger drive appears, not in its crude and unconditioned form, but with appetitive responses built upon it. The child is driven, to be sure, but not merely by hunger for any and every type of food; the hunger is specific, and the goal stimulus is clear. The hunger drive is altered in that the goal of striving has been defined by previous experience. The child's mouth waters, not for food in general, but for a particular kind of food. Perhaps most important, in this case, is the fact that the act of the leader determines the behavior of the follower only in the sense of eliciting an anticipatory response to a specific goal. The follower does not repeat all of the units of the leader's act; only the final response is matched. Nevertheless, the similarity in the goal responses of the two performers seems sufficient to justify classification of the behavior as imitative.

Case 1. Common Goal but Differing Responses

Ceci, at three and a half years of age, and her brother Mark, aged a year and a half, are in the kitchen late in the afternoon. Mark is to have Cornflakes for his supper. Until the previous month, Ceci ate with him, but more recently, she is supposed to have learned to eat with her parents instead, and to have become used to an adult menu. The observer reports:

Ceci saw the Cornflakes being prepared and immediately asked for some. She said that she wanted her supper at once. I said, "But Ceci, if you eat your supper now, you can't eat sup-

---

[2] It is emphasized that these are selected cases where analysis was possible because the history of the learning was fairly well known in each case. Other cases were found which were obscure or uncertain because the data to test our hypotheses were lacking.

per later, because you won't have any appetite; you won't eat anything if you eat now. We are going to have meat, gravy, potatoes, beans, and all the things you like. Why don't you eat with us instead of eating now?"

She said, "Want to eat now."

I said, "Look, Daddy is going to come out in just about two or three minutes. He is almost through talking to his friend now. Then I'll make you a ginger-ale cocktail. Would that be all right?"

She said, "Yes, but I want my Cornflakes."

I said, "You can have them for dessert tonight, if you want them. Will that be all right?"

She said, "Yes." She really is very exasperating in making these demands about having Cornflakes just as Mark does, when actually we know that this is really out of her pattern of eating now. She is accustomed to eating with us, and has been for the last month.

The drive in this case is a secondary one, i.e., an appetite for a particular food. Under the pressure of changed conditions, this drive is in the process of extinction. The older child has learned to imitate the younger child, but is now to be trained to a new secondary goal, i.e., "meat, gravy, potatoes, and beans" rather than Cornflakes. The attempt of the imitator could be diagrammed as follows:

	Leader	Imitator
Drive	Hunger plus appetite	Hunger plus appetite
Cue	Cornflakes plus meal situation	Brother eating Cornflakes
Response	Eating — same goal — dependent →	Request to eat
Reward	Reduction in hunger and appetite	Absent, punishment added

The drive in this case has two components. There is seemingly a direct and basic hunger component. Built on this drive is a secondary appetite for the particular food in question. This secondary drive is aroused by the cue stimuli of seeing the Cornflakes, seeing the plate, being in the kitchen, and seeing the brother eating. The stimuli in question have a double function: they induce increased appetition and they cue the time of the response.

What is to be seen in this case is a long-established imitative pattern. It happens to be one of the cases in which the history is completely explicit as to the circumstances under which the matched-dependent response was set up. The conditions of learning, i.e., having the children eat the same foods at the same time, had favored the development of imitative behavior. During the six months preceding the date of the observation recounted above, the children had eaten meals together five or six hundred times. Had they always been fed separately, one would not predict the behavior here observed. Ceci had been eating when Mark was eating and when she had seen him eating. The sight of Mark eating had thus acquired a secondary drive value, which served to heighten her appetite and to evoke in her anticipations of eating, too. These anticipations were now aroused when she saw her brother eating; she consequently began to want Cornflakes and to respond accordingly. Her response was not at first the goal response of eating Cornflakes (because she did not have them), but rather another response which has been repeatedly reinforced as part of the sequence leading to the goal. She asked her mother for Cornflakes. Thus, she responded somewhat differently from her brother, who was already eating. In this case, imitation determined the goal or sub-goal rather than the means by which the goal was to be reached. The mechanism involved was presumably that of the anticipatory goal response, as described in Chapter III, pages 49–53. The sight of her brother eating Cornflakes presumably elicited a tendency for her to make similar eating responses. These, however, could occur only in fractional form such as slight chewing movements or salivation. Through past experience, the stimuli produced by the fractional anticipatory responses of eating this particular food have become the cues to diverse responses of seeking it. One such response, asking her mother for Cornflakes, occurred.

The observer was mistaken about one thing. She assumed that this imitative behavior was no longer in Ceci's pattern and that she had transferred to the habit of eating with her parents. The mother wanted the situation to be this way. Actually, the new learning had not yet progressed to the point where the anticipatory response of eating with the parents was strong enough to compete with the immediate imitative responses. This is not surprising in view of the repeated practice and high reward which had fixed the response of eating with her brother. The mother was, indeed, compelled to introduce two new anticipatory responses into Ceci's hierarchy in order to make the anticipation of eating later the dominant one. First, she showed annoyance, which tended to raise anxiety in Ceci—an anxiety which competed with the response of "eating now." In the second place, the mother raised the anticipation of eating the desired Cornflakes later, thus adding this appetitive element to the delay of the eating response. The anticipation of food later, of Cornflakes in particular, and of punishment for persistence in wanting to eat now were sufficient to turn the scales in favor of delay.

The report shows that Ceci did wait and did eat with her parents, an experience which strengthened the tendency to imitate them rather than her small brother. She learned eventually to want to eat when her parents ate and to want the foods that they ate. Each time that she ate with them and her hunger drive was reduced, the concurrent stimuli gained increasing power both to stimulate imitative eating behavior and to cue the time when the response would occur. Similarly, refraining from eating with the little brother steadily weakened this imitative response, since it was persistently non-rewarded. The old habit retained its power for a long time, however, and would occasionally compete successfully with the habit of waiting to eat with the parents.

In this example, Ceci was receiving training to match behavior upward rather than downward in the age and status scale. The parents' reason for changing the conditions and permitting Ceci to eat with them was that this would enable them to train her in the beginnings of table etiquette and further to cultivate her speech responses. Both of these objectives are culturally defined as appropriate for people of the parents' social status. Once again it is clear that culture acts as a selective agent upon the hierarchy of innate and acquired responses, bringing some of them to the fore, rewarding them, and fixing them as social behavior.

The fact that many responses are learned under pressure of secondary reward has been a mystifying one to social scientists. It has been clear that a great part of social learning depends upon such secondary rewards rather than upon the direct reduction of primary drives. Without the concept of secondary reward, the scientist is unable to explain, for instance, the rôle of praise, prestige, or money in fixing social habit. In the following case, we see a very simple response being learned under conditions of secondary reward. The case suggests that imitative responses, like other social responses, can be established in this way.

Case 2. Secondary Reward

Tom, at thirteen months, and his mother are playing the familiar game of peek-a-boo. The mother puts hands over eyes, suddenly removes her hands, and says "Peek" in a high voice while smiling. When completely learned, the game is arranged in reciprocal series, first one and then the other initiating the action. Tom was standing near his mother when she reported:

Tom put his hands over his *ears* and buried his chin in his chest, lifted his head, said "Peek," and looked at me. I had not been paying much attention to him but looked up when he said "Peek," and said "Peek" to him.

Several days later the following behavior was reported:

During the last day or so, Tom has been playing his peeking game by covering his ears as he did one night not so long ago when he was playing with his father. Occasionally he has put his hands over his eyes, but some of the time it has been over his ears. Of course, he has several good models now because his father and I thought it was such a joke when he covered up his ears that sometimes we cover our ears instead of our eyes and say "Peek" to him. It is hard to know just what he does make of the peeking game.

It is obvious from the excerpt that the "peek" behavior is both matched-dependent behavior and *same* behavior. Tom will carry it out when someone stimulates him to do it and will also initiate the act independently. These mechanisms will be considered separately, beginning with the matched-dependent act. The latter may be analyzed as follows:

	Parent	Child
Drive	Unknown	Secondary—wish for parental attention
Cue	Sight of child plus other factors	Parent playing "peek"
Response	"Peek" behavior ----matched--- Playing "peek"	
Reward	Unknown	Relaxation at parental attention

(Response row: "Peek" behavior is linked by "dependent" arrow and "matched" to Playing "peek")

The "peek" game was first performed before Tom by his mother and was later taken up by the father. It was some time before Tom himself learned to carry out his part of the game, although he tended to respond from the first with laughter when the "peek" action was performed before him by someone else; the sudden appearance of the familiar face seemed to excite especial pleasure. He first learned to say

"Peek" without covering his eyes. He would say "Peek" and then smile just as if he were carrying out his part of the game alone. When he said "Peek," it seemed to give him something of the same satisfaction that hearing someone else say it did. It was probably this satisfying character of the word "peek" which led him to react with pleasure when he by chance hit upon it, or a word which sounded like it, in his own random verbal behavior. Once having heard himself say the word, he repeated it and learned it the better. It could then be introduced as a response in the game itself. The question arises as to why hearing his mother say "Peek" should have a secondary rewarding value, and this is, indeed, the crucial question.

There are two ways of answering this. The first one runs as follows: It is a matter of fact that in the several thousand or more reinforcing situations in which the mother has been the reinforcing agent, she has talked to him before and while rewarding him. Her vocalizations thus acquired a sub-goal or secondary rewarding character; they promised that he could coast home to reward with a high degree of certainty.

A second but closely related hypothesis would run as follows: Tom heard himself crying and babbling repeatedly just before major reduction of primary drive occurred. Hearing himself babbling, therefore, acquired a secondary rewarding character. Hearing someone else talk is sufficiently like hearing oneself cry or babble to tend to evoke the same relaxation responses. Thus, hearing his own vocalizations came to indicate to the child that the goal was in sight. The same logic also applies, of course, to the mother's footstep, the stimulus pattern of her voice, face, dress, and the like. Perhaps the word "peek," when uttered by the mother, profits by transfer from Tom's own vocal stimuli.

What seems likely from the foregoing is that the word "peek" had an acquired reward value by generalization from other vocalizations of Tom's own, as well as from similar vocal behavior by his mother. The mother's gestures and smiles, while uttering "Peek," similarly had a secondary rewarding value. When Tom himself produced the "peek" response, he

was rewarded in two ways: first, by all the stimuli (attention) associated with secondary reward and, second, by the
relaxing value of the "peek" stimulus which he gave himself.
Once produced, therefore, the response is still more reinforced with each repetition of the game. It is regularly dis-
sociated from conditions of punishment or lack of reward,
since parents do not, for instance, say "Peek" and then spank
a child. The conventional rules of the game represent the conditions of learning in this case.

Tom craves parental attention more or less continuously.
He has been hungry, cold, bumped, in the past; and these
strong drive stimuli have left their mark on him. Although
not frightened at the moment, Tom's reaction to the stimuli
about him is a vague tensing response which, in turn, produces stimuli of mild drive value. The absence of parental notice is a part of these anxiety-producing stimuli. On the other
hand, when the mother appears, talks, or smiles, these tensing
responses tend to drop out, and a rewarding state of affairs has appeared. One thing in particular he has learned;
namely, that when mother is following him with her eyes,
good things are likely to come. To have her look at him,
therefore, rather than at a book or out of the window, is to
him a stimulus which promises reward rather than trouble. Of
course, he does not formulate the matter to himself in this
way. Instead, he has learned to react directly to the cue of
being noticed by his mother.[3]

It was undoubtedly crucial that the game itself alternately
presents and conceals the mother's face, thus, as it were,
switching on and off her attention. The word "peek," being
uttered at just the point when her reassuring face is again
suddenly visible, is strongly reinforced. The structure of the

---

[3] That this type of response to parental attention is not instinctive but
does depend upon learning is shown by the fact that, under appropriate conditions, a child can learn to be anxious at parental attention and want to
escape from it. A child under close observation shows the following behavior: When he is hungry, cold, or otherwise driven, he desires parental attention and goes toward the parents. When he is free from noxious drive,
he tends to escape from parental attention where possible. This is because
unsolicited parental attention has often been associated with having his
nose wiped, being put to bed, or being segregated from the family.

game itself sets excellent conditions for immediate reinforcement of the word "peek."

The analysis of the case from the standpoint of imitation may be summarized as follows: The parent puts hands over eyes, suddenly withdraws hands, and says "Peek." Since Tom wants parental notice, this constitutes a reassuring state of affairs. On some one occasion, he happens to say "Peek," or something like it, to himself; he finds that hearing himself say this is rewarding; thereupon he repeats it and begins to stabilize the response. He then produces it in the game and is additionally reinforced, first by hearing the parent say it and second by saying it himself. In actual fact, another reinforcement was added in Tom's case. When he himself learned to say "Peek," his mother showed increased interest and played the game longer with him, thus increasing the secondary reward value of the game and more strongly reinforcing his uttering of the word.

At the time of the incident under discussion, Tom had not yet perfected the eye-covering part of the game and was still making random responses with his hands in the attempt to approximate his mother's behavior. When he covered his ears instead of his eyes, the gesture so amused his father that he rewarded it strongly and during one phase stabilized it as a desirable form of response. When Tom made the correct response of putting his hands over his eyes (or ears), he received fewer "no-noes" from his parents and a longer play period with its reassuring parental attention.

It will further be noted that the cues to which the parent reacted in initiating this game were not at all obvious to Tom. On the contrary, they were quite obscure and probably very complex. They would include Tom's appearance on the scene, a complicated series of cue-producing responses concerned with the proper behavior of a parent toward a small child in our society, possibly the absence of strangers, and the like. Tom had not learned to discriminate these cues and was therefore dependent on the responses of the parent to set him playing "peek."

Tom eventually assumed the initiative himself. The mother

was mildly neglecting him when he began the game—at least her attention was not fixed on him. Under the secondary drive to get her comforting attention, his response to the parental "peek" moved far forward in the series of responses, so far, indeed, that it eliminated the parent's part of the game entirely. What had been at first an imitative response became independent through generalization. The stimulus pattern of the parent's lack of attention then became a cue which elicited a mild anxiety response; this stimulated Tom to initiate the comforting "peek" game himself. When once he had tried out making the "peek" response outside the context of the game but in the presence of the neglectful parent, the result was rewarding; the anticipatory response was strengthened in its new position in the sequence and became stable and independent.

The parent, of course, plays an important rôle in the independent stabilization of the "peek" response by giving attention to the word "peek" immediately on its first appearance. The response is thus promptly rewarded and raised in dominance over competing responses in Tom's hierarchy. It cannot be urged too insistently that the parent, in selecting, rewarding, and fixing the child's responses, is not acting as an isolated agent, but is carrying on a practice old in our society; it is society with its culture which determines that "peek," and not some other possible response, is to be selected and fixed.

In the cases already considered, the follower has had as a cue the matched act of the leader. There is a class of cases, however, in which merely seeing the matched act is not enough. The follower must know whether or not it succeeds. Take, for example, the problem of whether or not to follow a leader child onto newly formed ice. The follower child will observe that the leader skates out onto the ice, but he will also note with greatest care whether or not the leader falls in. In the latter case, the total cue pattern will not have the effect of evoking a matched act, whereas if the leader skates freely and without danger, the watching child may follow. This state of affairs may be called testing. The leader tests a situation, and his success or failure becomes part of a total cue pattern which determines the occurrence or non-occurrence of an imitative response. This mechanism is exemplified in the following case.

Case 3. *Testing*

Mary and Bill (aged four and one and one-half, respectively) were playing near their mother, who reported:

Mary came over and said that she wanted to sit in my lap. I said, "Well, I want to read this book for a while. Leave Mommy alone." Mary nevertheless succeeded in climbing into my lap.

Then Bill came up as soon as Mary was on my lap. I said to Mary, "You see what happens. When you come up, he wants to come up; and when he comes up, you want to come up, and that means I don't ever have any chance to sit down and read my book."

It seems clear that in this case the learning of matched-dependent behavior is already completed. The response is evoked immediately on seeing the other child perform it. It is to be noted also that each child, according to the mother's testimony, tends to imitate the other.

In any case of human behavior where the history of total social learning is not minutely known, there are bound to be uncertainties in the analysis of any specific segments of it. The procedure here has been to study the specific incident, bring to bear on it any known material from the rest of the life history (without introducing this in detail), and make one clear-cut analysis of the case. It sometimes happens that several alternative solutions are possible and that no one of them can be ruled out. The drive, moreover, is frequently not merely a single secondary drive but several which operate concurrently and which are often exceedingly difficult to isolate and weight. Where there are alternative possibilities with regard to drive, we shall select one for the paradigm and discuss the alternatives later.

The behavior above reported can be analyzed in the fol lowing manner:

	Leader	Imitator
Drive	Secondary—to be held by mother	Secondary—to be held by mother
Cue	Mother	Sister's climbing and success
Response	Climbing on lap --dependent--> --matched-- Climbing on lap	
Reward	Being held by mother	Being held by mother

The essence of the dilemma diagrammed above is that the little boy, who is crawling, is constantly motivated to be picked up by his mother, but is often turned away. There is one situation, however, in which he is never refused, namely, that in which the sister is taken onto the mother's lap. In the particular household, taking up the second child is a culturally patterned act, "justice" being regularly done to the children by not withholding from one what is given to the other. It is this essential fact which sets the conditions for the imitative learning under consideration.

The situation with regard to independent cues is probably extremely complex. Certainly most of the cues furnished by the mother in the particular situation serve to elicit approach responses on the part of the children. Very likely these responses are more frequently successful when the mother is sitting down than when she is standing up and moving about. Probably the cue of hearing himself cry also functions as a part of the pattern which indicates to the child that he will be taken on his mother's lap. When responding to these independent cues, both children are occasionally reinforced. It seems to be a fact, however, that they are not always reinforced when responding to the independent cues, but since they are sometimes taken on the lap under these circumstances the behavior does not extinguish. On the other hand, if the additional cue element of the other child sitting on mother's lap is present, the response of asking to be taken up is regularly rewarded and hence strongly reinforced. The success of the other child thus provides the crucial cue to regular reinforcement.

The drive element selected for exposition, "being near the mother," undoubtedly plays an important part, whatever other drives may also be operating. At the age of one year and a half, Bill has already been fed some fifteen hundred to two thousand times by his mother and has experienced reduction of many other drives as well, such as escape from pain, while in her presence or being held by her. Her presence operates, therefore, as a secondary reward. The cues of being near the mother, in short, elicit less tension than the cues of being away from her. This relaxation presumably constitutes the reinforcement which binds the sight of the mother to the response of moving toward her. A sub-goal has been reached, and a secondary drive reduced. Of course, if the mother were to go away for six months, this mechanism could not operate so powerfully, and cases are frequent where the mother of a small child loses her sub-goal value. The reason is clear. If the mother does not continue to reduce primary drives, the secondary drive of wanting to be near her cannot be maintained. The deserted child will cling to the skirts of the person who has cared for him in the interim.

It is evident, further, that the fundamental learning had already taken place in the case under discussion. It was not possible to follow the slow development of the response. The record seems to show that Bill's response of crawling or walking to the mother was learned independently. The same is true of Mary's. This response presumably had once been tried by the boy just after his sister had been taken onto her mother's lap; upon reaching his mother, he, too, was taken up; and the connection was thereby fixed between seeing sister being taken up and his own response of walking toward the mother. With much repetition, a partial discrimination

was evidently established. When the leader child tried and
was not taken up, the follower learned not to demand to be
near the mother. When the leader succeeded, the approach
and demand habit was evoked and reinforced in the follower.

In the next and last example, the fact that imitation can be
elicited under the pressure of secondary drive will become
more clear. The wish to match behavior with another can itself become a secondary drive. When the conditions of learning are such that the behavior of others frequently points the
road to reward, such an imitative drive would be expected to
arise. The example further shows a rivalrous drive in operation. The wish is not only to do what the other person does,
but also to do it first.

Case 4. Secondary Drives of Imitation and Rivalry

Mary, at three and a half, has been playing in the snow
with her friend Jean, who is about the same age. The mother
puts Bill in his Taylor-tot (a small cart which can be pulled
by a handle). Mary had previously paid no attention to Bill
in this situation. The record reads:

Jean said, "I want to pull Bill."
Mary immediately said, "No, I want the first turn."
I said, "Well, you can take turns at it. Mary, you can take
the first turn, and then Jean." Mary pulled Bill for about fifteen feet and then dropped the handle and asked me to pull him.
I said, "Now it is Jean's turn." Jean pulled him up the driveway.

This situation is not clear as concerns Jean's motive. Her
history is virtually unknown, and we cannot, therefore, offer
any convincing presumptions as to how she had learned to
want to pull a little boy in a Taylor-tot. It must be accepted
as a matter of fact, for the purpose of this analysis, that she
did. It seems likely that she had learned to carry out such
behavior with her own little sister under pressure of parental
approval. This being conceded for the sake of the discussion,
the imitative analysis would proceed as follows:

	Jean	Mary
Drive	Secondary—desire for approval	Rivalry
Cue	Boy in Taylor-tot, mother, etc.	Jean's request to pull boy
Response	Request to pull boy	Request to pull boy
Reward	Unknown	Success in rivalry

(Jean's Response is "dependent" upon Mary's Cue; Jean's Response and Mary's Response are "matched.")

It would seem that Mary's tendency to match behavior with another has here become a secondary drive, which can be called a drive to imitate. Its history is very clear from the record of her previous behavior. She had learned that acts that other people carry out are very likely to be fun (that is, tension reducing). Examples would be eating, drinking, and carrying through the various appetitive drives based upon these. She had also learned that this fun occurred very frequently when she matched her acts with another's. She had repeatedly eaten, for instance, with other children, so that their eating behavior tended to become a cue stimulus for her own. The imitative drive by itself, however, carried her only to the point of stimulating her to do what the other child was already doing. Mary has further learned that there are some situations in which only one person at a time can make a desired response, and that the other person must wait. This applies, for example, to getting the first piece of birthday cake, to being picked up first by a parent, to being swung by an adult. There is also operative in the situation a cultural "first come first served" principle, in which the parents grant favors to those who make the first demand for them. Verbalized for Mary, the attitude would read like this: "If I get there first, I will get the most gratifying result the quickest."

Actually, Mary's reactions were probably more direct than such a formulation might imply. In many different situations she had been rewarded for striving to be first; hence in this situation she doubtless strove to be first without additional stimulation from thoughts about the probability of reward.

In families where there is an actual shortage of food, this rivalry factor frequently leads children to learn to eat very rapidly. The reward for quick eating is more of the scarce food.

It seems clear, then, that Mary had learned, before this incident was recorded, to make the response of repeating the claims of other children for a desired object or for permission to carry out a suggested line of activity first. The response was apparently readily generalized from the food and play situations to the novel but similar situation of cart-pulling. The perception of Jean carrying out the act of asking to pull the cart aroused a secondary drive in Mary. When a much smaller child, Mary had often responded to such a situation by asking permission to carry out the observed act after another child had performed it. Reward then entered to reinforce the imitative act. Gradually, however, the response of asking became anticipatory, and she would not wait until the other child had been tossed up in the air or gotten her lollypop, but would make her verbal demand immediately after the verbal demand of the other child. This anticipatory response was rewarded because frequently her claim would be considered more nearly on a parity with that of the person first demanding the good or service, and she would be allowed, though asking second, to enjoy the favor at the same time or even first.

Mary should, in principle, be less likely to react with rivalrous behavior in the next situation of the same specific kind. The reinforcement of her rivalrous action ended at the moment that she began to pull the cart. At this point there entered another factor, namely, fatigue. Mary found that it was laborious to pull the cart and that the fun element was relatively meager. Fatigue pressure soon became dominant over cart-pulling, and she dropped the handle of the cart after a few paces.

Jean, on the other hand, appears to have been much more strongly motivated. She pulled the cart "up the driveway," which is a far longer distance than Mary had pulled it; her act was also more effortful, since the driveway had a considerable slope. Whatever her drive may have been, it was evidently much stronger than the secondary rivalry drive in Mary.

It seems likely from the above discussion that competition or rivalry must frequently derive directly from the imitative mechanism, and that a rivalrous drive is built upon an imitative drive. Rivalrous behavior can, of course, be reinforced directly without the aid of the imitative mechanism. An acquired drive to imitate can become an acquired drive to rivalry when the conditions of reward are such that only one person at a time can make the response. Reward is then more rapidly secured if the imitator can beat the leader in making the suggested response. From the standpoint of the follower, matched-dependent behavior may seem merely imitative; from the standpoint of the leader, however, it frequently seems competitive. This is especially the case when the follower learns to make the matched response very rapidly upon perceiving the cue that the leader is in action, so that he threatens to beat the leader to the goal. In the case of *same* behavior, where both persons distinguish the environmental cue at the same moment, rivalry emerges in its clearest form. Then it becomes a question of which individual can make the correct response and reach the goal most rapidly.

Imitative versus Environmental Cues

Since so much importance is attached, in matched behavior, to the superior ease of following the imitative as compared with the environmental cue, it will be worthwhile discussing the circumstances under which an imitative cue is easier to discriminate than the environmental cue. It is obvious that the imitative cue will be easier to follow if the connection between it and the appropriate response is either innate or already partly learned. Our position is that if there are any innate connections between stimuli and responses of the imitative type, they are few and isolated.

If some response incompatible with the correct one is already attached to the environmental cue, this circumstance will favor the use of the imitative cue. The correct response is thereby greatly lowered in the initial hierarchy and in some cases partly eliminated. A child, for instance, who has been punished for attempting to walk down a particular stairway may respond with avoidance behavior to the pattern of cues associated with the stairs, but he may follow a trusted leader down these very stairs.

It is easier to learn to respond to an imitative cue than to an environmental cue if the former is more distinctive than the latter. Responses attached to less distinct environmental cues would be expected to generalize to other similar cues. These responses may be non-rewarded, and the effect of non-reward will generalize back to the indistinct cue. Furthermore, any responses incompatible with the correct one which may be already attached to near-by cues will be more likely to generalize to the indistinct environmental cue. It may be harder, therefore, to discriminate between the environmental cue and other similar cues than between the imitative cue and other similar cues. This state of affairs is exemplified in the behavior of a small child in the living room of a strange house. Four somewhat similar doors led from this room to the out of doors, and the child made a number of mistakes in selecting the correct door. On a second trial, he found it much easier to follow another child in seeking the correct door than to learn to find it himself. If the correct door had been painted red or had been of glass, it might have made the environmental cue sufficiently distinctive to be easily associated with the correct response, and might thereby have lessened the utility of the imitative response.

It is simpler to respond to an imitative pattern of cues when fewer separate habits are involved in the correct response to it than in that to the environmental cues. It is obviously easier, for instance, to follow the tail-light of a friend's car through the streets of a great city to an unfamiliar address than to poke along and find the way by the use of a street map.

Likewise, the attachment of the same response to a number of different cues is more difficult than its attachment to a single cue. If the independent stimulus involves five different cues, any one of which may be present, so that the subject must learn to respond to each of them, while the imitative response requires response to one cue only, other things equal, the imitative cue will obviously be the easier. This principle is exemplified by the case where a child must learn to withdraw from snakes, dogs, glass, high edges, and dirty objects (five different cues involved) as opposed to learning to withdraw when the parent withdraws (one cue involved).

That response will be more difficult to learn whose connection to a cue is mediated by the greater number of cue-producing responses. It is, for instance, easier to copy an answer from another student's paper than to use the calculus to determine it oneself. The response of imitating in this case is much easier than that of making the cue-producing responses involved in calculus, and the imitative cues will be easier to attach to responses than would be the environmental ones (i.e., those of the problem posed to student).

Analogous to the above principle is the following: If some of the required sub-units of a habit are already present, the total number of new stimulus-response connections to be learned will be reduced, and the habit will be easier to attach to a cue. If, therefore, many of the components of successful imitation (such as looking at the leader, putting one's hand in the same general region as his, or moving it up and then down) are already present as a result of previous learning, the learning of a new act as an imitative response to cues from a leader will be favored over learning it as an independent response to environmental cues. If, for instance, a boy has learned to watch and match, it will be easier for him to learn to throw a curve with a baseball by seeing how another boy puts his hand on the ball than by puzzling out the solution for himself.

The distinctiveness of cues, the presence or absence of competing responses, the complexity of the cue pattern itself, and the number of response segments already present will each and all influence the occurrence of the imitative as compared to the independent learning of a response.

These cases, it is hoped, suggest that complex social acts are susceptible to analysis from the standpoint of the principles and conditions of learning. They supplement the simpler cases where drive is direct and biological, reward is a reduction of primary drive, the cues are distinctive, and the response is of a gross muscular type. The possibilities of effective social analysis are greatly increased when it is realized that drive and reward can be acquired and complex, that cue patterns may be very intricate, and that responses may include verbal or other cue-producing types such as those involved in foresight and reasoning. Every principle and theorem of learning theory is doubtless involved at some time in some example of imitation. Mechanisms ranging from simple, almost reflex responses to the more elaborate responses which produce strong drives and distinctive cues all appear in examples of imitative behavior. Future expansions of learning theory will probably contribute to the analysis of examples of imitation which are now obscure. A theory of imitation, or of any other form of social behavior, can be no more effective than the general psychological and social theory from which it is derived. If the foregoing interpretations have been cogent for imitation, it seems likely that a similar pattern of analysis could be successfully undertaken for such phenomena as sympathy, suggestion, prestige, coöperation, and other social attitudes.

CHAPTER X

COPYING: THE RÔLE OF SAMENESS AND DIFFERENCE

THE dynamics of copying are more complicated than those of simple matched-dependent behavior. The essential additional elements characteristic of copying can best be brought out by the analysis of a concrete example.

This is the case of an adult who was so poor a singer that his friends considered him practically tone deaf. At an age when most people have already forgotten how they acquired the ability to match notes, he decided that he wanted to learn to carry a tune. The example involves two people: the copier and a teacher. The teacher served as a model,[1] singing the notes to be copied, and also served as a critic, punishing the copier when he failed to sing the right note and rewarding him when he finally succeeded in achieving a successful match. Because the pupil started out at such a low level of skill, all the details of the copying process were brought out quite clearly.

Interviews with the subject established the fact that he was motivated to learn how to sing because group singing played an important rôle in the parties of the primary clique to which he belonged. He thought singing would be fun, and experienced mild anxiety at being different from the other members of the clique. The first models whose behavior he attempted to match were his friends participating in group singing. They were also the first critics, verbally defining a non-match by saying, "You're way off key!" This practice, however, did not enable the subject to learn to discriminate the particular cues indicating that he was off key and to attach anxiety differentially to these cues. This was partly because the criticisms were relatively random, correlated more

[1] The term "model" apparently was first systematically used by Bernard (1926, p. 323).

with fluctuations in his friends' tolerance than with relevant
cues indicating goodness of match, and was partly because
the subject seldom made the response of singing on key so
that he could be differentially rewarded. Conditions for learning to match were poor, and little such learning occurred.
There was one response which was rather consistently rewarded in the group—that of stopping singing. This response was learned and ended the possibility of further trial-
and-error matching in the group situation. But the cue of being different from the group and the motivation which it
aroused persisted. Thus, when the subject was offered a
chance for special instruction, he accepted.

The task of learning to sing proved to be unexpectedly
difficult. First, the copier tried to sing a simple tune with the
model. The result was complete discord. The attempt to teach
the flowing melody of a tune was therefore abandoned, and
the task was fractionated into that of matching notes sung
one at a time. The teacher, acting as a model, sounded a note
and held it. The copier listened and then tried to hit the note.

The cues present to guide the subject may first be analyzed. When the model sang the first note, the pitch of that
note was present as a relevant cue. As soon as the copier
joined in with his note, certain additional cues were produced
affording a possible basis for a comparison of the two tones.[2]
These additional cues played a crucial rôle in the copying
process. When the two notes were of the same pitch, there
was a certain blending or smoothness of the total sound.
Somewhat similar blendings were produced by other combinations of pitches, especially by the octave. When the two
tones were not of the same pitch, there was a certain rough-
ness or grating quality to the total sound.[3] This cue was less

[2] All of these are cues resulting from the joint action of two sources of
stimulation. Such cues have long been emphasized by the Gestalt psychologists and often neglected, but not denied, by stimulus-response psychologists; they have recently been discussed by Professor Hull (1941*) under
the heading of *Afferent Interaction*.

[3] This cue may actually have been a complex pattern involving the result
of several different factors, such as physical beats between sound waves of
two different frequencies, the stimulation of disparate points on the basilar
membrane of the ear, or some more central mechanism.

distinctive at certain large intervals such as the octave, more distinctive at relatively close (dissonant) non-matches, and again less distinctive at very close non-matches. There were also present certain cues depending on the direction of the difference between the two pitches. To these the responses of "higher than" and "lower than" were later attached. These cues were more distinctive as the difference between the pitch of the two notes became greater.

The copier's responses to the cue of the note as sung by the model were very inaccurate. He had received enough previous training in speaking in the culturally acceptable range of pitch to come within three or four notes of the correct tone, but within this region his responses were exclusively those of trial and error. He did not know how to hit the correct note, nor even whether he was hitting it. He had no differential response to the cue of dissonance which was present when his note failed to match that of the model, and he could respond only to great differences of "higher than" or "lower than." In short, he had no specific responses to the cues indicating sameness or difference of pitch.

The teacher did have these differential responses and hence could act as a critic. In this capacity, the teacher continued to say "No" as long as simultaneous stimulation from the two notes produced cues indicating that a match was not close enough to be acceptable. Hearing the critic say "No" was a cue for the copier to react with responses which produced sharp little jabs of anxiety. From past experiences of failure, this verbal indication of disapproval had acquired considerable capacity to elicit an acquired drive. The tension was mild at first but mounted to an appreciable height as "No" was continually repeated. Because the copier already had considerable sophistication in the art of learning, the critic's "No" and the anxiety which it aroused acted not only as a drive but also as a cue to which the copier had learned to react by immediately varying his response. Stopped in specific responses by the critic's "No," but driven to continue responding by the motivation to learn, the copier varied his pitch in a random manner and felt rather helpless. During the course of these trials, the critic sometimes said, "That's too low, try a little higher," and discovered that although the copier could not discriminate any but major differences in pitch, he already knew how to tense his vocal cords to raise the pitch, and could do so to the cue of specific instructions. The introduction of this new cue by the critic cut the range of trial and error roughly in half, thus doubling the probability of hitting the correct note.

The critic next tried to limit the range of trial and error still further by giving instructions as to how much higher the copier was to sing. It was soon obvious, however, that the latter had never learned to attach appropriate responses to such suggestions as "go up two notes" or "go up just a little more." In the absence of proper habits of responding to such cues, these instructions were useless and were abandoned.

Finally, a tolerably correct note was hit by chance, and the critic said "Yes!" The copier felt relieved, held the note, and listened.

On succeeding trials, the copier gradually became able to reach the correct note more rapidly and to respond independently to the cues of sameness and difference. Previously he had been saying "No" to himself and responding with a twinge of anxiety after each "No" from the critic. He had also been saying "Yes" to himself, relaxing, and feeling pleased after each "Yes" from the critic. Gradually these responses began to become anticipatory,[4] so that the cue of dissonance (plus perhaps the cue of "higher than" or "lower than") tended to elicit anxiety responses and to cause the subject to vary the pitch of his note even before the critic said "No." Similarly, the disappearance of dissonance and the appearance of blending became a cue for a reduction of anxiety and thus acquired the capacity to reward the particular responses which had produced the match.

As would be expected, the copier's responses of saying "Yes" to himself and relaxing his anxiety tended to generalize from the cue of smooth blending produced by the actual

---

[4] See Chapter III for a description of the mechanism of anticipatory response.

match to the cues of similar blending produced by the octave
and other musical intervals. He had greater difficulty in attaching the response of "No" and mild anxiety discriminatingly to the less distinctive cues produced by these combinations than to the more distinctive cues produced by more dissonant combinations.

As discrimination was improved, so that the copier was almost certain to react to the cues indicating difference with responses producing acquired drive, and to the cues indicating
sameness with responses producing acquired reward, the copier became able to practice trial-and-error matching without
aid from the critic. This may be expressed in abbreviated
form by saying the copier could become his own critic. In a
much later stage of learning, he was able to use a piano as a
model, to serve as his own critic, and thus to practice improv-
ing his skill at matching without aid from the teacher.

The copier learned to respond to the cues of difference
with anxiety and to the cues of sameness with a reduction in
anxiety long before he learned to respond to the model's note
by immediately singing the same note himself. Thus the period of trial-and-error copying during which the subject was
his own critic extended over a considerable time. This stage
of the process, with the copier correcting his own trial-and-
error behavior by responding independently to cues of sameness and difference, frequently comparing his own responses
with the model, is perhaps the most commonly noted characteristic of copying (Park and Burgess, 1924, p. 346).

After the copier had learned to be his own critic for sameness and difference, there was a period when he had not yet
learned to respond differentially to directional cues. He knew
that he was off pitch, but he had no idea whatsoever whether
he should go up or down. The next stage was that of attaching the response of tensing the vocal cords to the cue of
"lower than" and the response of relaxing the vocal cords to
the cue of "higher than." This was learned partly by trial
and error and partly by anticipatory responses to the critic's
suggestions.

At the same time, the copier was also learning to limit the

range of trial and error still further by responding with a larger differential in tensing to the cue of a large difference in pitch. Verbal instructioris from the critic were inefficient in hastening the course of this learning because the subject had not already learned to make sufficiently specific responses to such instructions. He had to learn by sheer trial and error to make more and more accurate tensing responses to various amounts of difference in pitch. When this was learned, he was able to make more and more rapid approximations and corrections, so that his behavior lost that seemingly disorganized variability which characterized his first trial and error.

As his skill increased, the copier could respond with greater accuracy directly to the pitch of the model note, and make rapid sliding corrections on the basis of the direction and amount of difference between his own and the model's notes. In this manner he learned to match a single note.[5]

When the model sang a new note, its pitch, of course, was a different cue. As soon as the subject started to sing, however, the combination of the two notes produced cues of dissonance or blending similar to those previously present. Responses of anxiety or relief tended to generalize on the basis of this similarity, but because dissonances and blends sounded somewhat different in widely different parts of the scale this generalization was not perfect; the copier found himself less reliable as a critic in trying to match new notes. In like manner the relation of "higher than" or "lower than," and even the amount of difference, produced cues which were similar in different parts of the scale. Thus responses of tensing or relaxing the vocal cords an appropriate amount also tended to generalize. It became progressively easier to learn to copy new notes.

At last the subject had the units for copying single notes. It was discovered, however, that he still had to learn how to combine these units. When first trying to copy a melodic se-

5 In the interests of clearer exposition, the various stages of this learning are separated somewhat more than they were in the actual practice. The subject tried to copy new notes before he had thoroughly mastered the art of copying the first note.

ries he made mistakes, some of which he recognized (eliciting the response of "No," plus anxiety) and some of which he did not. It was necessary for the teacher to start functioning again as a critic, punishing the wrong combinations which the subject did not recognize. With additional training, the copier became more skillful at combining and recombining the units he had learned, until finally he was able to copy whole phrases of melody.

Eventually, the subject tried out his first song with an intimate clique. As he started to sing, he felt a slight undercurrent of anxiety, but, when he had finished, his friends reduced this anxiety by praising him. They said, "Yes, you sang on key," and he tended to repeat similar statements to himself. The coincidence of these statements with the praise and other social reward strengthened their acquired reward value when subsequently used either by the subject, serving as his own critic, or by the teacher. Through other similar symbolic transfers (some of which were probably verbally mediated and most of which are not yet well understood), the whole process of copying and responding to remote goals of self-improvement was strengthened. Occasional criticism from members of the clique kept up the anxiety-arousing value of the cues produced by failures to match.

The essential elements of the process of copying have all been illustrated in the example analyzed. The mechanism may now be compared with that of simple matched-dependent behavior. In both cases, the responses are connected to a cue from an independent subject or model. In both, likewise, the punishment of non-matched responses and the reward of matched responses eventually result in conformity of behavior between the leader and the follower. The essential difference between the two processes is that in matched-dependent behavior the imitator responds only to the cue from the leader, while in copying he responds also to cues of sameness and difference produced by stimulation from his own and the model's responses.

It seems probable that different types of imitation form a continuum ranging from pure matched-dependent behavior at one extreme to copying at the other. Between these two extremes lie responses which are chiefly dependent upon the cue produced by stimulation from the model's response alone, but are also slightly dependent on the cues of sameness and difference produced by stimulation from both responses. Once the sophisticated human subject has learned, as a part of his training in copying, to pay attention to cues of sameness and difference, he is likely to respond to such cues and use as many copying sub-units as possible in all of his further imitation. Thus, the children in the preceding experiments did not have to learn by laborious trial and error how to open the lid of the box that they had just seen the leader open; they used already acquired copying sub-units.

The response to cues of sameness and difference which characterizes copying is greatly facilitated by the critic, who punishes non-matches and rewards matches, and who often uses special techniques to single out correct responses.[6] It is also possible for environmental forces, such as the gravity that will pull one jarringly to the earth if the foot is not placed in the right spot, to serve in lieu of the critic. Once the cues of difference have acquired anxiety value and those of sameness have acquired reward value, the copier may act as his own critic, rewarding and punishing his own trial and error. When copying is progressing smoothly, the anxiety aroused by the cues of difference may be only minimal and serve merely as one of the cues to elicit well practiced habits of adjustment; but if the copier fails to succeed, anxiety is likely to reappear.

Often the criteria of sameness and difference are established long before the skill in matching is perfected. The student learns to feel uneasy about the fact that his handwriting differs from that in the copybook perhaps months or years before he can approximate the model. For the types of matches that play an important rôle in our lives, proper re-

[6] In the absence of a model, and hence in the absence of cues of sameness and difference, a critic may administer rewards and punishments which teach the pupil *same* behavior. Usually, however, critics compare the behavior of the pupil to some model, who, if not present, is described.

sponses are attached to the cues of sameness and difference at such an early age that most people take them for granted. It is necessary to detach oneself completely from one's accustomed environment in order to realize that responding appropriately to relevant differences has to be learned. But when one does encounter completely new situations, one may find that such responses are not innate. A young anthropologist discovered this to his sorrow when he attempted to join some adolescents who were beating a rhythm with sticks on the roots of a tree. He was considered to have an excellent sense of rhythm, by the standards of our society, and thought that he was matching the behavior of the adolescents perfectly. To his disillusionment, they politely requested him to stop and explained that he was so far off the rhythm that he was completely spoiling it. In learning those sounds in a foreign language which have no counterpart in English, the student invariably discovers that he does not have an instinctive capacity to make a perfect response imitatively on the first trial. Often he cannot at first even recognize the ways in which his responses differ from those of his model. It is only by getting completely away from the elements of their accustomed life that adults can approximate the experiences of children, all of whom enter at birth into an utterly foreign culture.

Though proper responses to sameness and difference may have to be relearned in completely new situations, there is a definite element of similarity in the sameness of widely differing pairs of matched cues. Likewise, there may be an element of similarity in the non-identity of widely differing pairs of non-matched cues. For example, Miller (1934) has demonstrated that if young children are trained to find candy under a yellow box placed with three red boxes, they will immediately look for candy under a purple box placed with three green boxes. Thus "difference in color" seems to function as a cue, irrespective of the specific color involved. Furthermore, as is well known, a difference in brightness is similar enough as a cue throughout the range of intensity so that an animal or child trained to go to the brighter of two dim

lights will also have a tendency to go to the brighter of two
bright lights. The same thing seems to be true of many differences, such as those in size, weight, and height. These results demonstrate that, within limits, sameness and difference
can serve as relatively constant cues irrespective of the specific stimuli being matched.[7]

The determination of just how different two pairs of
matched stimuli can be and still produce sufficiently similar
cues to elicit appreciable generalization from one match to
the other is a matter to be decided by further research in the
field of perception. The problem is complicated by the fact
that once different matches are both labeled with the word
"same," a verbal cue is introduced which, as will be shown in
the next chapter, can mediate secondary generalization.

During the course of socialization an enormous number of
skills in copying are learned. Some of these seem very humble
from the proud vantage point of adulthood. They include
putting one's hand in the same place someone else has put
his hand, turning a knob in the same direction that someone
else turns it, standing up when others are standing up in
church, and sitting down when they are sitting down. Though
the cues indicating a socially acceptable degree of matching
or non-matching may be different in these different types of
behavior, they all tend to be given a certain amount of functional unity because the subject is taught to respond to all
of them with a common word, "same," or with various synonyms of that word.

As a result of intensive training in copying with attention
frequently directed by means of language to the comparison
of themselves with others, people acquire tendencies to look
at the behavior and personal effects of others and to notice
any differences that may appear. This habit plays an important rôle in the diffusion of culture traits.

Individuals are likely to be punished for deviating too far
from the behavior of the rest of the group, and to be re-

[7] Because of this fact, one would expect the copying mechanism, elicited
by cues of sameness and difference, to generalize more widely than simple
matched-dependent behavior elicited by a more specific cue from the leader.

warded for conforming. A child moving into a new neighborhood did not have the skill to engage in sports, such as baseball, which were major activities of the playgroup. Not being
able to participate in the same way as the other children, he
suffered scorn and partial exclusion from the group. Lacking
group support, he was vulnerable to attack from aggressive
lower-class cliques lurking at the bottom of the hill and suffered pain from fists and stones.[8] Thus motivated, he learned
the skills enabling him to participate in the same sports as
his playmates, and was rewarded by social acceptance and
protection. As a result of such experiences, being different
tends to elicit anxiety and being the same to bring relief; an
acquired motivation to conform, or copy, is established.

In the case of the individual learning to sing, cues of a new
kind of non-match, the dissonance of tones, acquired a drive
value. For those whose musical training has been rigorous,
the socially unacceptable forms of non-matching can acquire
so strong a drive value that hearing someone sing or play
off-key can be a positively painful experience. It might be
ventured that the acquired drive value of dissonance can become so great that a sensitive musician could be taught to
run a simple maze, to press a bar, or to twist a dial in order
to escape.

The acquired drive to copy may have components other
than anxiety. The individual is often rewarded for copying
activities which his friends are enjoying. He may try new
foods that are delicious, may find that dancing, skiing, and
sailing are fun, and may escape summer heat by following
friends into the cool ocean. Through such experiences an appetitive motivation may be acquired to copy activities which
others seem to be enjoying.

Motivation to copy helps to produce social conformity. It
may not always be successful when the drives opposing conformity are sufficiently strong, but it does seem to be a stable
feature of social life. It is probably the basis of behavior
which Trotter (1917) has described as the "herd instinct"

---

[8] The onset of the bursts of pain elicited anxiety; their subsidence reinforced it.

and Sumner and Keller (1927) have noticed as "compulsions
of a moral order." It is possible that a more detailed analysis
would show that the mechanisms involved in copying are also
involved in that aspect of character, or super-ego formation
which the Freudians have described as "identification."[9]

When the external cues of sameness and difference are able
to elicit sufficient acquired drive and reward value directly
and without support from internal verbal cues, copying may
occur by unconscious trial and error. In many cases, however,
the cues of sameness and difference are able to elicit the responses producing acquired reward or acquired drive only
when operating as a part of a larger pattern. In general,
sameness is much more likely to be rewarded and difference to
be punished in situations which are verbally defined, first by
the critic and then by the subject himself, as copying situations. Thus the verbal definition of the situation, or what
might be called the intent to copy, may become an essential
part of the pattern of cues eliciting the responses involved in
copying. This is so-called conscious copying.

[9] In this connection, it is interesting to note that psychoanalytic observations seem to indicate that identification is most likely to occur with parents
or other loved, prestigeful people. These loved people with prestige are the
very ones who control the rewards and punishments which are most important to the child. They are thus in the best position to give acquired reward
value to conformity with their behavior, and acquired anxiety value to non-
conformity with their behavior. To deal adequately with this problem would
require a detailed analysis of the conditions of character formation. This is
beyond the scope of the present study.

CHAPTER XI

THE PRESTIGE OF MODELS: EXPERIMENTS ON CHILDREN

FROM the analysis of examples it has been found that one of the important conditions for the learning of imitation is the presence in our own society of hierarchies of individuals who differ greatly in the degree to which they have learned to make independently those responses which are most likely to be rewarded. Children of different ages form such a hierarchy. Because an older child knows better when, where, and how to respond independently to difficult cues in the environment, younger children are often rewarded for learning to imitate or copy older children.

But the same hierarchy which creates these conditions for the reward of imitation also creates conditions of differential reward for matching different models. If a child imitates an older, more sophisticated person, he is likely to be rewarded. If he imitates a younger, less sophisticated child, he is less likely to be rewarded; in fact, he may even be punished. Thus, in an earlier example, Ceci was rewarded for eating when her parents were eating and was non-rewarded in her attempts to eat when her little brother was eating.

People at various levels of the hierarchy are not only different in their ability to perform, in difficult situations, those responses which will be rewarded, but are also differentiated by more or less distinctive cues. Ceci's parents, who know the eating habits for which she is to be rewarded, are larger than she is; her younger brother, whose table manners are not acceptable, is smaller. The differences in size are distinctive cues. According to the principles of learning, the regular correlation of an important difference in reward with a distinctive difference in cues should tend to produce a discrimination. If differential rewards are persistently applied, Ceci should learn to match the table manners of her parents rather

than those of her little brother. But because Ceci has had so
many previous rewards for eating at the same time and in the
same manner as her little brother, a strong habit must be
broken down before this discrimination can be established.
Another factor interfering with the development of the discrimination will be the fact that she is sometimes rewarded
for imitating her brother in other situations. Thus the process of learning the discrimination may be slow, and her brother's table manners may continue for some time to exert a bad
influence on hers.

An analysis in terms of learning principles indicates that
the factor of generalization should play an important rôle in
the processes determining the degree to which any leader will
be reacted to as a prestigeful model. Generalization tends to
interfere with the first discrimination. To the extent that the
first good and bad models[1] are similar, the effects of reward
for matching the behavior of the good model may generalize
and produce a tendency to match the behavior of the bad
model; and the effects of non-reward or punishment for
matching the behavior of the bad model may generalize and
reduce the tendency to match the good model. If the cues are
quite similar, it may take considerable differential reward to
overcome these effects, and if the cues are too similar, a discrimination may be impossible. Conversely, of course, the
more distinctively different the cues characteristic of the two
models, the easier it will be for the discrimination to be
learned.

After a discrimination between two leaders is learned, it
should tend to generalize to other similar leaders. A leader
with whom the subject has had no previous experience should
be imitated to the extent that he presents cues similar to
other leaders whom the subject has been rewarded for imitating, and should not be imitated to the extent that he presents
cues similar to those of leaders whom the subject has been

[1] For convenience, the model which the subject has been rewarded for
copying will be referred to as a "good" model and the one which the subject has been non-rewarded for copying will be referred to as a "bad" model.
Good and bad will be used in a technical rather than a moral sense.

non-rewarded for imitating. Such generalization will not be expected to be entirely limited to the innate similarity of the cues, but should occur also on the basis of any acquired equivalence which may already have been learned for these cues.

At first, some of these generalizations will occur on the basis of similarities which are irrelevant, that is, which are not regularly correlated with reward or non-reward. If, however, the subject receives sufficient motivated, rewarded practice to learn to respond correctly to the new leader as a good or bad model, the effects of irrelevant generalization will be neutralized. Furthermore, the correct responses to relevant cues will be strengthened. Thus, as a subject learns to respond correctly to more and more good and bad models, the relevant cues should gradually be singled out to play an increasingly important rôle in further generalization to new leaders. The subject will be expected to acquire a better concept of the correct criteria for the goodness of a model, to be more judicious in the selection of his experts. This learning should be easier to the extent that the relevant cues are more distinctive.

Generalization from one leader to another has been considered. The two components of the discrimination should also tend to generalize from one situation to another. That is, after a subject has learned to imitate one leader and to non-imitate another in one situation, he should tend to respond with some of the same imitation and non-imitation in new situations. More generalization will be expected, of course, in proportion to the degree of innate similarity or previously acquired equivalence of the cues in the two situations. If both innate similarity and acquired equivalence are slight, such generalization as occurs may be overridden by other factors in the situation.

Finally, the discrimination may be expected to generalize from one response to another. After a subject has repeatedly been rewarded for imitating a response of one leader and non-rewarded for imitating a response of another, he should be more likely to use the first leader than the second as a model for other responses.[2]

If the responses produced by generalizations from situation to situation and from response to response are not rewarded, discriminations may be established on the basis of any relevant cues distinctively differentiating the two situations or the two responses. Under these conditions, a subject may be expected to learn to imitate a leader in one type of situation and not to imitate him in another, to imitate a leader for one type of response but not for another. For example, one may learn to copy the professor in the laboratory but not on the golf course. The more detailed deductions concerning such discriminations will be expected to be exactly the same as those already described for the discrimination between leaders.

The variables involved in learning to discriminate between models have been discussed with reference to the hierarchy of age-grading. The same variables apply to other hierarchies of individuals who differ in the degree to which they have learned to make independently those responses which are most likely to be rewarded. Social classes and specialized occupations are further examples of such hierarchies. These and other relevant societal conditions must be analyzed in detail before human imitative and non-imitative behavior can be understood. Before making this more detailed analysis of the conditions of human imitation, experiments will be described demonstrating that these conditions actually do produce the effects to be expected according to the principles of learning.

Experiment 7. Learning To Discriminate between Leaders[3]

The purpose of this experiment was to test the deduction that if two leaders are differentiated by distinctive cues and

2 Analogous to the so-called "halo-effect."

3 The authors are grateful to Mrs. Virginia Sheffield and to Mr. Fred Sheffield for intelligent work as research assistants in constructing the apparatus and conducting the experiments described in this chapter.

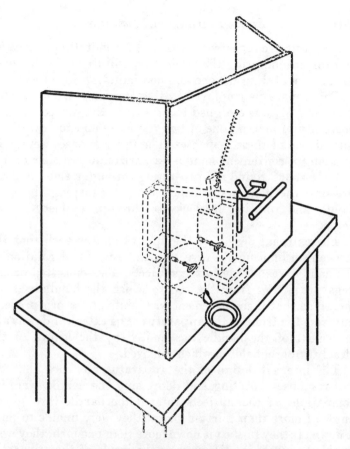

FIG. 11. APPARATUS FOR TESTING PRESTIGE
OF A LEADER AS A MODEL

The handle may be either rotated clockwise through the ninety
degree angle allowed by the pegs or depressed the six inches allowed by the slot. The internal parts of the apparatus, represented in dotted lines, make these two responses incompatible.
After a correct response is made, an assistant experimenter,
concealed behind the screen, can drop candy through the funnel
out into the dish. The back of the slot in the front screen is covered by a sliding shield not shown in the diagram.

On trials with the handle, the two stirrup-shaped rings were
absent. On tests for generalization, they were inserted into the
apparatus in the position indicated.

the subjects are repeatedly rewarded for imitating one leader and for not imitating the other, they will learn the discrimination of imitating the one and non-imitating the other.

The apparatus employed in this experiment, represented in Figure 11, was designed to present to the subject the opportunity of making one of two responses and to reward the correct one of these responses. The two responses were: (1) grasping a convenient handle—a horizontal crossbar on the end of a short, round rod projecting through a slot—and depressing the handle six inches, or (2) grasping the same handle and rotating it clockwise through a ninety degree angle.

The external design of the apparatus was such that the mechanism limiting the direction and amount of rotation of the handle was visible to the subjects. This consisted of two pegs projecting from the rod to which the handle was attached so that their movement was limited by a peg projecting from the front of the apparatus. The extent of downward movement of the handle was limited by the length of the clearly apparent slot in which it moved.

The internal design of the apparatus was such that the two responses, rotating and depressing the handle, were incompatible. If the subjects rotated the handle through an angle of more than thirty degrees, they were unable to push it down; if they pushed it down more than one inch, they were unable to rotate it. A spring on the inside of the apparatus exerted just enough force to return the handle automatically to its initial raised and horizontal position.

Gumdrops, serving as reward, were dropped into a dish from a small tube emerging from the front of the apparatus. Whenever the subject made the correct response, a piece of candy was dropped into the tube by an assistant experimenter who sat concealed behind the apparatus. The same assistant experimenter also recorded the subject's responses.

The subjects were twelve fo rth-grade boys of normal intelligence from one of the city schools.[4] The leaders to be dis-

4 The experimenters are grateful to Mr. Allen J. Hickerson, Director of Teachers' Training at the State Teachers College in New Haven, to Miss

criminated were a third-grade boy from the same city school and a male student from the Yale University Graduate School. These leaders were selected for difference in size and age, because these are two of the distinguishing cues involved in discriminations of models learned during socialization.

The procedure was divided into five stages, partly to bring out more clearly some of the processes involved and partly to facilitate the learning of the discrimination. In the first stage, all of the subjects were trained to perform the same responses as the leader. For purposes of subsequent control, half of the subjects were rewarded for imitating the large leader, and half were rewarded for imitating the small leader. In the second stage, subjects who had been rewarded for imitating the large leader were rewarded for non-imitating the small leader, and subjects who had been rewarded for imitating the small leader were rewarded for non-imitating the large. The third and fourth stages were repetitions of the first and second, respectively. After these preliminary stages, the training in discrimination was completed by presenting the subjects with the large leader and the small leader in an unpredictable order. The details and results of each of these stages will be discussed in sequence.

Step 1. Learning to imitate a leader. While the experimenter was bringing the subject to the vacant schoolroom in which the experiment was conducted, he asked the child whether he liked candy. All did. Before each subject entered the room, the assistant experimenter signaled for either a rotating or a downward motion, giving the leader the cue for his response.

In the experimental room, the subject and the leader were both made to stand directly in front of the apparatus. The experimenter then gave the subject the following instructions: "If you do the right thing, you will get candy. If you do the wrong thing, you won't get candy. You will get quite a few turns. Try to learn to get candy each time. You can either eat your candy right away or keep it in this bag. He

Mary J. Mooney, Principal of the Barnard School, and to the teachers of the Barnard School for their coöperation in making these subjects available.

gets a turn first; then you get a turn." Then the experimenter said to the leader, "All right, your turn." After the leader had made his response and gotten his candy, the experimenter said to the subject, "All right, your turn."

If the subject made the same response as the leader, he got candy. If he did not make the same response, no candy appeared, and the experimenter said: "No candy. You must have made a mistake that time." Since the subjects always either rotated or depressed the handle as far as it would go, it was easy to determine when the subjects had made a response. As soon as the subject had made one response, either correct or incorrect, he was taken out of the room.

While the subject was out of the room, the assistant experimenter gave the leader his cue as to which response to make on the next turn. If the subject had made a mistake, the leader always was instructed to repeat the response that he had just made. Thus the subject was exposed to the same cues until he finally made a correct response. Each trial consisted of one or more similar turns always ending in a correct response.

The leader's response for the next trial was always determined from a list which progressed in an unpredictable sequence.[5] On all trials after the first, the experimenter gave no further instructions except those incidentally needed to get the subject out of the room and to indicate the leader's first turn, which was immediately followed by the subject's turn. Each subject was given trials until he reached a criterion of three correct first turns in succession. Then he was given two test trials.

In this situation, the initial tendency of eleven out of twelve of the subjects was to imitate on the first trial. Eleven out of twelve subjects also imitated on the second trial. These results were presumably produced by the training in imitation which the children had already received as a part of their socialization before entering the experiment. Because of

[5] Rotate, down, rotate, rotate, down, rotate, down, down, rotate, down, rotate, down, rotate, rotate, down, down. Then, if learning was not complete, the same sequence was repeated.

this strong initial tendency, the criterion was reached very rapidly; the average number of trials required to reach the criterion of three was 3.3. The average number of errors made was .42. In the two test trials after the criterion, the subjects made an average of .04 errors. This demonstrates a statistically reliable tendency to imitate; but because the initial scores were almost as good, it does not demonstrate statistically reliable learning of imitation during the experiment.

Step 2. Non-imitation of the second leader. After the subjects had been tested for learning to imitate the first leader, the second step of the experiment was begun. This second step was introduced without any break in the procedure. No new instructions were given. Two important conditions, however, were different. While the subject was out of the room after the last trial of the preceding stage, a leader of different size was substituted; and on trials behind this leader, the subjects were non-rewarded for imitating and were rewarded for non-imitating. In short, the subjects who had previously been rewarded for imitating adults were now rewarded for non-imitating children, and the subjects that had previously been rewarded for imitating children were now rewarded for non-imitating adults. Training was continued on this procedure until subjects had reached a criterion of three successive correct trials, after which they were given two test trials.

All the subjects began by imitating the new leader on the first turn of the first trial. On the first turn of the second trial, six of the subjects imitated. In an average of 4.4 trials, after having made an average of 13.4 errors, the subjects reached the criterion of three successive correct trials. On the test trials, they demonstrated conclusively that they had learned to non-imitate the second leader. Eleven out of twelve non-imitated on the first turn of the first test trial, and all twelve on the first turn of the second test trial. The difference between the first trials and the test trials was of a magnitude to be expected by chance less than one time in a thousand.

This demonstrates that the generalized habit of imitation can be broken up by arranging conditions so that only non-imitation is rewarded.

Steps 3 and 4. Relearning to imitate the first leaders and then to non-imitate the second leaders. After the subjects had been tested for learning non-imitation of the second leaders, the training in discrimination was carried on, with no break in procedure, by giving them a series of trials in which they were again rewarded for imitating the first leader. After they had reached a criterion of three successive correct first turns, they were given a series of successive trials in which they were rewarded for non-imitating the second leader.[6]

Step 5. Discrimination of leaders when presented in unpredictable sequence. As a final step in learning the discrimination, the subjects were given a series of trials in which shifts were made from leaders of one size to leaders of the other size in a rapid and unpredictable manner, and in which the response (rotate handle or depress it) made by the leader was also shifted in an unpredictable order.[7] In this final procedure, the subjects were consistently rewarded for imitating one leader and for non-imitating the other.

Leaders were shifted while the subject was out of the room. No new instructions were given. Subjects were given trials until they reached a criterion of six successive, errorless first turns, three behind a child leader and three behind an adult

[6] On the first trials, in relearning to imitate only five out of twelve started by imitating the first leader. This is reliably less than the same subjects exhibited at the beginning of the experiment and thus represents generalization from the preceding training to non-imitate a second leader. The criterion of three successive correct first turns was reached in an average of 6.1 trials after having made an average of 3.2 errors. In the relearning of non-imitation, the subjects reached the criterion in an average of 4.4 trials after an average of 1.4 errors.

[7] Letting *A* stand for adult, and *C* stand for child, *R* stand for rotate, and *D* stand for depress, so that *AR* symbolizes a trial on which an adult leader rotates the handle and *CD* symbolizes a trial on which the child leader depresses it, the sequence of trials was: *AR, CD, CR, AR, CD, AD, CR, CD, AD, AR, CD, AR, CR, AD, CR, AR, CD, AD, CR, CD, AD, AR, CR, AD.* If more trials were needed, the same sequence was repeated.

leader. They reached this criterion in an average of ten trials after making an average of 1.8 errors. After reaching it, they were given four test trials.

Had they been responding by chance alone they would be expected to make an average of two errors on these four trials. They actually made an average of .3 errors on these four trials. The probability of securing so small a proportion of errors by chance is less than one in a thousand. Thus the results of this experiment conclusively confirm the deduction that if two leaders are differentiated by distinctive cues, and a subject is repeatedly rewarded for imitating one leader and for not imitating the other, he will learn the discrimination of imitating the one and not imitating the other.

Experiment 8. The Generalization of Prestige or Lack of Prestige to New Leaders

The purpose of this experiment was to test the deduction that after the subject learns to discriminate between two leaders as models this discrimination will tend to generalize to new leaders, so that subjects will imitate those resembling the previous good models and non-imitate those who are similar to the previous bad models.

The subjects used were the twelve children from the preceding experiment. Six of these had just learned to imitate an adult leader and to non-imitate a child leader; the other six, to imitate a child and non-imitate an adult. In order to test the degree to which this discrimination had generalized, new adult and child leaders were used. There was no interruption or other change in the procedure from the previous experiment; a new leader was simply introduced while the subject was out of the room between turns. The sequence of trials employed was a mirror image of that used in the previous experiment.[8]

The subject's performance on the first turn with a child leader and the first turn with an adult leader were used as tests for the generalization of the discrimination. On the first

[8] In other words, *CD, AR, AD,* etc., instead of *AR, CD, CR,* etc.

turn with the new child leader, eleven out of the twelve subjects performed the response which had been correct with a leader of this size in the preceding discrimination. For six of these, the correct response was imitation and for five it was non-imitation. Similarly, on the first turn with the new adult leader, eleven out of twelve of the subjects also performed the response which had been correct with a leader of this size in the preceding discrimination. Since the probability of securing by chance as high a proportion as eleven out of twelve is only .003, these results are statistically highly reliable.[9] They demonstrate that when new leaders were introduced into the situation, the subjects immediately responded to them as good or bad models, basing their discrimination on similarities in size to leaders they had been previously rewarded for imitating or non-imitating.

After these tests, the subjects were brought to a criterion of six successive correct responses, three to an adult leader and three to a child leader. After reaching this criterion, a third pair of leaders (another graduate student and another third grader) was substituted for the preceding pair without any change in the procedure. The sequence of trials behind these leaders was changed back to that used for the original leaders. The first two trials of this sequence, one following an adult leader and the other following a child leader, were used as tests of the further generalization of the discrimination. On the first of these trials, ten out of twelve of the subjects immediately performed the response which had been correct in the preceding discrimination. On the second trial, eleven out of the twelve performed the correct response. There are less than two chances in a hundred and three in a thousand, respectively, of securing proportions as high as these by chance alone.[10]

[9] Calculated from the Binomial Expansion (Thurstone, 1928, p. 132).

[10] According to learning principles, one would expect the subjects' generalization to this third pair of leaders to be still more accurate than the generalization to the second pair of leaders. Actually, the generalization was slightly poorer. This difference, one more error, has an exceedingly low statistical reliability, however, and so does not constitute a dependable trend in the wrong direction. That no reliable difference in the expected direction

The results on the tests with both of the new pairs of leaders confirm the deduction that, after an individual learns to discriminate between two leaders as models, this discrimination will generalize so that the individual will tend to imitate new leaders if they are similar to previous good models, and to non-imitate them if they are similar to previous bad models.

Experiment 9. The Leader's Prestige as a Model Generalizing from One Response to Another

The purpose of this experiment was to test the deduction that after the subject has been rewarded for imitating one leader and non-imitating another in one type of response, he will show a greater tendency to imitate the one than the other in different types of response. The subjects were the twelve children used in the preceding experiment. After they had been tested in that experiment they were brought to a criterion of six successive correct responses in order to make certain that they had thoroughly learned the discrimination of imitating one leader in operating the handle and non-imitating the other. Then the subjects were given tests to determine whether this discrimination would generalize to two different situations in each of which a new type of response had to be performed.

In the first test situation, two boxes similar to those used in Experiment 5 were placed on pedestals approximately 34 inches high and 8 feet apart. The subject and leader were made to stand side by side at a starting point approximately 6 feet from each box. The new response was opening the lid of the correct box. The following instructions were given: "See those two boxes, there and there? You can go either to this one or to that one. If you go to the right one, you will get candy; if you go to the wrong one, you won't get candy. He gets a turn first; then you get a turn." After this, the ex-

of improvement was found may perhaps be explained by the fact that the subjects generalized so well to the first pair of new leaders that the amount of improvement possible was too small to be detected with statistical reliability in a group of only twelve subjects.

perimenter said to the leader, "All right, your turn." After
the leader had returned from making his choice, the experimenter said to the subject, "All right, now, your turn."

The first trial was behind an adult leader, who had previously been told to go to the right-hand box. On this trial
seven out of twelve subjects responded correctly, that is,
went to the same box as the leader if they had been rewarded
for imitating him in operating the handle and to the other
box if they had been rewarded for not imitating him. The
second trial was behind a child leader who had previously
been told to go to the left-hand box. On this trial seven out
of twelve subjects also responded correctly. These results are
in the direction to be expected from generalization, but the
trend is so slight that it could easily have been produced by
chance.

In order to train the subjects for the next test, correct responses were rewarded and incorrect responses non-rewarded
until the subjects reached a criterion of six successive correct
trials, three following an adult leader and three following a
child leader. These trials occurred in an unpredictable sequence similar to that used in the previous experiments.

After the subjects had learned to imitate one leader and to
non-imitate the other, in the situation in which the response
was opening the correct box, they were tested for generalization in a new situation in which the response was pulling on
the correct ring. The apparatus was that used in the original
experiment. The handle was turned out of the way, and two
rings were inserted in the positions illustrated in Figure 11.
Each was at the end of a rod which could be pulled out two
inches before being stopped by a collar at the other end, on
the inside of the apparatus.

Each subject was brought into the room and directed to
stand beside the leader immediately in front of the rings. The
experimenter said: "See these two rings? You can pull out
either this one or this one. If you pull out the wrong one, you
won't get candy. He gets a turn first, then you get a turn."
Then the experimenter said to the leader, "All right, your
turn." After the instructions, the leader, who had been given

his cues as to which ring to pull out before the subject had entered the room, pulled out one of the rings and got his candy. The experimenter said to the subject, "All right, now, your turn." If the subject generalized correctly to the new situation, he received candy; if not, he was given no candy. Each child was given one test behind a child leader and then one test behind an adult leader.

On both of these tests all twelve of the subjects made correct responses, that is, those who had been rewarded for opening the same box as the leader immediately pulled out the same ring, and those who had been rewarded for opening the other box immediately pulled out the other ring. The probability of securing by chance twelve correct responses out of twelve is less than one in a thousand. These results confirm the deduction that the leader's prestige as a model can generalize from one type of response to another.

The Verbal Responses of the Children

During the course of these experiments, many of the children spontaneously said in effect, "You do the same as the big leader and different from the little leader."[11] The rest of them made similar statements when asked what they had learned to do. These statements indicate that the children were responding to some criterion of sameness and difference. Thus their behavior was not merely matched-dependent, but rather copying. The simple copying units involved in rotating or depressing a handle, going to a box, and pulling out rings had, of course, already been learned by the children. Their task was not to learn how to copy these simple manipulations, but to learn whom to copy or non-copy.

Their verbal responses probably helped the subjects to learn whom to copy and then to generalize from one type of copying to another. The manner in which these verbal responses probably functioned may be suggested in a vastly oversimplified sketch. The statements made by the children

11 Half of the children, of course, made the opposite statement, indicating "same as the little leader and different from the big leader "

indicate that while they were learning to respond properly in the handle-rotating situation they were also learning to respond to the big leader with the word "same" and to the small leader with the word "different." Actually, they may have been responding with synonyms for each of these words, with sentences, or even with nonverbal cue-producing responses, but for simpler exposition all of these will be referred to by the words "same" and "different." Previous experience with doorknobs, water faucets, etc., had already taught the children to respond by turning the handle themselves to the cue of hearing the word "same" plus the cue of seeing someone else turn the handle. Similarly, they had learned to respond by not turning the handle themselves to the cue of hearing the word "different" plus seeing someone else turn a handle. First the words were said by another person; then they were probably repeated by the child, eventually being abbreviated to subvocal form. Thus, as soon as the subjects learned to respond to the leader with the appropriate word, a cue was present eliciting the correct response.

Responding with the aid of verbal cues involves less new learning in this experiment than responding without them. In order to learn to respond to the large leader correctly without the aid of verbal cues, the subject must acquire a connection between the sight of the leader turning the handle and the response of turning it himself; he must also acquire a connection between the sight of the leader depressing the handle and the response of depressing it himself. If, however, he learns a verbal response to the problem, he only has to acquire one new connection, that between the sight of the leader and the response of saying to himself the word "same." Learning the simple habit of responding with the correct word provides a cue mediating previously learned, more complex habits. That is why many of the subjects probably first arrived at a verbal solution (hypothesis) and then suddenly started to respond correctly.

A similar analysis applies to the box-opening situation. The words "same" and "different" would be expected to be more thoroughly learned as responses to the big and little leaders after the additional rewarded practice in this second situation.

When confronted with the new situation in which the task was to pull out the correct ring, the children would be expected to generalize their habits of responding to the big leader with the word "same" and the small leader with the word "different." But because of their previous experience with handles on gum-vending machines, drawers, etc., they had presumably already learned to respond by pulling out the same handle to the pattern of hearing the word "same" plus seeing someone else pull out a handle, and, similarly, on hearing the word "different" to respond by not pulling out the same handle. Thus saying to oneself the word "same" or "different," upon seeing the big or little leader, should act as a cue tending to elicit the new correct response of pulling or not pulling the same ring. Because the word "same" has, during the socialization of the individual, had so many different copying acts attached to it as a cue, it can serve to mediate generalization from one type of copying to another.

It is possible that a certain amount of transfer may have been mediated by cues produced by nonverbal responses. For example, if in connection with choosing the right box, the children had learned to look toward the place where the big leader went and away from the place where the small leader went, they might have transferred this response to the ring situation. Then the response of looking in the right direction would be expected to furnish cues tending to favor the response of pulling out the correct ring.

Summary

These experiments have confirmed the deduction from learning theory that an individual can learn to discriminate between leaders as good and bad models. He learns to copy the leader whom he is rewarded for copying and to non-copy the leader whom he is rewarded for non-copying. Once such learning occurs, it generalizes to new leaders, so that there is a tendency to copy the new leaders who are similar to those whom the individual has been rewarded for copying and to non-copy the new leaders who are similar to others whom he has been rewarded for non-copying. If a leader has acquired prestige as a good model for several responses, he is likely to be copied in other new responses; and if he has acquired "negative prestige" as a bad model for several responses, he is likely to be non-copied in other new responses.[12]

[12] A similar analysis could probably be applied to other forms of prestige, such as that involved in compliance with suggestions and obedience to commands.

CHAPTER XII

THE SOCIAL CONDITIONS
PRODUCING IMITATION

IMITATIVE behavior, we have argued, is learned and follows the laws of learning. It will tend to appear when it is rewarded and tend not to appear when it is non-rewarded or punished.[1] When, then, is it likely to be rewarded? Where, in social life, should imitative behavior be expected to appear frequently or even inevitably? This question can be put perhaps in a more telling way: When are social conditions appropriate for imitative learning? How must the social maze be arranged so that imitative behavior is rewarded?

The particular social conditions under which imitative behavior is most likely to occur, and in which, indeed, it may be predicted, seem to be, in general, those of hierarchy or rank with regard to specific skills and social statuses. It is true of learning in general, as well as of imitation in particular, that the superordinated teach the subordinated and the latter learn from the former. What, then, are the forms of social superordination and subordination which favor imitative learning?

There seem to be at least four classes of persons who are imitated by others. They are: (1) superiors in an age-grade hierarchy, (2) superiors in a hierarchy of social status, (3) superiors in an intelligence ranking system, and (4) superior technicians in any field. Each of these groups will be discussed in detail in its turn. All societies seem to rank

[1] Since reward and punishment are not the only factors involved in learning, exceptions to this tendency may be produced by the operation of other variables. Imitative behavior may fail to appear, although it would be adaptive, because it has never been tried as a response or because the cues designating the situation in which it would be adaptive cannot be discriminated. Similarly, imitation may appear, although it is maladaptive, because it has not yet extinguished or because it is supported by generalization from highly similar situations in which it is rewarded.

people, formally or informally, according at least to some of these criteria.[2] The reason why imitation occurs in these situations is clear. Superordinated persons recognize the cue stimuli which designate the nearness or presence of important goals. The subordinated, seeking these goals, often find it easier to depend upon cues given off by the activity of the leaders. The superiors can act as models and critics to aid their inferiors in perfecting the desired habits.

Age-Grade Superiors

The grading of people into age groups is undoubtedly one of the major circumstances under which imitation can take place. Age-grading is implied in our own society in such terms as "infant," "child," "adolescent," "college student," "grown man," "man in the prime of life," "old man." Although such grading is not as sharp in the American as it is in some other societies, it does nevertheless designate roughly what behavior may be expected from a person in any particular age-grade and how he is to be treated by others (Linton, 1936, p. 118). Such events as getting one's first long trousers, making a debut, or beginning to earn one's own living mark turning points in the treatment of the persons concerned. It is further useful to note that an age-grade system constitutes an approximate skill and prestige hierarchy. Up to a point (perhaps old age), freedom and privilege increase with the advancement through different phases of the age-cycle. As children moving up in the age-cycle are allowed or taught to make the responses of those in the next age-grade above them, and find that these responses lead to reward (for example, being permitted to stay up later and play longer), those above them acquire prestige—that is, they become lead-

[2] Terman (1904) found in a study of leadership that student leaders were larger (perhaps evidence of generalization from the fact that persons in higher ranking age-grades are generally larger); better dressed and of more prominent parents (quite surely evidence of higher status); brighter in school (certainly evidence of higher intelligence); and more fluent and better readers (evidence of superior techniques). It is presumed that where leaders led, followers of lower rank in the above traits followed and imitated.

ers and models for matched-dependent and copying responses of wide range and variety. Rewarded matching or copying of particular responses institutes a tendency to match the behavior of superordinate persons over a wide range of responses. The tendency to match behavior with a superordinate person or group does not need to be conscious, willful or intentional. It can occur, and does frequently occur, automatically and without verbal aids. The imitative response is directly connected to the cue of the other person's behavior without intermediate mental links of response.

The general evidence for the existence of tendencies to match lies within the experience of every person. Children are notorious for their tendencies to copy the behavior of older siblings and adults. Parents achieve prestige with their children by the means shown in Chapter XI. Their behavior cues the proper matched responses; and children learn rapidly to copy the novel responses of their elders. Younger children want to stay up at night as late as older brothers and sisters or parents. The little boy wants a bicycle when he is "too young" to have it. He wants to eat with his parents on formal, as on other, occasions. The little girl wants a real electric stove just like her mother's so that she can "cook for Daddy." The youth wants to drive the family car though he is still below the legal age limit. Children play at keeping house, at being parents, at teaching school, and at all the multitudinous activities of adults, when they cannot actually carry these out in fact. They enjoy handling the cigarettes, books, pots, and pans of their elders (which have become subgoals by virtue of frequent association with the rewarding parents). Children are, of course, specifically rewarded for these tendencies to copy their elders. Often by matching behavior with those above them in the age-cycle, they reach important goals which would otherwise be inaccessible. They get food, rest, and relief from pain, as well as praise, by following the cues provided by adults' behavior. They match, and copy if they can, the more adaptive responses of their age-grade superiors.

It has been emphasized in another connection (Chapter

IX) that imitation occurs between children of slightly differing chronological ages who are within the same age-grade. If children, for instance, are accustomed to eat together, the one slightly younger can stimulate the older to want to eat quite as readily as *vice versa*. It is unknown at this time whether more imitation occurs within an age-grade or between children of different age-grades, but it is quite sure that imitative action occurs in both situations. Imitation between age-grades seems to occur because, as a group, the older have superior privileges, skills, and techniques for reaching goals.

This superiority of the older group undoubtedly has several roots. Older children have superior learning ability for straight biological reasons. They certainly have had more practice in specific fields of response and have connected a larger number of relevant responses to cue stimuli. They also have superior privileges accorded them by society.

It should not be overlooked in this connection that the age-grade also limits imitation. The small child in our society may, or even must, wash his hands like his parents but may not smoke a cigarette. He may copy the table manners of his older brother but may not go to bed as late as his brother. In many such cases imitation is punished rather than encouraged by the structure of the social maze, and one would not expect it to appear as regularly. Where imitation is forbidden to the group below, the imitative tendencies are likely to appear in two forms: first, in mimicry of the behavior of the superior group, as in the way small girls play at having a grown-up tea party; second, in a fervent desire to get into the group above, manifested in efforts to meet the conditions of membership in the superior group, as by working hard for grades in school.

Imitative action can and does occur where it is not adaptive. The younger child, rewarded by the parents for keeping his hands clean like his older brother, learns to go to the washroom at the cue of seeing his brother go there to wash his hands. He notices also that the brother has a pocket watch and tries to imitate him in this detail of behavior also.

The younger child appropriates his father's pocket watch and drops it. and as a consequence is punished. In this instance, he had falsely generalized from one rewarded similarity of response to another.

The rigidity and complexity of age-grading in our society is only barely indicated by the foregoing discussion. Our intention, indeed, is only to suggest the reality of the variable of age-grading rather than to do it complete factual justice. Adults have passed through most of the routines of age-classification and hence tend to forget the detail of the training through which they have come. The sense of great achievement which accompanied First Communion, high-school graduation, and the first money earned are forgotten. The special satisfactions of being allowed to listen to stories told by the older boys, to go on hunting expeditions with "the bunch," and to take part in an uncensored adult conversation have all faded, and the keenness with which they were once desired is lost. Some can recall setting great store on reaching the age of twenty-one and being able to vote. Many more will remember the age-grade dilemma in the form of the problem of calling older men "Sir," and more particularly of reaching that degree of maturity where this form of self-subordination was no longer appropriate. Being called "Miss" or "Mister" oneself is another mark of change in age-grade status. Each of these events has been part of the routine of entry into a superior rank with its new privileges, duties, and rewards. Each such superior rank has been a goal for those who have occupied the status just beneath it, evoking in them tendencies to mimic and to participate.

Age-grading has, in our own society, a certain informality and lack of precision, although these in no way detract from its reality. In many primitive societies the outlines of the system are much sharper. The age-grades constitute distinctive groups whose members are specially identified. Definite ceremonies mark entry into and exit from each such group. Behavior appropriate to the members of each is defined and sometimes ritualized. The age-grades themselves are organized into a clear hierarchy, with the privileges appropriate to each precisely specified. The mimicry of behavior up the age-grade system is observed among primitives as among ourselves. Although varying in degree of distinctiveness, age-grading is present in all societies in some form, and apparently it always has the characteristic result of engendering imitative tendencies.

Imitation of Superiors in Social Status

American society seems to be organized in a series of ranked participation groups (Warner, 1941*), (Davis and Dollard, 1940, pp. 256–262). While sharing many traits in common, these ranked gradings have also their distinctive modes of behavior, which are themselves evaluated as "higher or lower." It is, for example, better form to use grammatical than ungrammatical English, to wear a hat than cap, to have clean than dirty fingernails, to be polite and self-controlled than undisciplined and "vulgar." Specific items of this kind become associated with social rank and are viewed as the mark of the superior person.

The arrangement of social classes is not an accidental or irrelevant phenomenon. The members of these classes have differential access to the goods and services of our society—the higher the class, the more and better the access. Possession of symbols of superior rank gives superior control of direct reinforcements, such as softer beds, better food, better drinks, more desirable sex objects, less laborious work, better medical service and therefore less pain—and, most important of all, greater security in the continued possession of all of these. To seek higher social status and the symbols evaluated as "superior" in the society is, therefore, no idle quest for mere prestige. People learn that to be superordinated in rank brings a richer and more secure life. The symbols of superior rank thus acquire a secondary rewarding value. Once they are possessed, the owner or bearer can afford to relax somewhat.

The question might be raised as to why people tend to imitate those above them rather than those below them in social status. To account for this, it must be kept in mind that imitators can discriminate between cues which indicate reward and those which do not. For instance, children can distinguish between large and small leaders, can match behavior with the former and do the opposite of the latter. Age-graded groups are likewise distinguished by cues which mark their superordinate or subordinate character. The child learns that he is rewarded for imitating the "boy who wears long pants," but not the "small boy who cries every time he falls down" and is still in the baby category. Social classes, similarly, have their characteristic stigmata, which constitute a set of cues for those in subordinate class groups. Indeed, people of superordinate status are popularly referred to as "*big* shots."

Once imitation of social superiors has been rewarded in one situation, it tends to extend to other stimulus situations and other responses. Such generalization of imitation is frequently seen as "aspiring" or yearning for higher status. Social inferiors are rewarded for some types of imitation of their superiors but not for others. For instance, they are frequently rewarded for adopting the political opinions of their superiors—a fact which is important in maintaining the channels by which superordinated persons control the political life of the society. On the other hand, imitation upward can sometimes be maladaptive. If a person drives a better make of car than he can afford, following some social superior, he may be punished by being told that he evidently thinks himself "too good" for his friends. Provided cues are distinctive enough (and they are usually made so), subordinates in the social hierarchy will learn just which responses of their superiors they may match and which ones it is inadvisable to match. Those to be matched will be rewarded, and those to be avoided will be punished.

It seems that, as a general rule, imitation in a class hierarchy takes place between juxtaposed classes rather than between those which are socially distant from one another. Individuals in lower-middle class are quite aware of the privileges and social characteristics of those immediately above them. The stimuli of the behavior of upper-middle-class persons are close at hand, and the rewards attendant upon upper-middle behavior are more accessible to striving. By contrast, lower-middle-class people may have no conception at all of upper-class life, with its select schools, debuts, ancient family heir-looms, memories of distinguished ancestors, and the like. They do not, therefore, show a tendency to imitate upper-class behavior.

The members of all sub-groups below the topmost in a society slowly learn that they are subordinated in the privilege hierarchy. The tendency to strive for the symbols of superior status is therefore an inevitable one, although it is checked in many ways by social punishments and by ignorance. Socially mobile persons are those who undertake the actual struggle for superior symbols of rank. Through the proper expenditure of money and the acquisition of skills, they attempt to alter their positions in the society by acquiring the behavioral attributes of the group superordinated to them. Even among the individuals, however, who do not attempt social mobility, the perception of status differences remains as a crude stimulus to change of position. It is rather the inability to discover any means of changing status than the lack of any secondary drive to do so which accounts for the stability noted in many subordinated social groups. It seems to be one of the dreams of our society, a dream toward which we have steadily progressed in the last hundred years, to distribute the symbols of social rank according to the actual social utility of the individuals concerned.

Many who exhibit an acquired drive of imitativeness have presumably developed it in the course of movement from one age-grade to another. Children are rewarded for striving to make their responses approximate those in the age-grade next above them. This striving exists as a strongly reinforced tendency and, with many people, generalizes into the sphere of social class. Those who have been particularly successful in winning advantages by matching behavior in the age-grade cycle are likely to carry over into the arena of social class the effort to approximate the responses of those above them. Often they are so steadily punished or non-rewarded for this striving that mobility tendencies extinguish, and the individuals concerned "settle down" and accept their lot in a particular segment of the status structure. If, on the other hand, their efforts are reinforced, such individuals continue to be ambitious, for they have been rewarded for being dissatisfied with lower status and for attempting to do something about it. Social climbing can thus be strengthened or weakened by the appropriate conditions of learning.

Persons subordinated in a hierarchy have great difficulty in fully approximating the behavioral symbols of those above them. It requires a long period of specific training to change social habits completely and most people, even those who are most mobile, rarely find themselves in a really adequate learning situation. As a result, copying from below upward is likely to be fragmentary and transitory. However difficult it may be, however, copying is probably always more efficient under social conditions than the attempt to hit upon the habits of superordinated people by trial and error. Without the early acquired technique of matching behavior by copying, which serves to identify cues and limit trial-and-error behavior, it would be virtually impossible to make correct discriminations and produce the right responses in most social situations.

While Negroes in America, for instance, have learned some of the social habits of Western civilization under direct reward and punishment, they have learned much more by matching and copying the superordinate whites. They have imitated the manners and customs of the superior white caste in techniques of child rearing, preparation of food, form of family, grammar, and in many other particulars and would do so even more fully if they were not specifically punished for the attempt in some social spheres. By and large, Negroes may not imitate a white man in staying at a white hotel, in marrying a white woman, or in competing for the highest political offices. If a Negro does try these responses, he is punished for getting out of his "place," which is always sure to be near the bottom.

Great numbers of lower-middle-class girls imitate the clothes and personal fads of Hollywood stars. The stars themselves exhibit, in their pictures as well as in their personal lives, a glamorous and successful life with full achievement of many primary goals, such as avoidance of tedious work and the realization of romantic goals. Imitating them in any partial sense gives the copier the feeling of being nearer to escape from drudgery and burdensome sexual tension. Frequently, too, the copied behavior does actually achieve results. The girl is, in fact, more attractive to her boy friend when her hair is arranged like that of the current Hollywood favorite.

Under hierarchical conditions, subordinated persons show a marked tendency to mimic the speech, clothes, and attitudes of those better placed, but it must be remembered that it is only a tendency. Not all lower-class people imitate in all particulars the middle-class people whom they know. In many cases they have habits which compete with the preferred trait. Class-typed habits of speech, for example, cannot be uprooted readily. Moreover, a person wishing to copy must have sufficient contact with the model to enable him to make a fair seeming copy. Again, he may have been partially extinguished in previous imitative attempts, so that his drive to imitate has been weakened.

The superordinated in a class structure do not welcome the cheapening of their precious symbols of status by sharing them too widely in the society. The values for which high status can be exchanged are limited. The more widely these symbols are shared, the less the return to each holder thereof. The superordinated have various means of defense, which are, in fact, means of punishing those who attempt to move upward in the hierarchy. They call mobile persons "climbers," thus calling unpleasant attention to their former inferior status. They label as ridiculous the partial approximations of their own habits which are achieved by subordinated persons, as, for example, white people frequently ridicule the attempts of Negroes to speak correct English. They comment that so-and-so is "getting above his station," that he is "too big for his trousers," and so forth. They may protect their residential area by the stipulation that no property may be sold to Negroes—a form of caste defense—or that no house may be built there which costs less than, say, twenty-five thousand dollars—a class defense. They may employ pointed jibes or innuendoes to intimidate those who would copy them too exactly, informing the subordinated by implication that their social antecedents are irretrievably bad or their existing habits vulgar and unacceptable. These caste and class defenses tend to limit mobility with its persistent copying and matching.

There is another form of punishment which tends to discourage social imitation upward. It comes from the members of the mobile person's own class. They react to the attempt of one of their members to leave the group with various jibes and sneers such as that "so-and-so thinks he's too good for us now," or "his wife is getting awfully snobbish," and so on. Thus, the person who tries to be mobile and fails will find himself less comfortable upon his return to his own class group. In spite of limitations, however, our American "open" class system presents a set of social conditions under which imitation is often rewarded and in which a tendency to imitate may safely be predicted.

Imitation of the Intelligent

There is another hierarchy within which imitation is likely to occur. Within any age-grade or social class, people are distributed on some kind of a continuum of intelligent social adaptation. Those toward the lower end of this continuum tend to imitate those above. Intelligence means, among other things, the ability to read rapidly the environmental cues and to produce or improvise (by recombination of response units) adaptive responses to them. The stupid are incompetent at both. They do not read the social cues as well nor produce the adaptive responses as certainly or as rapidly as do their brighter fellows. They have, however, a resource which can save them much of the trouble of discovering the correct responses. They do know how to copy, having learned this habit in various situations of primary reward and punishment. By copying, they are relieved from the burden of improvising an adequate novel response and connecting it with the proper cues, if, indeed, they are capable of doing so in complex situations. Copying is therefore especially convenient, since it provides a technique for organizing response units and producing the total habit so that it can be reinforced. This being the case, it can safely be predicted that the less intelligent will frequently employ matching and copying techniques to make their behavior adjustive. By watching those with superior intelligence, the less gifted can learn when significant cue stimuli are present and can watch and copy the adaptive responses carried out by the intellectually superordinated.

The bright child who can tell time recognizes that he is late for school and begins to run. The dull child who cannot tell time must cue his behavior to the brighter one and copy his response, if he wishes to avoid the punishment for being late. This kind of situation is not alone characteristic of children but may also be observed in the reactions of adults. It serves to differentiate the behavior of people within age-grades and class groups as it is known in fact to be differentiated. The intelligence continuum crosscuts all the other forms of ranking.

It seems very likely that intelligence differences between individuals are, in part, biological, but it seems equally probable that social variables play a part in nearly all cases of specific differences in intelligence. Some children learn more rapidly or effectively because of favorable social circumstances, which increase drive and thereby facilitate learning, or because their parents have more efficiently, though perhaps unwittingly, applied learning principles.[3]

Imitation of Technicians

A modern society, by virtue of its division of labor, is composed of many specialized groups. Each group of specialists

---

[3] The space here devoted to intelligence ranking is not a measure of the authors' estimate of the importance of the topic in comparison with the three other variables here listed. Less attention is given it since the point will, perhaps, be so readily granted.

is characterized by special responses cued to particular stimulus configurations and has a sort of monopoly on adaptive behavior in the field of its specialty. A scientist, for instance, knows how to set up an experiment so that a decisive result will be secured. A plumber has his responses ready at the stimulus of a leaking faucet. A football coach can diagnose the novel play of an opposing team and find a defense against it. A doctor can forecast the course of many diseases from the symptoms of the present day. In all these cases, the layman, as far as a particular skill is concerned, must depend on the technician to discern reality for him and to indicate the adaptive response.

The technician has organized a large number of connections between particular responses and stimuli into complex habits. If one wishes to learn his skill, it is much easier to bring copying units into play to establish the proper connections between responses and stimuli than to attempt to hit upon them by random behavior. Copying is learned by everyone in the course of socialization and can be brought forward as an aid to new learning in any dilemma. The technician acts as both model and critic. Even in copying, to be sure, there is always an element of trial and error. One may not have mastered all the units which are to be reorganized under the guidance of the technician. In this case, copying serves to limit the field of response, and trial and error intervenes where copying must perforce leave off. If the necessary units are not present, copying is no easier than trial and error. If, for instance, the son of an American missionary in New Guinea tries to learn from a native how to make a drum, the boy may get little help from his teacher because he cannot follow the language cues which ordinarily guide copying, because he is unfamiliar with the materials, and because he cannot handle the primitive tools with the manual habits acquired in a workshop at home. In such a case, he might be as well off to take the unfamiliar tools and, understanding the goal, try to invent a solution for himself.

The category of technicians cuts across age-grading, social class, and intelligence hierarchies. An older, better placed, and more intelligent individual may imitate a person subordinated to him in all of these categories but not in some specific skill. A smart city lawyer on a fishing trip may learn from a stupid farmer lad which are the most promising pools in a given creek. The President of the United States, no less than others, vaccinates his children against smallpox when the epidemiologists show signs of alarm at an approaching epidemic. The subordinated in a skill hierarchy must necessarily trust to the superordinated to identify reality and to suggest the adaptive response. Imitation inevitably occurs unless one wishes to attempt the impossible task of amassing all arts, crafts, and sciences at the same time.

A skill specialty results from extensive practice in a given field. Concurrently, a specialist must relinquish the chance to practice in many other fields and, in return for his very high talent in one field, must be content with a much lower general level of adaptiveness in others. Social division of labor, however, seems to be highly functional just because it saves multiple learning by many individuals and promotes a higher level of technical efficiency. One skill under each skull seems to be the ideal of our current society, as compared with the pioneer ideal of many skills under one skull. Under these circumstances, widespread imitative behavior, both matched-dependent behavior and copying, is bound to occur.

Technicians acquire prestige according to the mechanisms already outlined. We imitate them at some one point and are heavily rewarded for so doing. The tendency to imitate generalizes to other behavior of the technician, even though it is maladaptive. Biological scientists, for instance, may be excellent models to follow in regard to the use of adrenalin, but their views in regard to child training may be quite worthless. A politician may reward a large number of people by showing how to clear out a slum area and rebuild it properly. His followers tend, therefore, to approve and follow his opinions on other matters. He may, however, be a very inaccurate predictor as to the outcome of a foreign war. This faulty generalization of response is known as the "halo effect."

Non-Imitation

It has already been noted that social conditions may be so set up as to bring about the negative of imitative behavior, doing the opposite. This phenomenon has been frequently noted in the case of mobile individuals, who very carefully avoid the habits characteristic of their former social status. Mobile persons must change their cliques in order to achieve mobility. Successfully mobile persons are careful to dissociate themselves from their former cliques and the ways characteristic of the former social level. They definitely do not imitate the friends of their adolescence or early adulthood. Middle-class Negroes take great pains to be different from lower-class Negroes and to stress these differences. They do not, for instance, "shout" in church. They emphasize their educational advantages over lower-class Negroes and are careful to refer to the latter as "ignorant and dirty" (Davis and Dollard, 1940, p. 136). By so doing, they are stressing the negative of imitation of the religious and personal habits of the lower class. They know well that they would immediately be punished by relegation to lower-class status if they showed too many traits characteristic of the lower class, and they also know that their hold on middle-class status is tenuous and can easily be lost. They are, in fact, easily confused with lower-class persons by the topmost people in their own group and by the entire white caste. They struggle all the more vehemently to make themselves stand out as stimulus objects differentiated from lower-class persons.

In age-grading and class-typing, it was seen that there are punishments that attend the attempts of individuals to imitate *all* of the behavior of those superordinated to them. It was further observed, in the case of intelligence differentials, that the response performed by the leader may be too difficult for the follower to copy; imitative behavior would not be predicted in this case. Similarly, in the question of skill differences, it was observed that competing habits may make the acquisition of another skill difficult or that differential social rewards for specific skills may make it inexpedient for a person with a skill of superior social value to copy the skill of an inferior. (The banker may find that it "does not pay" to do his own plumbing.)

The question arises as to whether sex-typing should be included in a list of the social conditions favoring non-imitation. It is known that parents are aware of the biological sex differences of their children and that they respond differently to each sex from earliest infancy. The new father is invariably asked, "Is it a boy or a girl?" The name itself is chosen according to sex. Although considerable parallelism prevails in the treatment of boys and girls for a period after birth, by the time a child reaches his second year sex-typing has already begun. It becomes more marked as the years go on and is very apparent in the behavior of small boys and girls by the age of five. The apparent strategy is to provide children with a set of mental and social habits which will match their biological sex. Since these habits are incompatible at many points, although not, for example, in table manners or grammar, differential training conditions are set up. The little boy is punished or at least not rewarded for playing with dolls, but he is encouraged to be interested in trains, hammers, and the like. He is usually not permitted to wear girls' clothes, but he is allowed to take more risks and to be more expressive in a physical sense. The play of girls and boys is modeled (by the toys given them) according to sex, and the stories read to them emphasize the differential behavior of boys and girls. Punishment and discouragement prevent the boy from learning a girl's rôle and keep the girl from adopting masculine habits.

One would expect, in such a case, that there would arise a tendency not to imitate the other sex, to behave in an opposite or at least different manner. Life-history studies reveal, indeed, that this tendency is deep-rooted and vigorous, and that it remains throughout life a serious affront to accuse a man of effeminacy or a woman of masculinity. The punishments meted out to adults who actually exhibit such tendencies tend to maintain and strengthen the sex-typed habits acquired in childhood. Under these circumstances, imitation of the habits of the opposite sex would hardly be expected to be the rule. It does occasionally occur, however, and the exceptions are no less instructive than the usual behavior. In those cases where the own-sex rôle has been made to seem particularly dangerous or difficult, imitation of the opposite sex rôle may occur. Such individuals frequently learn to escape corrective social punishments by secretive behavior.

The conditions of learning in the cases referred to above, it will be noted, parallel closely those in the previously reported experiments on children. The children were subordinate in age, status, and intelligence hierarchies. The experimenters, who were superordinate, set the conditions of learning; that is, they determined the nature of the problem, the response which would be successful, and the placing of the rewards which fixed the desired behavior. There seems every reason to believe that the same conditions are operative wherever imitative behavior is learned, although in real life the superordinated who do the teaching may not be consciously aware that they have set up such conditions. They are unwittingly following the routines of their culture.

It seems clear also that all three kinds of imitative learning respond to the same hierarchical conditions. *Same* behavior follows the general laws of learning and is taught by "superiors" to "inferiors." Matched-dependent and copying behavior are notoriously an expression of the permanent or temporary subordination of some persons to others in age, status, skill, and intelligence hierarchies.

It is characteristic that matched-dependent behavior occurs where there is a model, but no critic to guide and limit response. The model functions merely as a stimulus to elicit the response of the imitator. This situation is frequently faced by the socially mobile individual. He can see what others are doing, after a fashion, but has no one to guide him in the minute definition of the appropriate cues and responses. The matching in matched-dependent behavior is, therefore, bound to be only approximate. Frequently, for instance, the imitator will hit upon the correct response but will not know when to make it, and must depend upon cues from others for the timing of the response. For example, the imitator may know that there are some occasions on which he ought to wear a pearl-gray tie but he will not know exactly when these occasions are to occur. He must consequently match with those who do.

The situation is quite different where the imitator has learned to copy. In this case, both model and critic are provided; the model demonstrates the response and the critic limits the range of practice. A boy going to a good "prep" school, for instance, will not be allowed by mere chance to hit upon the behavior expected of a boy in the school. He will be specifically instructed by teachers and older boys. In the family, likewise, the child is expected to copy the behavior of the social models. In addition to the other types of more basic training which the family administers, it also teaches the child the behavior appropriate to its social class. The family critics who are responsible for the cleanliness, sex, and aggression training of the child function also in regard to his speech, manners, and dress.

The conditions of life of our own society, and perhaps of many others, conspire to reward an acquired drive to match and copy. Such a drive seems to be a common American attitude. It probably derives strength from the fact that doing the same as others is rewarded in a multitude of situations, whereas the perception of being different is a signal for punishment. In the course of the socialization of the child, he soon learns that the safest line of behavior is that which is being carried out, or can be carried out, by someone else of the same age-grade and status. It is safe in one environment to shout "Wop!" at another child, or to fight the teacher, or to eat with one's knife, because age- and class-mates are seen carrying out the same behavior. The child has a sense of well-being when he has mastered his family's technique of table etiquette; punishment occurs only when he deviates. He is not likely to be corrected for items of speech behavior when others use the same words and expressions; the jarring cor-

rections come only when the child deviates from the familial
or clique model. In the course of time, people become very
conscious of when they are doing the same and when they are
behaving differently from others. This awareness of being
different is particularly clear in the case of mobile persons
who are attempting to change the first culture of childhood to
a second set of habits found in later life to be preferable.
Such persons, for instance, find themselves getting red about
the ears when they answer a telephone and say, "This is him,"
to someone who will certainly recognize a grammatical error.

In an adult clique, the members exhibit similar manners,
styles of clothes, standards of living, modes of child rearing,
and many other characteristic details of life. Cliques also exercise considerable control over their members in regard to
their moral, political, and recreational behavior and opinions.
Divergence draws punishment in the form of unfavorable notice, ridicule, and possible exclusion from intimate association. Punishment for difference in behavior is frequent
enough so that the mere perception of difference constitutes a
stimulus which excites punishing responses, i.e., anxiety. The
perception of sameness, on the other hand, constitutes an af-
firmation that not punishment, but eventual reward, is in
sight, and this, in turn, induces relaxation responses. It is not
necessary that these anticipations of reward or punishment
be conscious in either case. The discomfort of mobile individuals is undoubtedly explained in part by the fact that
they are so acutely aware of differences between their own behavior and that of other people. Persons well trained in a
particular position are likely to be stable and comfortable
since they experience constant reassurance in the persistent
matching of their behavior with others. It is the perception
of difference that rouses anxiety and sets the copying drive in
motion.

There is nothing innate or inevitable about the anxiety-
raising capacity of perceptions of difference. Exactly the
opposite result can be reached under appropriate conditions;
that is, perception of difference can be a secondary reward.

This is the case when a law-abiding citizen compares himself with a criminal, a member of a superior society with a "barbarian," or an upper-class person with a social inferior. In such cases perceptions of sameness are punishing, while knowledge of difference brings self-satisfaction.

CHAPTER XIII

IMITATION AND INDEPENDENT LEARNING: EXPERIMENT ON CHILDREN

IMITATION can hasten the process of learning by forcing the subject to respond correctly to the proper cue more quickly than he otherwise would. In this way, a preliminary phase of imitation or copying is often useful in teaching a subject to respond independently to the proper environmental cues. In fact, one of the chief functions of copying as it is commonly used in the schoolroom is to get the subject to the stage where he can make the socially appropriate response independently and in the absence of a model. This use of the mechanism of imitation is of enough practical importance to deserve special attention. A more thorough understanding of the details of the process may suggest when imitation should be expected to be of great aid, of little aid, or a positive hindrance to independent learning.

The manner in which a subject learns to copy a melody has already been discussed. After the subject becomes adept at matching notes with a model, he can follow a new melody through, note by note, after the model. Thus he is able to make the response of singing the correct melody on the first trial. In this case, the contrast with unaided trial-and-error learning is tremendous. The probability of the subject's hitting upon the correct melody by chance through an independent parallel invention of the same tune is obviously so low as to be out of practical consideration.

One of the chief functions of copying, in the example analyzed, was to get the subject to make the responses involved in singing the correct melody. This was possible because the cue of hearing each note had been connected to the response of singing the same note. The correct response could have been produced in other ways. If the subject had also known how to read music, he could have been presented with the stimuli of a series of notes on a musical score; or if he had learned to respond to the names of the notes (E, D, C) with the appropriate pitches, he could have been induced to sing the correct melody on the first trial by verbal instruction. In all of these cases, the techniques used by the teacher will be effective only if the subject has already learned the proper units for reacting to each stimulus from the teacher—the heard pitch, the note seen on the staff, or the name of the note —with the response of singing the correct note. In the case of copying, the stimulus from the teacher and the note sung by the pupil are perceptually similar. In the other two cases, there is no similarity between the stimulus presented by the teacher and the response made by the subject, but the function of all three techniques is exactly the same: to induce the subject to sing a correct melody on the first trial.

When the subject is copying the melody for the first time, the crucial cues for producing the correct response are the notes which he hears the model sing. At the same time, part of the stimulus pattern is just having heard himself and felt himself sing the preceding note. Thus, by generalization there is a tendency for the subject, on the second trial, to respond appropriately, not only to the stimulus of hearing the model's note, but also to the stimulus of hearing the preceding note in the melody and, in the case of the initial note, to the stimulus of the situation, the name of the song, or the thought of the name of the song. Because responses are weaker in situations to which they generalize than in the original situation in which they were rewarded, it will be easier for the subject to sing the tune on the second trial with the aid of hearing the model than it will be if the model does not continue to sing. As soon as the generalized tendencies become strong enough so that the correct response will occur in the absence of the model, this generalized response can be rewarded, and the subject is on his way to independent learning.

Copying plays an exceedingly important rôle in the learning of language. A few examples may be analyzed. A little boy, aged four and a half, is with his mother in a department store. While she is busy with other merchandise, he becomes fascinated by the BB guns on an adjoining counter. As soon as his mother is free, he drags her there, points to one of the guns, and asks, "What's that?" His mother answers, "A BB gun," and explains to him what BB's are. He then repeats the word "BB" several times while looking at the guns. That night, he asks his father to buy him a BB gun. By first imitating his mother, the child has now learned to use a new word independently.

In this case, the motivation is probably some complex blend of acquired drives. One factor is presumably the desire to be able to ask the father for the BB gun as a present, similar requests having sometimes been previously rewarded. It may also be that much prodding and rewarding on the part of the parents have established a slight anxiety at seeing an object which he cannot name and have given the response of being able to name the object a slight acquired reward value. Two of the distinctive cues are the sight of the gun and hearing the mother say "BB." The response is saying "BB."

The child has already learned to respond to the cue of hearing the mother say "B" with the response of saying "B" himself. The double stimulus "BB" from the mother is able to elicit the double response "BB" in the presence of the gun. The units are of necessity old. Two things are distinctly new about the response. The first of these is the combination of the units, the occurrence of the second syllable "B" as a response to the cues produced by just having said the first syllable, also "B." The second is the occurrence of the whole response in the presence of the gun as a cue. This new pattern of response seems to have been strengthened by the acquired reward value of the child's knowing that he can ask his father for a gun. For this new response subsequently to occur independently, it is necessary that generalization occur from the situation in which the cues involve both the sight of the gun and the sound of the model word as pronounced by the mother, to the situation in which only the sight of the gun is present. In this case the new word generalized still further to situations in which only words or thoughts about the gun were present. Presumably, these words and thoughts were also present as cues when the child was first imitatively practicing the new word.

A similar example occurred earlier in the life of the same boy, when he was taken to the snake house in the zoo. He saw a huge, colored snake coiling and rearing behind the glass. He seemed fascinated and asked, "What's that?" He was told, "It is a snake." After hearing this, he repeated, "Nake, nake," and was rewarded by being lifted up to get a better view. Afterwards, he asked to go back and see the "nakes."

In this case, the connection between the cue of hearing someone else pronounce an initial *s* before a consonant and making the response of pronouncing the initial *s* himself was not present. Independent evidence for this conclusion comes from the fact that the little boy was mispronouncing all words beginning with *s* before a consonant—was, for example, saying "mells" instead of "smells." Because the matching of this unit had not already been learned, the response elicited imitatively was, of necessity, imperfect. Thus the response elicited by generalization to the cue of the object alone, in the absence of the mother's pronunciation of the word "snake," was also imperfect. Although imitation did not produce the independent learning of a perfectly correct response, it nevertheless speeded learning by immediately eliciting a closer approximation than would be expected after thousands of purely random responses.

The imperfection of the child's speech in this example emphasizes the point that imitation cannot be used to produce either a sound or a novel combination of sounds in a new situation, unless the component cue-response matchings have already been learned. This demonstrates also that there is no general unlearned capacity to imitate, a fact which is painfully obvious to a stranger trying to learn the unfamiliar phonetic elements of a foreign language.

Such emphasis upon the necessity of learning units for

copying specific elements of the language[1] before imitation can aid independent learning raises the question: Why would it not be as easy to establish the independent learning directly in the first place? As has been suggested, the saving comes in the imitative *combination* of units. For the sake of illustration, let us arbitrarily assume that, out of the sounds which a child makes, "da" occurs by chance one time in a hundred, and "dee" also one time in a hundred. Then the proud parent who is trying to get the child to say "da" after he himself says "da" will have to repeat this cue only approximately one hundred times before the correct response will occur and can be given that crucial first reward which will increase its subsequent probability of occurrence to the same cue. The same will be true of "dee." It may be expected that a total of two hundred trials will be required to get out the first correct response units to each of the cues separately. Assuming that there is no initial positive or negative tendency for the syllable "dee" to follow "da," the chances of the combination "daddy" occurring at any given time are $1/100 \times 1/100$, or only one time in ten thousand. Thus it will be much harder to start learning the combination than the elements. There will be a saving in learning the elements separately and then combining them imitatively.

In the attempt to make this analysis simple, several complicating factors have been omitted. The first of these is a purely statistical one. The assumption was made that the two elements were uncorrelated. Actually, the syllable "dee" may be higher in the innate hierarchy of responses to the cue of

---

[1] For the student in a phonetics course whose teacher rewards him for learning a language in the most logical manner possible, these units are the phonemes of the language and certain difficult combinations of phonemes. Units learned by the child may be much less discrete. They are probably embedded in simple words from the very beginning, because it is words, not single phonemes, for which the child is rewarded. After being repeatedly rewarded only in the cue context of the rest of the phonemes of a given word, a child may need considerable practice in a number of different contexts before a given phoneme becomes a unit readily elicitable in any context of cues. What the functional units actually are for different children and the details of the process by which these are learned are questions beyond the scope of the present investigation.

just having said "da" than are other syllables. A positive correlation of this type will, of course, increase the probability of the specific combination occurring. Unless the correlation approaches 1, however, the specific combination will be considerably less probable than the elements.

A second complication is the fact that the elements may not be rewarded by the adult members of society if they occur separately, but only if they occur in some meaningful combination. Since reward is essential to the learning of a habit, the more frequent occurrence of the elements separately than of any given combination will not aid learning unless the occurrence of the elements to a given cue is rewarded. Because certain combinations are rewarded more often than the phonemic elements embedded in them, they may be learned more rapidly than the simpler elements by themselves.

A final complication is that the process by which the child learns to make a given sound to the cue of hearing that sound may not be entirely through trial and error. The fact that the child is exposed to the cue of hearing himself make a sound at the same time that he is making the responses which produce that sound may allow the child to acquire a slight tendency to imitate himself. This may generalize to other people. According to the hypothesis followed in this book, such learning can occur only if motivated and rewarded. A detailed discussion of the conditions which might motivate and reward such learning will be found in Appendix 1, which presents a revision of Holt's theory of imitation.

The factors mentioned in these three qualifying paragraphs may produce effects which serve to complicate the simple analysis of the difficulty of learning a combination in comparison with the difficulty of learning the units of that combination. Even after these complications are taken into account, however, the conclusion seems to remain essentially the same. It will be more difficult to teach the child, as his first word, a combination of many units, such as "hypochondriacally," than the combination of a few frequently occurring units, such as "mama." It seems improbable that in any culture the first word learned by the child is a complicated combination of ten or more units.

It is a well-established fact that once the imitation of simple units is learned, these units play an extremely important part in the further learning of language.[2] Once the component units have been mastered, the teacher has at his disposal a means of eliciting, in specific situations, combinations of responses which would practically never occur by chance.

The function of imitative copying as a stage in the process of the learning of independent responses is, of course, not limited to language. Imitation also facilitates the learning of manual responses. In one observed case a parent was teaching a child how to open a door that tended to stick. The mother demonstrated in detail the way the child should grasp the door handle with both hands and should brace himself to pull hard. In this case, as in the majority of cases observed, the parent, being interested in getting the child quickly to try the response which would be rewarded, did not rely upon demonstration and copying alone. At the same time that the parent was trying to elicit the proper responses by demonstrating them, she was also trying to elicit the proper responses by describing them. Thus verbal and visual cues may be summated to the same end. The joint action of the cues from the model and the cues of language actually did elicit a successful combination of responses which, up to this point, had failed to appear in the trial-and-error behavior of the child. When rewarded in this situation, the response generalized to the situation in which the imitative and language cues were absent. The sticking door by itself became a cue to try these responses; the child learned to open the door independently.

In the interest of producing the correct responses, parents usually supplement demonstration with language. In the cases studied to date, pure examples of demonstration without language seem to be the exception. One example of inad-

2 References on this point are summarized by Dorothea McCarthy (1933, p. 338).

vertent teaching by pure demonstration may be cited. A
mother was accustomed to keeping small gifts for her children in a cabinet which could be reached by a short stepladder. On one occasion a child observed the mother climb on the
stepladder to get a small present out of the cabinet. At this
age, imitation had already been established as a means of securing various rewards, and the specific units—climbing,
reaching, opening—had already been learned as matched behavior. Thus, almost immediately, the child tried climbing up
to the cabinet. Subsequent occasions demonstrated that his
one trial of imitation had helped him learn a habit which
could be performed independently.

No one has yet made an exact determination of the importance of imitation relative to other techniques of learning.
But it is certain that in both child and adult life, imitation is
a means to many important types of learning. Athletes pick
up new points on form, new tricks of play, by watching other
athletes. Experimentalists pick up apparatus hints by watching mechanics at work. Socially mobile individuals learn how
to behave in strange social gatherings by observing the behavior of others. Every time such learning is rewarded, the
component copied responses are strengthened.

The conditions under which imitation can hasten the process of learning independent responses may now be listed:

1. The cue-response connections producing the units of
matched behavior must be present, if example is to be useful.
Because he has more units, a mechanic learns more by watching another mechanic perform a mechanical operation than
does a layman. One of the purposes of elementary education
is to supply proper units of behavior. The individual must
have these copying units, be they fundamental dance steps or
the phonemes of a new language, before he can use copying
as a short cut to further learning.

2. The model must be correct. If the model is wrong and
the person has a tendency to imitate, this tendency must be
extinguished before a correct, rewarded response will occur.
If the response performed by the model is one which gives a
smaller amount of reward or a reward diluted by unnecessary

fatigue, the dependent subject may fail to hit upon a better response, which would perhaps have occurred had the inferior response not been elicited and strengthened through reward, and had the drive not been partially reduced.

3. The subject must generalize from the situation in which the model's cue is present to the situation in which it is absent. This is more likely to occur when the environmental stimulus is a relatively distinctive component of the total stimulus pattern. If responding to the cues from the model directs the dependent subject's sense organs and attention toward the proper environmental cue, this may enhance its distinctiveness. If, on the other hand, responding to the cues from the model directs the dependent subject's sense organs and attention away from the proper environmental cue, he may not be exposed to it at all. In this case, no generalization will occur, and there will be no benefit from imitation.

Experiment 10. The Rôle of Direction of Attention in Determining Whether Imitation Facilitates or Hinders Independent Learning

According to the preceding analysis, one of the important variables determining whether or not a stage of imitative behavior will facilitate the learning of independent behavior is the degree to which the subject is exposed to the relevant environmental cues during imitative behavior. Thus, the more the act of imitation helps to direct the imitator's attention toward those of the environmental cues which are relevant and so makes them distinctive while the correct response is being performed, the more likely the imitator is to become able to perform independently, in the absence of the model. And conversely, the more the act of imitation directs the imitator's attention away from the relevant environmental cues, the less likely the imitator is to learn the cue-response connections which will enable him to perform independently, in the absence of the leader. The purpose of the following experiment was to test these predictions.

In order to test for the effect of directing attention toward or away from relevant cues in the environment, two situations were compared. One of these situations was set up so that the subjects who imitated were vividly exposed to the relevant cue, whereas the subjects who did not imitate were not exposed to this cue. After responding in this situation, one would expect the imitators to have progressed further toward learning to perform the correct response independently than the non-imitators. The second situation, employed for control comparison, was the same as the first in every respect except that the response of imitation did not expose the subjects to the relevant environmental cue, while the response of non-imitation did vividly expose the subjects to this cue. After trials in this situation, one would expect different results: The subjects who had not imitated should have progressed further toward learning how to perform the correct response independently. Since the degree to which imitation directs the subject's attention toward the relevant environmental cue is the only factor in which these two conditions are different, positive results would confirm the theoretical expectation that this factor is important.

The subjects used in this experiment were the same forty first-grade students who had just finished Experiment 6. Half of them had learned to imitate and half of them had learned to non-imitate in going to one of two boxes for candy. In the present experiment, the imitators and non-imitators were each divided into two subgroups. For purposes of reference, the first pair of these subgroups, ten imitators and ten non-imitators, to be used in the first situation, may be designated as Section I, and the second pair of subgroups, ten imitators and ten non-imitators, to be used in the second situation, may be designated as Section II.

The physical setup of this experiment was, in general, quite similar to that employed in Experiment 5. The starting point of the subjects was marked on the floor. Ten feet from the starting point and ten feet apart two chairs were placed on the corners of the base of an imaginary equilateral triangle, of which the starting point was the apex. On each chair was a box with a hinged lid. These were similar in every respect to those employed in Experiment 5, except that each had a quarter-inch hole drilled through the center of the lid. This hole was one and one-half inches from the front of the lid and slanted down toward the center of the back at a forty-five-degree angle. Into either of the boxes could be placed a small portable flashlight lantern.[3]

The problem for the subjects in Section I was to learn that candy was always to be found in the box containing the light. The flashlight lantern was placed in the bottom of the front of the box with its lens facing up. The candy was placed directly on top of the lens. The lid was closed, and a small beam of light was unobtrusively visible shining out through the quarter-inch hole in the top as the relevant environmental cue.

On the first trial, the leader was given his turn first. He always went to the box containing the light and the candy. When opening it, he was careful to stand so that the additional light, which otherwise would have been visible with the lid of the box up, was shielded from the subject. After the leader had his turn, the dependent subject was given his turn. On these turns, each imitator, because of his previous training, went to the same box as the leader. Upon lifting the lid of the box, each imitator was vividly exposed to the cue of the light while reaching for the candy. The non-imitators, on the other hand, went to the other box. Upon lifting its lid, they were not exposed to the light and did not get candy. For both groups of subjects, the first trial contained only one turn. This was necessary in order to prevent the non-imitators from correcting their response and being exposed, in the same way as the imitators, to the light as a very distinctive and vivid cue.

On the second trial, the light and candy were shifted to the box in the other position in order to determine what independent learning had occurred as a result of the first trial. The subjects were given this second trial without any leader.

Because the light was the only cue that was shifted when the reward was shifted, the presence of light in one box and

[3] A two-cell flashlight lantern with a lens two and one-eighth inches in diameter; trade name, Niagara Junior Guide No. 12.

absence of light in the other box was the relevant cue. Other cues, such as the position of the boxes, were irrelevant in that they were not correlated with the reward. In this case, the presence of the light in the correct box was more striking and distinctive as a cue than the absence of a light in the other box because lights are not to be found in most boxes of this kind, and because the difference in illumination between the light in the one box and its background was greater than the difference in illumination between the shadow in the other box and its background.[4]

Since the response of the imitators, opening the lid of the correct box, vividly exposed them to the light as a distinctive relevant cue at just the moment that they were reaching for the candy, one would expect the goal response of reaching for the candy to be attached to this cue. On the test trial, one would expect this response to generalize to the situation in which only a little light was shining through the hole in the top of the box. This generalization would be expected to be facilitated by previous experiences in which feeble lights seeping out through holes have been associated with bright lights behind obstacles such as doors and by the complex verbal responses learned during such experiences. Therefore, on this test trial, one would expect the imitators, who were vividly exposed to the correct cue, the light, as a result of having followed the leader, to be more likely to respond to the light in the absence of the leader and hence to make a correct choice. Conversely, one would expect the non-imitators, who, as a result of not following the leader, had not been vividly exposed to the light as the correct cue, to be less likely to succeed.

In order to demonstrate that any such success was the result of being exposed to the correct cue, Section II was used as a control group. The problem for these subjects was to learn that candy was always to be found in the box opposite to the one containing the light. In all other respects the procedure was the same. On the first trial, the leader had his turn

[4] Contrast with background is a factor which has been emphasized by Gestalt psychologists.

first. He always went to the box opposite to the one containing the light. After he had had his turn of going to the correct box and getting his candy, the dependent subject was given his turn. On these turns, the imitators, because of their previous training, went to the same box as the leader. Upon lifting the lid of the box they got candy but were not exposed to the relevant cue, the light. The non-imitators on the other hand, because of their previously learned tendency, went to the opposite box from the leader. This trial was, of course, an error. But upon lifting the lid of this box they were vividly exposed to the relevant cue, the light. Thus the extinction resulting from non-reward was attached to the response of going toward a light. Since the subjects were already sophisticated and knew that eliminating an error was a step toward candy, it is probable that, in addition to the effects of experimental extinction, the effects of turning away from the light were strengthened by the acquired reward value of eliminating an error.

On the second trial, the light was shifted to the other box. The problem still was to find the candy, which was in the box without the light. In order to test what independent learning had occurred as a result of the first trial, the subjects were given a second trial without a leader. On this trial, one would expect the non-imitators, who had been vividly exposed to the relevant cue while turning away from the box not containing the candy, to tend to respond to this relevant cue again. The imitators, not having been exposed to the relevant cue, would be expected to respond on the basis of position or other irrelevant cues which would lead them to make errors. Thus the non-imitators should make more correct responses on the trial without a leader than would the imitators.

The results confirm the deductions. When the conditions were arranged so that imitation facilitated and non-imitation hindered the subject from exposing himself to the relevant cue, the imitators did better than the non-imitators in the test for independent learning. On the other hand, when the conditions were arranged so that imitation hindered and non-imitation facilitated the subject in exposing himself to the relevant cue, the imitators did more poorly than the non-imitators in the test for independent learning. Under the first set of conditions, 90 per cent of the imitators and only 40 per cent of the non-imitators made correct responses when tested for independent learning. A difference of this magnitude would be expected by chance only approximately one time in a hundred. Under the second conditions, 30 per cent of the imitators and 100 per cent of the non-imitators made correct responses when tested for independent learning. A difference of this magnitude would be expected by chance less than one time in a thousand. Thus, it is conclusively demonstrated that the degree to which responses of imitation or non-imitation facilitate or hinder exposure to the relevant cue is a crucial factor in determining the extent to which they will facilitate or hinder the course of learning to respond independently.

Incomplete Imitation

In the preceding experiment, imitation interfered with independent learning when the response imitated caused the subject not to notice the relevant environmental cue. Since the complete response of the leader involved looking at the relevant environmental cue, the response that the follower imitated was an incomplete copy of the leader's response. The leader looked at the light in the first box and then went to the second box. The follower looked at the leader and then went directly to the second box without first looking for the light. Since conditions were such that an imperfect copy of .this kind would be rewarded, the imitator learned this imperfect copy. But this imperfect copy was effective only when the model was present. Thus the subject was unable to perform independently.

In this experiment, the crucial response omitted was the first response in the leader's sequence—looking at the relevant environmental cue. In more complex examples of copying, it is possible for other crucial responses to be omitted. In the schoolroom, the copier may start by looking at the same question in a test as the bright student in the class, but may omit the intervening cue-producing responses of working out the problem and then may merely look at, and copy, the model's answer. If he is rewarded for this, he will tend to learn to copy his model. But this habit will not help him to solve the problem independently, because it is an imperfect copy with several crucial links omitted. Had the copier been able to observe and match all of the mental processes of his model, so that exactly the same responses were rewarded, his copying might be expected to help him to learn something about independent problem solving.

In summary, imitation can greatly hasten the process of independent learning by enabling the subject to perform the first correct response sooner than he otherwise would. Imitation is particularly important when (in cases involving combinations of a number of different units, such as the notes of a song or the syllables of a long word) the occurrence of the correct response would otherwise be exceedingly improbable. In order for imitation to elicit the first correct response, the essential units of copying or matched-dependent behavior must already have been learned.

When the subject is rewarded for performing an incomplete copy of the model's responses, independent learning will be retarded if practice on this incomplete response lessens the probability that the total correct response will appear. A reward for an incomplete response may lessen the probability of the total correct response occurring by keeping drive at such a low level that the individual is not in a learning dilemma. The incomplete response may also interfere with the correct response by being incompatible with some crucial link of the correct response. Experimental results demonstrate that such incompatibility, if present, is important. When watching the model prevents the subject from copying the model's response of looking at the relevant environmental cue, imitation delays the process of learning to respond independently. When watching the model directs the subject's attention toward the relevant environmental cue, imitation hastens the process of learning to respond independently.

CHAPTER XIV

CROWD BEHAVIOR

THE general conclusion of the studies of crowd behavior could be stated in parallel to the old quip, about as follows: "People in a crowd behave about as they would otherwise, only more so." It is nevertheless true that this "more so" exists and is at times extremely important. Crowds and crowd-mindedness constitute a continual danger to an orderly social life, since they tend to suppress that rational canvass of alternative responses which makes possible an intelligent social policy. Even if crowds are occasionally useful in the survival of a society—as in fund-raising rallies or war emergencies—they are as patently dangerous a great part of the time—as in revolutions, riots, and lynching mobs.

The data used in this examination of the mechanisms of crowd behavior are not, and need not be, original. Several generations of sociologists and psychologists have examined the problem and have made available a body of facts and principles. The most obvious and certain of these conclusions will be analyzed here (Bernard, 1926, pp. 438–451; 1931, pp. 612–613), (Ogburn and Nimkoff, 1940, pp. 272–303), (Young, 1927, pp. 627–690).

The first consideration will be the nature of the patterns of stimuli which evoke and increase the agitated behavior of crowds. Most students of the matter agree that a common stimulus is necessary, that is, a stimulus noticed, and responded to, by a large part of the crowd. This stimulus may have drive value in itself, as the feeling of a hot deck underfoot, or may have acquired drive value, in that it is not itself a drive but does evoke a response which, in turn, produces stimuli of drive-like intensity. Such a cue stimulus might be the quietly spoken word "fire" in the absence of direct evidence as to the existence of fire. Both of these types of stimuli will be referred to as drive stimuli. Drive stimuli mobilize responses which give the first intimation that something is amiss in the environment and that further responding is in order.

To be differentiated from such common responses to common drives are responses to the behavior of others once the common responses have been set off.[1] The behavior of people in a crowd is a kind of interpretation of the drive stimulus. If they feel the danger to be great, for instance, their common responses to drive are more energized; they run faster, clamor louder, boo harder. Each of these responses of any one person is perceived by others in the crowd and may become a stimulus to them, further activating the behavior of these individuals. In past situations, each individual has been rewarded for reacting more strongly when others also were reacting strongly. In various danger and competitive situations, it has been found expedient to rush toward a goal which others are seeking or to scamper faster from a common danger because others are running. In this way, the agitated behavior of others acquires power to evoke a stronger response in any one individual.[2] If A runs faster, B, C, and D tend to run faster, too, although the drive stimulus itself has in no way increased for them. Crowd stimulation is added to the actual excitation of the drive as the individual member of the crowd at first perceives it.

Together these two stimuli—drive[3] and crowd—determine

[1] "The joyful ecstasy of a jubilant crowd remains a feeling of joy; a panic of fear is fear; the hatred of a lynching mob is hatred. . . . In all of these instances, and innumerable others, the *specific emotion experienced is not of crowd derivation*. What is common in the above situations is the crowd psychology: through a summation of stimuli, and through imitation, the emotions become intensified" (Goldenweiser, 1922, p. 373).

[2] Hull has demonstrated by an ingenious experiment that a watching subject shows a demonstrable tendency to lean forward when observing another subject strongly leaning forward (1933, p. 41).

[3] The writers recognize an annoying dilemma in the proper naming of these drives. Actually, crowd stimuli are drive stimuli, i.e., acquired drive stimuli, and are built upon primary drive. The real line of distinction is between what happens to the individual as a result of the stimuli received before his presence in the crowd and what happens to him after he is in the crowd. Such alternatives have been considered as "crowd-drive" stimuli and

the strength of the responses which will be made by individuals in the crowd. If the drive stimulus is weak, as in the case, say, of an aggregate watching an excavation, no very vital crowd stimulus can be added to it. If the drive is strong, as fear of fire in a theater, crowd stimulation can build up the total stimulation to great heights. Responses in the one case will be the weak ones of mere looking; in the other, they will consist of frenzied efforts to escape.

Drive stimuli can presumably be so strong as to account for panic behavior in a crowd without involving the factor of crowd stimulation. Some situations are so dangerous, so frustrating, or so aggression-provoking that they stimulate a common mass action which does not rely on crowd stimulation. In this case, the responses to the drive are common, immediate, and powerful. There is a large element of such direct mass response to drive stimulus in the panic aboard a sinking ship or the stampede in a theater fire. Indeed, it has been well observed (Faris, 1937, p. 77) that individuals can show panic responses when alone. The case is at hand of a tenderfoot lost in the Maine woods who, after a day of wandering, became so disoriented that he twice crossed a well-rutted wagon road without noticing it and, when finally found, hysterically resisted his rescuers. In his case, an anxiety drive had been so powerfully aroused as to energize primitive escape responses at the expense of all others. The case of the drowning man who fights off, or even strangles, his rescuer is a classic from folklore and from actual experience.

In the discussion which follows, three variables will be constantly watched, namely, drive stimulus, crowd stimulus, and strength of the response to the two. *Drive stimulus* refers to the excitation which the individual experiences under similar conditions when out of the crowd; *crowd stimulus* denotes the provocative strength of the stimuli given off by other per-

"non-crowd-drive" stimuli, "individual-drive" stimuli and "social-drive" stimuli, or "pre-crowd-drive" stimuli and "crowd-drive" stimuli. Various neologisms have been considered. All seem objectionable from one standpoint or another. The names selected seem the least objectionable in a choice of evils.

sons in the crowd; and *strength of response* is a measure of
energization of action under the impact of the two kinds of
stimuli. If drive stimulus, for instance, be held constant,
strength of response should vary directly with increased
crowd stimuli if the data generally accepted by sociologists
are facts.

If drive stimuli are raised to an inordinately high pitch, it
may not be possible to distinguish the effect of crowd stimuli
in bringing about powerful mass responses. This circumstance makes it difficult to discriminate between the strengths
of drive and crowd stimuli wherever the primary drive stimulus is particularly strong, as in the case of panic before an
oncoming flood. It is important not to confuse the two types
of stimulation, however difficult they may be to analyze;
much that is often attributed to the effect of the interaction
of the crowd itself is undoubtedly due to the direct effect of
a primary drive stimulus. If the individual can be thought
very likely to do by himself what he is known to do in the
presence of others, his behavior cannot be laid to the stimuli
given off by other persons in the crowd. There are, without
doubt, cases where the sheer effect of crowd stimuli guides the
behavior of an onlooker. A friend, for instance, idly wandering on the Vatican grounds one day, observed a troupe of
perhaps two hundred people moving rapidly into one of the
smaller chapels. Crowd-attracted, he joined the group and
was rewarded by seeing the Pope and being a part of the
group blessed by him. A trace of an acquired drive can be detected in the fact that the friend wanted to "see the Vatican"
and was therefore alert to any signs that would indicate at
what places or times the most interesting sights could be seen.

In addition to drive stimuli, crowd stimuli, and strength
of response, another itemization of variables has been made
which seem, by general agreement, to be involved in the behavior of crowds.[4] One of these is *interstimulation*. If all of

[4] The chapter on crowd behavior from Ogburn and Nimkoff (1940, pp.
272–303) has been used as a guide to the identification of the variables commonly recognized by students of crowd behavior. The systematic discussion
from the standpoint of learning theory is added by the authors.

the people in an aggregate were blindfolded, bound, and their ears filled with wax, it would be next to impossible for crowd behavior to occur because the individuals could not readily stimulate one another. It is just the nudges and pushes, the cries, and the sight of the gestures of others which constitute the main avenues of crowd stimulation. Each person's responses become stimuli, not only to himself, but to all other persons within the range of sensibility. This is what we have called the crowd stimulus.

A second circumstance in crowd behavior closely related to interstimulation is that of *proximity*. This may be physical proximity, which has its special advantage, or "social proximity"; but, in any case, individuals must be within signal distance of one another. Other things being equal, the nearer together persons are, the greater should be the effect of crowd stimuli and the more modalities of stimuli should be operative. The most powerful stimuli are presumably those given off by face-to-face contacts, because individuals have learned that others are more useful or dangerous when they are actually present and less so, for example, when heard over the radio or pictured in the movies. Books may, however, be the stimuli which initiate a crowd-like type of reaction. This is stated to have been the case with Harriet Beecher Stowe's *Uncle Tom's Cabin*, which created a ferment of discussion and a kind of stampede to the Abolitionists' position all over the Northern states of the United States. (The responses it evoked in the dissimilarly trained individuals of the Southern states were quite different.)

It is known since the Orson Welles broadcast (Cantril, 1940) that the human voice over the radio can lead to crowd-like types of interaction among large numbers of people. In the case of long-distance communication, of course, the leader is separated from other members of the crowd, and they may be (at first) separated from one another. The moving pictures likewise seem to aid in building up crowd-like conditions in the cases of spread of fashions in clothes, house decorations, and political opinions. In books, one deals with words without voice or gesture. It may be that the stimuli are increasingly effective as visual stimuli are added to aural stimuli. In any case, these mass communication inventions serve to broaden the areas within which people may be brought into such contact as to make possible crowd-like reactions. In the past, the size of a crowd was limited by the range of a human voice and the reports of it, or by the span of sight of a man from a hill or tower. Modern crowds may be world-wide and may receive stimuli which initiate crowd reactions with almost the same effectiveness as they can be received when within actual earshot.

It is generally believed among scientists familiar with crowd behavior that *numbers* are an important feature in crowd action. It seems that as few as two people can exert on one another the type of influence which has been described as crowd stimulation. The effective portion of a group for any one person is that part of the aggregate which is able to stimulate him. The importance of numbers seems to be partly based on the fact that people have learned that larger groups are safer models than smaller ones. Just as in the experiment reported in Chapter XI, where a large individual acquired prestige, so numbers can become the cue of a prestigeful model. A large number of people performing a response evoke it more strongly in any single individual, and similarly a large number of people avoiding a response can evoke avoidance tendencies in an individual.

Many individuals in each crowd have been separately punished or not rewarded for doing acts with only one person or none as model, whereas they have been frequently rewarded for acting as large groups of others act. They seem to behave on the presumption that forty million Frenchmen *can* be wrong, but that they are not as likely to be so as one Frenchman or two. Children in school, for instance, are punished if they fall out of line when other children are marching or if they get off the tune when other children are singing, while they are regularly rewarded for conforming to the behavior of others. Although, to be sure, they are sometimes punished when carrying out acts with other people, the great balance of reward seems to be on the side of doing what others do and avoiding what they avoid. It is probable, for this reason, that sheer numbers have an effect in producing matched behavior in individuals in an aggregate.[5]

Individuals tend to feel secure in crowds when they are acting as the crowd acts. This feeling of security can be explained in terms of the analysis of copying as a secondary drive. Acting the same as other people cues non-punishment and relaxation, thereby rewarding conformity. Noticing that one is acting differently, on the other hand, elicits anxiety responses. It is these anxiety responses which set the acquired drive of copying into action. The individual, apprehensive at observing the difference between his behavior and that of others, tries to notice carefully what they do and attempts a copy. If he succeeds, he is rewarded by a reduction in anxiety, as well as by the avoidance of the real punishments which frequently follow deviation from group models of behavior.

It is often urged that individuals are *anonymous* in crowds just because of the numbers of persons involved, and that, as a result of this anonymity, individual responsibility is blotted out. There are undoubtedly many types of crowd situations where this is the case. The learning involved here seems to be very simple. The individuals have found that they are rather more likely to be punished for any specific act if their names and identities are known, and if others can lay hands on them whenever they wish. Punishment is much less certain when name, address, and identity are unknown. A single individual provides cues which are much more difficult to discriminate when many similar individuals are present.

The rôle of the leader in a crowd has been repeatedly emphasized as important, usually under some such designation as the *prestige factor*. We speak here of an actual leader, rather than of a system of beliefs or "leading idea," which may dominate the crowd. The leader functions both to pre-

[5] The fact of "numbers" may be important in another way. With increased numbers the chances are greater that deviant individuals will be present in the crowd who will make exaggerated responses to the common drive stimuli; examples would include hysterics in a theater crowd or sadists at a lynching. Deviant responses produced by such persons increase the volume and quality of stimulation in the crowd.

sent and to interpret the drive stimulus. He may call attention to a danger and make his hearers aware of its full extent. He may extol a particular patent medicine or indicate an offending individual. If his speech is impassioned, his gestures intense, he will operate as the same kind of stimulus to members of the crowd that they do to one another. If he has prestige, individuals in the crowd will heed his warnings, discriminate dangers as he sees them, and generalize copying responses to him.

It is worth pointing out a number of the attributes of the leader in a crowd situation. He centers attention on himself, which many in the crowd would hesitate to do. He stands alone—often on an elevation—and frequently he alone speaks. Each of these stimulus patterns has acquired authoritative potential for the individual members of any crowd. Parents and teachers have presented their behests and distributed their rewards while exhibiting exactly the same behavior—by centering attention on themselves, standing alone and above, talking alone, and the like. Obedience to such persons is a well-learned habit for every normal person, however it may be modified after childhood. Crowd members generalize to the leader the responses of obedience which they have learned toward parents, teachers, older persons, larger persons, and superordinated individuals generally, just as the children in the experiments reported in Chapters VIII and XI generalized imitation. In some cases the leader arouses expectations of reward and punishment; in others he elicits automatic habits of obedience. Through this secondary power to reward and punish, he is able to suggest to the crowd the response that he wishes from them and to suggest also that he, like those more primary symbols of authority, has the power to reward the behavior that he wants. Conversely, he can specify and taboo the responses which he does not want.

This secondary rewarding power of the leader is integral to the process of suggestion. To be able merely to suggest the response is not, however, enough. The suggestion must be accompanied by the implication that carrying out the response will be reinforced. For this reason, suggestions from inferiors or non-leaders are often not heeded. Suggestion is effective only in cases where the following state of affairs prevails: namely, where one person is superordinated to another, and where the former is able, or is supposed to be able, to reward the responses that he wants and punish those that he does not want. Each person learns as a child that if he obeys his parents, he gets rewarded or is at least not punished. The child learns to generalize "doing what he is told" far beyond the primary situation of parental control. When he makes subordination responses to superiors outside the family group, he is frequently rewarded for this behavior also. Thus it comes about that a leader in a crowd, who may never have rewarded or punished the particular persons in the crowd, can nevertheless achieve authority.

The size of the crowd is not to be regarded as a substitute for the prestige of a leader; rather it supplements the leader's prestige. Response to the size of the crowd is probably a matter of separate conditioning. People are trained in one set of circumstances to "follow the leader" and in another set of circumstances to "follow the crowd." People have learned in one case that deferring to, admiring, and following the behests of a leader is behavior which more regularly leads to reward and escape from punishment; in the other case, they have learned early that doing what many other people are doing is safer and more profitable.

The leader or leaders of a crowd may also liberate the members thereof from anxiety about carrying out antisocial responses. Members of the crowd may be led not to expect punishment in the crowd situation for acts which would ordinarily be punished. For example, if the sheriff, who would have to arrest you for a murderous response, is in the crowd himself, there is less reason to fear legal retribution; if the district attorney, who must indict you, or the judge and prospective jurymen, who would have to pass sentence on you, are behaving with the crowd, the danger of punishment for antisocial acts is lessened. This is especially the case when crowd members control these individuals by election, or when the local mores permit the antisocial act even though the

wider culture enjoins it. Recognition of sameness and difference is accessory to this behavior since one must recognize
that one's own act is the same as the sheriff's and will merit
punishment as little as does his.

Repetition of stimuli seems to be a variable in crowd behavior. It is thought that such repetition increases suggestibility. Taken by itself, the importance of repetition (as
apart from rhythm) would seem to be that it increases the
volume of stimulation and hence of the crowd drive. Repetitive stimuli tend to summate and increase the total pressure
of stimulation from the acts of others in the crowd. Thus one
vocal stimulus, e.g., saying "Boo" to an unpopular crowd
leader, is still ringing in the ears when the next appears. The
same contention could be made for stamping the feet or clap-
ping the hands.

Closely allied to, but not identical with, repetitive stimuli
are *rhythmic* stimuli. The importance of rhythm has to do
with the ease of making a mass response. Rhythmic responses
are apparently easier to tie together than non-rhythmic responses. Uneven or unconventional periodicity of response is
much more difficult to learn. In the case of rhythmic responses, one can tie one's second response to the stimulus
trace of the first. For instance, the second mass utterance,
such as "Hold that line!" can be cued to the first. The crowd
can act together more decisively and thereby produce a
larger volume of stimulation when it stamps or claps in
rhythm.

The mounting excitation and climactic nature of crowd responses have been the subject of frequent comment. In explanation of this fact, the importance of the *circular reaction*
or interaction of the members of the crowd has been noticed.
The mechanism of the circular reaction seems to be a special
case of interstimulation. Two members of a crowd begin by
responding to the drive stimulus with a certain level of intensity, depending on the strength of this stimulus. At this
point the crowd variable may set in. The first individual notices the response of the second, and the stimuli given off by
this response operate to intensify his own response. The first

person is now responding more vigorously than he would to the drive stimulus alone. The second person, in his turn, is stimulated by the intensified response of the first, and increases the vigor of his own response. This process continues, following the conditions of the particular situation of crowd excitation, until it is terminated by some goal response which reduces stimulation. The reciprocal exposure to stimuli activates summatively the behavior of each person. Whispering becomes more intense and widespread under these conditions, talking turns to shouting or booing, walking becomes running, striking or batting becomes tearing, cleaving, or smashing. The behavior is obviously imitative, of the matched-dependent type.

The question remains as to how it comes about that the response of one person is energized by seeing another making the same response with energy. The now-familiar reference to the conditions of socialization of the members of the crowd seems to provide the answer. Children have learned that when others are running toward the same goal, it is advisable to speed up, if the goal is to be reached. They are frequently rewarded, in such situations, for running faster when they see others run. The response of running faster when others run is therefore fixed to the stimulus of seeing the other person run. The same type of situation occurs hundreds of times in the history of all normal children.

The question of the *kind of responses* which can occur under crowd conditions is worth discussion. Responses evoked by crowd excitation are ready-made. Apparently, no considerable amount of learning of new responses takes place under crowd conditions. Persons who do not have the requisite responses do not react to crowd stimulation. The responses which are ready at hand in the crowd situation have, as has been repeatedly stressed, a history—they are learned. A man who does not know how to speak English can hardly learn it under crowd conditions, let alone intensify his performance under crowd stimulation. Persons who do not understand the market mechanism, at least the simplest aspects of it, cannot participate in a market boom. It requires a whole arsenal of ready-made skills to take part in a gold rush, and those who did not command at least some of them would not have been found among the hosts of miners who stampeded, at one time and another, to California or South Africa. Crowds are most likely to react, therefore, with common mass responses which have been learned individually by everyone. Such common responses as running, striking, pursuing, fleeing, jeering, and copying are found in the arsenal of responses of most persons in a crowd. A group of people can become a crowd by performing together some· highly technical and difficult response pattern as well as by performing some simple response such as running; but such patterns will be definitely limited by the skill demands of the situation. Musical crowds can, for example, by their interaction momentarily inflate the value of a specific singer. Faddist movements rage in all the arts, from time to time, and are apparently partly built up by individuals noticing the favorable responses of others and reacting to them.

It has been well observed by Faris (1937, p. 76) that persons with habits opposed to those of the crowd are not affected by crowd stimulation. This again stresses the point that the responses with which individuals come into crowds have already been learned in previous socialization and are merely evoked and intensified in the crowd situation. Graduate students, for instance, are often taught to scoff at certain intellectual movements, and it would seem that scoffing increases as others are seen to do the same. Such a reaction is known to have occurred with regard to Freud. Freudian analysts, on the contrary, are not stimulated to jeer by such a reaction on the part of other scientists. The jeering stimuli call out, rather, defense reactions in them. Similarly, totalitarian affirmations often produce responses of defense of democracy in those trained in the latter. Lynch mobs raise protest, not conformity, in the visiting Yankee in the South. One must actually begin to make a response in a crowd before this response can be further excited by crowd stimuli; and to begin to make the response in question, one must have learned how to make it.

It can safely be repeated that men act in crowds the same as they do when alone, but, under some circumstances, more so. Crowd behavior is often surprising because we have such a poor idea of how individuals can act when they are alone. Under the surface of everyday social conformity, we do not ferret out the presence of the antisocial responses which can be mobilized and released, under some circumstances, in the crowd. This principle holds as well for socially valuable as for socially damaging types of response. Individuals at a fund-raising rally are often willing to give much more money to a cause than they can really afford. The more one can know of the diverse responses to which human beings in our society are trained, the less mysterious will any type of crowd behavior seem.

It has been widely noted that the interstimulation and responses occurring in crowds are likely to be of an *emotional* type. This emotionality of crowd behavior seems to be shown in the strength of the responses aroused in crowds. Strong responses may be a result, as has been noted, of a strong drive stimulus affecting all members of a crowd. Strength of response may also result from the circular conditioned stimulation of the crowd situation, which increases the strength of the response to primary drive. It seems to be a fact that strong responses to primary drive are frequently aroused in crowds, e.g., terrific anxiety at the danger of being burned, powerful aggression against the attacker of white womanhood, or strong greed for sudden riches. It is the degree to which strong responses are present that makes the difference between an idle aggregate of onlookers, an organized crowd, and a mob bent on action or destruction.

These considerations do not yet, however, explain the emotional character of the crowd. The most satisfactory theory seems to be that crowd emotion is a response-produced drive of the type described in Chapter IV. Response-produced stimuli summate, as a strong response series continues, and act as a drive. It is this drive that we recognize as emotionality. Differing emotions apparently take their peculiar character from the fact that different strong response series in operation give off stimuli characteristic of each. The emotion of anxiety, for instance, is characterized by stimuli aroused by strong visceral responses to a context which signals pain; that of anger is characterized by the stimuli from internal responses accompanying approach and attack. Individuals are "excited" when they are making such strong responses, and this excitement is labeled as emotion in any of various different specific cases. It should be noted that the stimuli given off by strong responses have the properties of strong stimuli, that they do, in fact, drive the person experiencing them to further action. Once the first strong response has been made, perhaps to a cue stimulus which is weak, internal stimulation is built up which leads to an ever stronger progression of responses. This "emotional build-up" accounts for part of the rising crescendo of action in a crowd.

Crowd leaders all have a crude empirical knowledge of this principle. They do not use statistical and rational cue symbols when dealing with a crowd, except incidentally. What they do use are verbal stimuli which set off strong common responses, such as "rape," "mad dog," "defense," "Would you want your sister to marry a nigger?" It must be repeated that there is nothing instinctive about the responses to these cue stimuli. The words have been integrated, in former learning, with powerful primary responses. Once the response, e.g., to the word "rape," has been made, strong internal stimuli are evoked, and these constitute the emotion of rage which drives the individual to more violent action.

Passionate primary responses to cues such as "rape" are apparently fixed in the socialization of all individuals. Where they do not appear, it is because other training has supervened, and other habits have overlaid them. Man is given to crowd behavior in the sense that a strong response is frequently functional in gaining his ends and that the crowd offers the conditions where such responses may unroll. It is quite possible to set up habits of counter-suggestibility as far as crowd behavior is concerned. Most people have learned by experience not to go to the longest line in front of a ticket window, but rather to "use their heads" and go to the line where the fewest people are waiting. Others have learned, in case of a theater fire, to notice where the most people are struggling and then go to the opposite exit. The crew of a boat has learned, in case of a panic, to tell people not to jump overboard but to go to their lifeboat stations and wait. This is to say that the primary, common, strong responses can be opposed by others which do not favor the mounting excitation of crowd behavior but instead bring about a disciplined response to a strong drive stimulus. Under these circumstances, one would not expect the summative excitation of crowd behavior, because the circular imitative reaction does not begin. The behavior of others in the group stimulates to discipline and orderliness rather than to the undisciplined and disorderly unrolling of the common strong responses.

It has frequently been alleged that individuals in a crowd tend to respond *uncritically* to the stimuli of others. It is important, therefore, to examine this problem and to decide what a critical response is as compared with its opposite. "Criticalness" seems to be the act of waiting, when under drive stimulus, so that alternative lines of response may be rapidly and symbolically canvassed. In the meanwhile, the most direct or obvious response to a stimulus is held in check. This is a kind of behavior which must be learned, since it involves delay in attempting to make a goal response. Individuals must be punished for making the quick and obvious response if the habit of being critical is to be established. Children are told, "Look where you are going, and you won't 'bump your head." They are asked: "Why didn't you stop to think when the boys asked you to play hookey? Then the teacher wouldn't have punished you." When the child makes too ready an answer, he is asked, "What other ways are there of solving the problem?" When, after a canvass and the discovery of an ingenious solution, the child is rewarded, this fact tends to stabilize the "stop and think" response. He is able, with such training, to resist the pull exerted by the example of others and to select the ticket line with the fewest people or the exit not crowded by others.

Impulsive adults have learned that it is not always expedient to make the first response which occurs to them. Other persons will punish the hasty act or the careless impromptu word. In this way, the opinion of others becomes a factor in checking impulsive action. Anxiety responses are developed as to what other people will think, and these serve to hold first responses in check so that alternative lines of response may be canvassed. It is at this point that the influence of the crowd becomes important. A person does not have to fear criticism for making his own impulsive response when many others are making the same response. The anxiety over criticism for impulsive action is reduced, and the quickest and most primary response to the drive is elicited. Thus the individuals in a crowd tend to respond less critically than they otherwise might.

Debate in an open forum also provides protection against the quick or imitative response. Debaters are likely to be punished for hasty and overstrong responses, so that response tends to be confined to the verbal level. The technique of debate makes certain that if a debater does not think of alternative responses, his opponent will think of them and will bring them out as stimuli for the audience. With individuals in the audience battered by stimuli suggesting conflicting responses, there is less possibility for accumulative pressure to carry out one line only. Audiences are compelled to experience the stimuli to competing response series, and it is therefore difficult to convert them into crowds or mobs. Totalitarians deplore this aspect of democracy. In a debate or scientific discussion the audience is characterized by the fact that both strong responses (those which build up high internal response-produced stimulation) are prohibited and that conflict between opposing response series is engendered by the very structure of the situation. Circular stimulation never gets going to intensify the stimuli to a given line of response.

Learning theory, in summary, seems capable of clarifying the variables which have been recognized to contribute to crowd reactions. The importance of interstimulation, proximity, numbers, anonymity, prestige of the leader, repetition, rhythm, circular reaction, type of response, emotionality, and uncriticalness seems to be emphasized rather than diminished by a closer analysis. These factors are seen to be operative through various combinations of three primary variables, i.e., drive stimuli, crowd stimuli, and the strength of response to each.

CHAPTER XV

ANALYSIS OF A LYNCHING

SCIENTISTS may take a crowd apart and analyze the factors functioning in a crowd situation; it is not always so easy to put the factors together again into an account which does justice to the concussion of extreme crowd excitement upon an individual. In order to show how group response varies with drive stimuli and crowd stimuli, we have chosen the case of a lynching mob where all three factors are strongly present. The effort will be to isolate the factor of crowd stimulation and show its rôle in producing the violence of mob response.

The mechanisms underlying a crowd in action can be shown from the behavior of the mob which lynched Arthur Stevens on June 20, 1933.[1] To be proved is the proposition that crowd stimuli increased the strength of the aggressive response by the mob over and beyond the strength of such response attributable to the stimulus of the crime itself. An over-all view of the event will be presented first. Then the detailed behavior will be analyzed.

McCord County, in a state in the Deep South, was suffering a depression in 1933, along with the rest of the country. It is, moreover, an area chronically poor in comparison with other sections of the nation. The Negroes and whites of the lower and lower-middle classes had been in steady competition for a declining number of jobs. Upper-middle and upper-

[1] The structure of fact in this case has been drawn from a report of the National Association for the Advancement of Colored People. We are greatly indebted to the N.A.A.C.P. for permission to use and paraphrase its findings. The facts were secured for the N.A.A.C.P. by a highly qualified white investigator, who interviewed in the area after the lynching. All names of persons, places, and institutions used in this account are pseudonyms. In no instance does a name refer to any person, place, or institution now existing, or having existed in the past. Slight details of fact have been changed when they might be identifying, but the essential social and scientific meaning of the case has not been altered.

class whites tended to favor Negroes because of their greater
subordination and the cheaper wages for which they could be
hired. Lower-class whites responded with severe rivalry and
hostility toward their Negro competitors.

Arthur Stevens, a lower-class Negro, aged twenty-three,
had grown up in Belfast, in McCord County, across the road
from the farm of a white family named Durfee. He had
known the Durfee daughter, Iona, and, according to the best
evidence available, had entered into a sexual relationship
with her. When she tried to break off the relationship on
June 10, 1933, he murdered her in a brutal manner and concealed the body. The girl was found the next day, and evidence was discovered which seemed to implicate Stevens. He
was arrested and interrogated and allegedly confessed his
guilt.

Sheriff R. E. Ingle, fearing mob violence, moved Stevens
first to the Fairlee jail, twenty miles away, then to Mentone,
thence to Nashua, and, finally across the state line to Edgar.
Informed of the last move, a hundred men from the Durfee
neighborhood drove two hundred and ten miles, stormed the
Edgar jail, secured Stevens, and brought him back to a spot
within a short distance of the Durfee farm.

There Stevens was tortured, mutilated, and killed by the
nuclear mob and then additionally assaulted by the larger
mob to which his body was turned over. His mutilated corpse
was then hung from a tree in Longwood, the neighboring
county seat, where it was viewed by many.

The mob, however, did not stop with lynching Stevens. It
came into Longwood and created riotous conditions in the
town for a whole day. Negroes were attacked and chased out
of town, without regard to age, sex, or physical handicap. A
search for Negro maids was made in the upper-class section
of the town. Many of these were defended by their employers.
The riot was not suppressed until troops were sent into the
town late in the afternoon of June 21.

In general, people in Longwood seemed to approve of the
lynching as the best way "to keep the nigger in his place."
Deputy Sheriff T. V. Brown stated in the local newspaper on

the day of the lynching that "the mob will not be bothered, either before or after the lynching." Widespread, if not complete, community connivance in the crime was indicated.

Analysis of the Lynching

There are two variables operating to produce the vehemence of response actually observed in this crowd. One is the news of the reputed rape and murder, to which each white person in the mob would probably react with some degree of aggression toward Stevens. The other variable is the interstimulation of the crowd, which is believed to have strengthened the total aggressive behavior. Under ideal conditions, other variables would be held constant, the crowd factor altered, and the relative strengths of response (with and without it) compared. An attempt will be made to carry out this operation. The attempt will necessarily be crude, since the lynching did not take place under experimental conditions and since we are depending upon an observer whose report is necessarily incomplete. The testimony of some witness who had not expected to participate in the crowd but had been drawn in and, under crowd conditions, showed vehement aggressive responses would be very desirable; unfortunately, such testimony is not available, although there is a good probability that such an event did occur. One of the writers has himself felt the morbid rise in interest and tendency to go along and at least watch, which was aroused at the perception of a lynching mob in action. Without this experience, he would have affirmed that he could show only unqualified horror at such a sight.

Control of the variable of crowd excitement can best be secured by constant reference to what an individual similarly stimulated would do if alone. This is an inexact criterion, but better than none. To put the question in the concrete: Would a person who had heard about the murder of the Durfee girl and perhaps seen her corpse have reacted with the extreme outburst of aggression against Stevens which was characteristic of the nuclear mob? Would a person similarly exposed run amuck for a day attacking Negroes wherever they could be found? The best judgment of the writers is that the answer is "No." But the question must be fully and fairly put to the reader also. This will be done in the following analysis.

The Drive: Fear

The drive mobilized by this incident is fear. The fear takes three closely allied but separable forms: fear of economic rivalry, fear of sexual assault on white women, and fear of bodily attack to white men or women. Each of these will be considered separately.

Fear of the economic rivalry of the Negro is an old story in this area. Lower-class and lower-middle-class whites have experienced it for over a hundred years. Ultimately, this fear is based on yet more primary fears, such as fear of starvation, of cold, and of exposure to pain by illness. The lesson has been learned that there are too many people, white and black, for too few jobs. Upper-middle and upper-class whites have utilized the Negro to the partial exclusion of the white man. The Negro's inferior caste status has made him more docile and more amenable to lower wages and less deferential treatment than whites would accept. The aggression of these whites has flared out, not against their superiors in the white caste structure, who are, after all, primarily responsible, but against the Negroes, who are being utilized by these better-placed whites. In recent years, the lower-class whites have steadily put increased pressure upon the Negroes for jobs, and have, for instance, dispossessed them from several types of work which were traditionally the property of the Negro caste. Just before the lynching occurred, a parade of white people was organized in Longwood to demand the "purification of the FERA rolls." Presumably the real demand was that Negroes should be put off government relief rolls and whites allowed to take their places. In this struggle for subsistence, white workers actually rival one another as well as Negroes. But the Negroes, marked off by color and debased by inferior caste status, are ready targets for aggression. The ancient fears of "no food, no house, no doctor" are mobilized chronically in this area.

Fear of sex relations with, or rape of, white women by Negroes is a powerful one. Fear of the rape of in-group women is, indeed, not limited to the case of Negro men and white women.[2] Sexual jealousy is a painful drive everywhere in our society. Negroes living in the vicinity of the Stevens home knew or suspected that Stevens and Iona Durfee were having sex relations. The whites seem not to have been so clearly aware of the fact, although there is some evidence that certain white men had their suspicions. It is hardly likely, however, that the whole white community knew of the relationship. If they had, they would probably have taken action against Stevens, although the impulse to kill him would have been weakened if the woman were known to have given her consent. Rape of the murdered woman was certainly posited by the lynching mob, although no direct physical evidence on this score was publicly produced. Suspicion of sexual relations, or rape, aroused passionate responses of resentment in the community. Sexual equality is, after all, a step toward social equality. If Negroes were allowed sexual privileges with white women, it would be difficult to exclude them from the family group; and, if the Negro were included in the family group, it would be impossible to maintain his subordinated status. According to Stevens' confession, which, to be sure, was extorted from him, Miss Durfee attempted to break off the sex relationship on June 10, and further threatened to "tell the white men on him" if he refused. At this, Stevens is believed to have become enraged and frightened, and to have killed the girl.

The third of the fundamental fears is that of physical attack or murder done by Negroes on whites. This fear was also mobilized in the incident. The details are certainly horrible enough. The local newspaper printed the father's account of the state of the murdered girl. She had been "choked so hard her eyes were coming out of their sockets." Her head had been violently bashed in, her arms had been broken, and she was otherwise lacerated. This report made the whole com-

[2] In the Oedipus complex, Freud seems to have the best explanation of its source.

munity a witness to the facts of the murder as the father saw them. Iona's sister added to the picture of the crime. She stated, in the Longwood newspaper account, that she had never seen anything so brutal and hoped that this would not happen to her. She wished that every resident of the community could have seen the body of her sister and remarked, with hate, that no form of punishment could be bad enough for the murderer.

These, then, were the primary cues which aroused violent anxiety and anger responses among the neighbors of the Durfees. The factor of crowd interaction was soon in action. Word of the event went from person to person throughout the enraged community. It seems doubtful that an exact account could be transmitted in this way, and it is very probable that the story grew as it circulated. Certainly Mr. Durfee's "bunch" immediately went into action. They promised him a first share in the punishment of Stevens, once the mob had located him. Although the data are not contained in the record available, we would predict that as the story went about it was exaggerated, that threats were made, that old memories of other lynchings were evoked, that it was said that the "niggers are getting out of hand" and that an exemplary punishment ought to be made in the Stevens case. These reactions would serve to build up and fortify the crowd response. Imitation of Stevens by other Negroes would be anticipated, and the reaction would run, "If one Negro can thus rape and murder and get away with it, other Negroes will try the same thing." This reaction, in turn, would enhance the old fear of the South, that of a Negro insurrection with "all of us killed in our beds."

The Secondary Response: Aggression

When people are frightened, there are two possible lines of response. One line is to run away from the threatening agent; another is to attack and attempt to destroy it. The adults of this community had undoubtedly learned to suppress aggression in some cases and to express it in others. They had often been rewarded in various situations for being aggressive

toward Negroes. Under aggressive pressure, Negroes were
known to give up jobs, to get off the sidewalk, and even, in
occasional cases, to abandon their own women to the advances
of white men. Such rewarding situations and many others
had fixed the pattern of aggressive response in the case where
a frustration was imposed by a Negro. The frustrating fears
described above, consequently, being caused by a Negro,
aroused a secondary drive of anger against him.

Some part of the anger mobilized against Stevens may not
actually have been due to frustrations which he himself imposed. The economic frustrations resulting from competition
have been mentioned. In this particular, Stevens merely sym-
bolized his race and was, undoubtedly, the object of a certain
amount of displaced aggression. Similarly, other frustrations in the personal lives of the whites concerned may have
resulted in aggressive responses which were displaced to
Stevens. Not displaced, however, were the responses stirred
by the rape and murder. These strong responses were directed toward Stevens quite proportionately and legitimately
in the eyes of the community. Death of a kind more horrible
than that stipulated by the law is believed to be necessary to
keep men like Stevens in line.

It is pertinent to ask why the aggression mobilized by economic frustrations is not more persistently and violently expressed toward Negroes. The answer seems to be that it is not
conventional to kill a Negro, let alone torture him, for taking
a white man's job. Apparently only the cues of sexual, physical, or social assault ("sassing" a white man) will justify the
ultimate in revenge behavior. Southern children presumably
receive the same training against intra-family aggression as
do children in other parts of the United States. Their aggressive responses must be curbed, at least when directed
against family members. Presumably, there is some generalization from this training to all types of human beings, although, as between adult lower-class whites in the South,
there may be a greater freedom of aggressive expression than
is common in the West or the North. Certainly, such a difference in aggressiveness can be noted among the social classes

in the white community; in the middle class and above, as a general rule, there is less direct aggression permitted either to children or to adults than in the lower class. The taboos on murderous aggression against any human being would, in Stevens' case, be lifted by the insupportable aggression of the Negro.

The frustrations which arise from economic rivalry between lower-class whites and Negroes do not suffice to elicit direct aggression because the culture pattern for aggressive responses is determined primarily by the leading whites. Upper-class whites are not frustrated by economic rivalry from Negroes, but are, in common with other classes, threatened by sexual or direct personal assault from Negroes—from their servants, for instance. They profit, in fact, from the lowly economic state of the Negroes. Therefore, to upper-class whites aggressive retribution seems permissible for sexual or personal assault, but not for economic damage.

Permissiveness

The question must be asked: How are the taboos against in-group aggression lifted so that such behavior as that characteristic of this mob could be actualized? One may notice first the general cultural pattern. Aggression between whites, man or clan, is much more likely to be tolerated, even legally, when the provocation is a sex offense or a direct attack. The relevant legal concepts are those of "the common law," in the case of a sex offense, and "self-defense," in the case of physical assault. Each of these provocations justifies a degree of direct counter-aggression even between white men.

In the case of Negroes, the same permissive patterns prevail, but with added force. The lynching of whites has been known in the South for seventy-five years, but has declined in recent times, so that lynching is now a punishment reserved almost exclusively for Negroes. The individual Negro is not only an offender in his own right; he also symbolizes his caste. At the news of his assault, fear rises sharply that his behavior, if not punished, will initiate a wave of rapes and murders against white persons. To this collective threat the white community responds collectively. Thus, in the Durfee case, the "bunch" of a hundred (the nuclear mob) got into its automobiles and started to ransack jails in search of the criminal.

Despite all this, lynching is outside the law. The North and the West are opposed to it. There is always the danger that the Federal Government will exert coercion upon state and local authorities. There is also anxiety aroused by the emergence into daylight of powerful aggressive impulses. These two factors impose a need for justification and for concrete permission by the community. It is here that the mechanism of the crowd is significantly involved. Under the cover of crowd and communal permissiveness, the most deadly of angry phantasies may be acted out. The wider society may admonish and threaten; the local community signalizes permission.

In the case of the Stevens lynching there were a number of cues which would convince individuals in the crowd that no punishment for participation in the lynching would ensue. "A prominent businessman" of Longwood arranged with a friend in Nashua to notify him the moment that Stevens was removed to the Edgar jail, in the neighboring state. If a "prominent man," who is unlikely to be punished, participates, surely lesser men may safely join the mob. Legal compliance in the lynching was seen by the people in the fact that Stevens was removed from the strong jail in Nashua to the country jail at Edgar, a building easily stormed. It was said to be well known locally that some of Longwood's prominent businessmen and citizens themselves participated in the mob. Such individuals are likely to control the machinery of punishment and to be able to obstruct it if they choose. Certainly they would choose to do so if they themselves participated. A deputy sheriff stated on June 20, the day of the lynching, that "the mob will not be bothered, either before or after the lynching." As one of the individuals who would have to carry out arrests and legal punishments, if there were to be any, his published statement would tend to diminish fear at participating in the lynching. The Longwood *Press-Jour-*

nal gave, on June 20, an account of the mob which did not condemn the mobsters. Plainly, the conscience of the community had not been aroused against the lynchers, at least as expressed in the daily paper. The Ku Klux Klan symbol was brought forward. A prominent Longwood citizen is said to have advocated its revival "to protect the honor of womanhood and champion the oppressed." The Klan is itself a symbol of righteous activity in the South, and the mob was compared, by implication, with a group of clansmen defending their homes and women. On Friday, the twentieth, a near-by radio station broadcast news of "a lynching party to which all white people are invited." Surely, one may argue, if the radio invites citizens to a lynching, it is unlikely that punishment will follow for participation, since radio stations do not advocate forbidden activities.

Even some of the Negroes of Longwood, in their terror, gave tacit approval to the lynching of Stevens. One wrote to the daily paper on June 16, "But I am writing to let you know that we leave it to you all to do what you all see fit to do with him." Since this message implied that no counter-aggression would be manifested by Negroes, it might have served to keep the anxiety of the white participants low. The white visitor who secretly investigated the lynching and gathered the facts here brought forward came to the community a short time after the actual lynching. He found it difficult to ask direct questions about the crime. There was a kind of conspiracy of silence in the community to keep the details from prying outsiders. This protective atmosphere would help to guarantee participants against retaliation from the outside and would therefore tend to reduce anxiety as regards participation in the lynching.

The rioting of the mob ended only when crucial punishment symbols were again invoked. Order was not restored in Longwood until Saturday afternoon, June 21, when guards with guns arrived. A Negro attacked by a large mob on Saturday was saved only when white men pointed a machine gun at the mob. A mob does, indeed, respond to the positive value of punishment symbols just as it responds to the permissive value of cues indicating the improbability of punishment. One of the important functions of the crowd variable was to provide these signals of non-punishment.

Strength of Response of the Nuclear Mob

The news of the murder of Iona Durfee rang like a gong through the Belfast community. The powerful emotion of anger was aroused against Stevens. A nuclear crowd formed, consisting, by inference, of the immediate friends of Mr. Durfee. This mob, "grim, determined, silent, and efficient," pursued and captured Stevens with the apparent connivance of the law. Be it noted that "grim, silent" behavior can be a stimulus to aggression no less effective than excited clamor. Grimness and determination frequently precede successful aggressive acts, and each member of a small mob can stimulate the others to additional determination and anger by such behavior.

The aggressive responses manifested toward Stevens were of almost incredible strength. He was taken to a spot within four miles of the Durfee farm at Belfast. The first plan had been to bring him directly to the site of his crime and to punish him there. The nuclear mob, however, decided against this plan. A very large crowd was gathered in the field where the Durfee girl's body had been found. The smaller mob feared two things: first, that the large mob might kill Stevens too quickly and thereby spare him the suffering he was thought to deserve, and, second, that the large mob might get out of hand and start shooting, and that someone in it would be hurt.[3] An isolated lynching by the nuclear mob was therefore decided upon. It is to be noted that the nuclear mob feared that the large mob would "get out of hand," meaning that crowd stimulation would build up an angry excitement so strong that it could not be controlled. Apparently the vari-

[3] There are occasional examples of a large mob getting so far out of control that promiscuous shooting at the victim has begun. In some such cases, others than the victim have been hit. This situation occurred at the burning of Lloyd Clay at Vicksburg, Mississippi, May 14, 1919.

able of crowd excitation was recognized (though as a danger) by the nuclear mob.

The nuclear mobsters decided on a protracted torture for Stevens. This is said to have lasted for some ten hours during Friday, June 20. It is amazing that Stevens could have lived through so many hours of pain. To make the punishment fit the crime, Stevens was castrated, and, to add horror, he was compelled to eat his own genitals. Red hot irons were plunged into his body at various points. To make his suffering more intense, he was several times promised a swift death; each time he was given a simulated hanging in which life was almost choked out of him, but he was then cut down and tortured more. His belly and sides were sliced with knives, and fingers and toes were cut off. Finally, he was "just killed." His body was tied behind a car and dragged to the Durfee farm, where the larger mob was waiting.

The strength of these aggressive responses toward Stevens seems to suggest unmistakably the variable of crowd excitation. It is difficult to believe that a hundred individuals could be found in this community who would, by themselves and without crowd excitation and permission, have carried out such extreme torture upon the Negro. An occasional sadistic individual might be capable of such an act. Many more people could doubtless "think" of it. Without the effect of mutual interaction, however, it seems hardly credible that any hundred such perverse individuals could be discovered in a single, small community. The only alternative inference is that crowd permissiveness released aggression and that crowd excitation increased it.

Strength of Response of the Larger Crowd

The larger crowd also responded strongly to the appearance of the (mercifully) dead body of Stevens, which was dragged into its midst behind an automobile. The rope dragging the body was cut, and the corpse was left with the crowd. There is no reason to believe that the nuclear mob continued to assume leadership in the larger crowd.

A roar of exclamations greeted the appearance of Stevens'

body, which had been dumped in front of the Durfee house. The crowd saw "a woman come out of the house and drive a butcher knife into his heart." Members of the crowd rushed toward the body. Some kicked it; others drove their cars over it. Children came and drove sharpened sticks into the body. Thereupon, the larger crowd went on a rampage. One of its first acts was to burn down the house of Stevens' mother, which stood across the road from the Durfee home. Stevens' body was dragged into Longwood at the back of a car and hung to the limb of a tree. Its naked, mutilated surfaces were viewed by large numbers of citizens. The body was photographed (postcards were subsequently sold in the community). After these aggressive acts, the mob subsided for the night, but only part of it dispersed from Longwood.

Stevens' body was cut down at eight o'clock the next morning (Saturday). By this time, the Negroes in Longwood were in that state of terror characteristic of the aftermath of a lynching episode. They kept to themselves as much as possible, and many avoided the town, though it was Saturday, a market day. A part of the larger mob hung nascent and excited about the streets of the city. At noon, under circumstances unknown, a white man struck a Negro. The latter tried to defend himself, and a crowd gathered rapidly and "flew into a frenzy." The Negro ran to the courthouse, where he was protected by a group of friendly white men, who held his pursuers at bay with a machine gun. This incident led to a new outburst of aggression, and riotous scenes prevailed throughout Longwood for the rest of the day. This city mob is said to have been led by a young man of "good family," that is, an upper-middle or upper-class man. Such leadership would probably have a permissive effect on all persons subordinated to him in social status. The mob attacked Negro men, women, children—even some that were blind. A large number of Negroes were driven from the town afoot and in terror. Individual Negroes were pursued and beaten, but, strangely enough, none was killed on this day.

The mob met resistance from many well-placed white employers of Negroes. Men and women defended their trusted

servants against the mob. The police of Longwood were not
in evidence during the rioting. Where they were no one knew,
but an element of alarmed white people could find no one to
oppose the mob. An attempt was made to deputize certain individuals (unknown), but they refused to serve. Finally, National Guardsmen entered the city at 4.30 in the afternoon
and quelled the riot. The mob dispersed, growling, with
threats to return and repeat the incident on the following
Saturday. There were signs of mob action even the next Saturday, but an increased police force (and a heavy rain) suf-
ficed to prevent another outburst.

The Case for the Crowd Variable

In the reaction of the larger mob, at least four variables
seem to have played a part: (1) direct anger over the fact of
Stevens' crime; (2) the interpretation of the crucial events
by word of mouth and newspaper, which increased enraged
feeling, both before and during the mob's congregation at the
Durfee farm; (3) the frustration of the larger crowd by the
long wait for the lynching, which would serve to increase the
anger drive; (4) the permissive effect of the sight of successful aggression already wreaked on Stevens. Two of these
variables (1 and 3) would presumably determine a given
strength of response for each person in the crowd without
reference to the other persons present. But both of the other
variables (2 and 4) would increase the strength of the response through the presence of the crowd. Any one of the
adults in the crowd might, for instance, have killed Stevens
for murdering the Durfee girl; but it seems hardly possible
that they would behave as they did, or go to such extremes,
without the presence of crowd excitation.

The sight of Stevens' damaged body apparently evoked
two types of response in the crowd: (1) increased excitation
to anger; (2) drop in punishment expectation. It became
clear that people might act aggressively toward Stevens and
other Negroes without fear of punishment, since the hundred
men in the nuclear mob had already done so. Stevens' body
bore testimony to the tortures inflicted upon him, and no one

was at hand to punish the torturers, many of whom, if not all, must have been known by some persons in the larger mob. The deliverance of Stevens' body to the larger group was a specific cue to non-punishment.

The fact that aggression had already been carried out against Stevens would tend to increase the angry excitement in the larger crowd. Since presumably they had individually learned that aggressive responses are most rewarded when performed in concert, the aggressive act of any other person would stimulate additional strength of aggressive response in the witness. Without these assumptions, it is difficult to understand why the members of the mob allowed nearly ten days to pass before attacking Negroes generally. If, moreover, there were no crowd variable as an excitant to the anger drive, it is hard to see how children, who ordinarily are compelled to suppress aggressive responses, would have driven their pointed sticks into Stevens' body. It is further difficult to understand why the crowd should not have been content with working its vengeance on Stevens alone. If there were no crowd variable exciting aggressive responses and signalizing non-punishment, why should the house of Stevens' mother have been burned down and the general attack on Negroes in Longwood have been undertaken? Although direct response to the fact of the crime and the frustration of the crowd in waiting and being cheated of the sight of the actual lynching undoubtedly played a rôle in its running amuck, it seems highly probable that the behavior of the nuclear mob excited aggression in the larger mob, which then ran its course through a day of riotous behavior.[4] It should further be noted that strong responses themselves produce stimuli

[4] It might be urged that the larger mob and smaller mob as well, having been just rewarded for aggressive behavior toward Stevens (by drop in their anxiety about Negro competition, etc.), would become still more aggressive. If this condition were true, it should apply particularly to the nuclear mob which, having been at the actual scene of the torture, should have been most rewarded by its anxiety-reducing aggressive expression. So far as we know, however, this was not the case. In fact, the mob in Longwood seems to have been under other leadership than that of the actual lynchers.

which drive behavior and give momentum to any series of responses which is under way. It is very likely that this response-produced drive functioned, in addition to crowd stimuli, to perpetuate for a time the behavior of the mob.

The conclusions are, therefore: (1) that the discussion and interpretation of Stevens' crime by word-of-mouth report served to increase the strength of aggressive response; (2) that the grim behavior of members of the nuclear mob increased its ferocity; (3) that interaction in the waiting larger mob built up the strength of aggressive response; (4) that the dramatization of the aggression of the nuclear mob (revealed by Stevens' body) excited additional strength of anger drive and weakened anxiety over punishment of aggressive responses (thereby making them differentially dominant in behavior); (5) that the riot in Longwood resulted in part from the variable of crowd excitation as sketched above.

One preventative of mob behavior of this type is to keep the members from gathering where they can interstimulate one another. This is apparently done by the military whenever martial law is imposed. Such restrictions are clearly aimed at the variable of crowd excitation, which can elicit aggressive responses in the separate individuals and make them manifest far beyond their strength in isolation. A further preventative is, of course, to increase the strength and certainty of punishment to be anticipated for carrying out aggressive acts. The riot in Longwood itself was finally arrested by the appearance of a determined punishment organization, i.e., troops with guns. The various forms of Federal anti-lynching bills which have been proposed represent other ways of increasing punishment expectations with regard to a lynching. If such a bill imposed a money penalty on the county as a whole, it would undoubtedly be fairly effective, since it would strike at the pocketbooks of the managerial group in the community. At the present time, this group certainly derives an indirect benefit from lynchings since they tend to subordinate Negroes, to make them more docile, and to make them accept any level of livelihood which is imposed upon them in return for the privilege of existing at all.

The factors of crowd behavior as described in the previous chapter seem, in most cases, to be operative in the crowd which lynched Arthur Stevens. The matched-dependent mechanism and rapid copying are both in evidence, while *same* behavior is shown in the common responses to the primary fear drive.

The common *stimulus* responded to by a large part of the crowd is obvious; it was Stevens' crime. There was the *interstimulation* of the stern lynchers, intent upon their crime, and the *proximity* of members of the huge crowd awaiting the lynching. The factor of *numbers* cannot be easily discounted. Belfast itself is a town so small that it is not even shown on an automobile map, and yet the crowd which gathered at the Durfee farm numbered, by various guesses, from three to seven thousand people. Such a large number of people must have conveyed a powerful impression of community approval for the aggression under way. Among such numbers, too, the factor of *anonymity* would play a rôle. The *prestige* factor is present in the case of the "prominent citizens" who took part in the mob action. *Repetition* of the stimuli to aggression appears in the numerous newspaper references to the progress of the lynching mob and, undoubtedly, in the local conversation about Stevens' crime. The *rhythmic* element does not seem to have been present in this case. The *circular reaction* is shown in the cumulative behavior of the larger mob in response to the appearance of the smaller mob dragging Stevens' body. Powerful responses were evoked in individuals by the news of Stevens' crime, and these responses admittedly gave rise to a high *emotional* state. The emotion could be described as anger or revenge. There seems little doubt that the local community, turned into a mob by the stimulus of Stevens' crime, reacted *uncritically*. It did not insist upon trial by jury. Even after the hasty investigation, it was not absolutely certain that Stevens had committed the crime. Once the powerful aggressive responses were produced it was impossible to impose a waiting or delay response strong enough to compete with them. The obvious competing set of responses—arrest, arraignment, and trial by jury—could not be attempted in this case, although the sheriff evidently made an effort to protect Stevens from mob violence. Critical responses can only be enforced in such a case by penalties which make it advisable to wait, see, examine, deliberate, try, and judge.

CHAPTER XVI

COPYING IN THE DIFFUSION OF CULTURE

BY the word "diffusion," anthropologists identify the process by which culture traits pass from group to group and filter over wide areas from a common point of origin. An extensive and valuable literature has accumulated around the subject. Older workers were inclined to attribute similarities of culture to independent inventions by different peoples. The modern view is that the alteration of a culture is much more likely to result from borrowing traits and habits than from inventing them. It is known, for instance, that the use of tobacco has diffused from a single source in Middle America to much of North and South America and thence to Europe, Africa, and Asia, albeit with many local changes in the function and form of using it. In the face of such evidence, it is needless to presume the repeated independent invention of the trait of using tobacco, even though the fact of such use be discovered in widely separated parts of the world. No attempt will be made here to discuss the many and complex methodological problems of diffusion as they have been perceived by a host of workers. Attention will rather be centered on the social-psychological problem involved in diffusion.

From the psychological standpoint, diffusion is a process of copying. It can include any transfer of habits, simple or complex, from some skill in using a trade object, such as a gun, to skill in both using and in producing the object; from the mere idea of an object or process to the total technique of its preparation.

Diffusion is seen as the transfer of habit from one individual to another within a group or from one group to another. Such transfer must accordingly involve the laws of habit formation and, in particular, that special complication of the principles of learning which we call copying. To be diffused, a habit must find its place in the recipient society. This "place" may be in the habit systems of all members of a group or only in those of special categories of persons, such as those differentiated by sex, age, or class participation (Linton, 1940, pp. 471–472). Copying, as we have seen, differs from dependence matching. In dependence matching, it is not necessary for the imitator to know that his behavior is the same as that of the model, while in copying it is essential. Copying may be conscious or unconscious; that is, may occur with or without verbal aids.

Copying has been recognized by various anthropological writers under different terms, such as borrowing, taking over a trait, etc. All seem equivalents of the word "imitation," as loosely used. Kroeber, indeed, has asked for a better understanding of the types of mechanism through which the "generic diffusion process operates" (1940, p. 20). Wissler has assumed imitation as instinctive (1923, p. 206). Other writers by various allusions have indicated their understanding that the tendency to copy is not innate but is in some way learned, thereby inviting a discussion of the type launched here.

No adequate treatment of invention from a sociological standpoint can be given in this framework. From the psychological standpoint, it may be said that invention involves trial-and-error learning in a dilemma situation. The inventor is in a dilemma when he is behaving under high drive but without a habit adequate to reduce drive. He must bear the tension of drive while new responses or response series are organized and tried out. It may, indeed, take centuries or millennia for the proper unit skills which compose an invention to be collected and organized in the response arsenal of a single inventor. Undoubtedly, men spent thousands of years enduring exhausting pressures of fatigue while collecting plants and hunting animals before the domestication of plants and animals was perfected. Invention is a complex process of the recombination of response units; the efficient responses must be put into the right order, must be brought forward at the right time and place, and must be connected to the right cues. Anthropological authors (Wissler, 1923, p. 122), (Kroeber, 1923, p. 239) seem to agree that this process is much more difficult than copying. Their psychological colleagues stand firmly with them on this score.

Copying is enormously economical in that it is a technique for getting the correct response to occur rapidly. The model offers a solution which has already proven successful. If tried out, it is much more likely to be rewarded than any given inventive or trial-and-error response or response series. By bringing early reward, the copied response cuts down the time of bearing drive and is therefore differentially reinforced. In those societies where copying is strongly and differentially rewarded, it should become dominant over the competing inventive or creative patterns. If, however, copying is not rewarded, is only rewarded in some situations, or ceases to be rewarded, inventive habits are sufficiently reinforced to reappear in a dilemma situation.

Psychological Conditions Bearing on Diffusion

A degree of drive (see Chapter II) seems to be a necessary condition for copying by any society. Drives may be of a primary or secondary type. The primary drives seem qualitatively the same for all societies, and each society has a technique for reducing each basic type of primary drive. The presence of the biologically founded hunger, fatigue, pain, and sex drives provides motive forces for activity among men everywhere. They serve as chronic internal stimuli which set the human being in search of responses to reduce these stimuli. Such responses may be forthcoming by the onerous technique of invention or by the more rapid means of copying.

The importance of drive has been repeatedly, though often inadvertently, recognized by writers on diffusion. Linton (1940, p. 481) calls attention to the intolerance of societies at any modifications which leave any of the group's needs even temporarily unprovided for. He says, further (1940, pp. 481–482), that the stimuli to culture change lie in the discomfort or discontent of a society's members. Malinowski

(G. E. Smith, *et al.*, 1927, p. 28) assigns an important rôle to nutrition and sex drives in the attempt by man to master his surroundings. It may be inferred from Sayce (1933, p. 19) that he viewed the introduction of the horse to the Indians of the North American plains as a means of reducing fatigue and hunger drives. Dixon (1928, pp. 36–37) notes the importance of need as a spur to modification of a culture. Wissler (1923, p. 113) comments that fear drove the indigenous Europeans to take over the horse from Asiatic nomads so that they might meet the "savages of the steppes on anything like an equal footing." Dixon (1928, p. 107) notes further that the Eskimo blubber lamp, while needed by the Eskimos, did not meet a corresponding drive among the neighboring Indian tribes to the southward, who had wood for fire and light. In the latter case, the presence of low drive among the Indians seemed not to favor copying.

Secondary or acquired drives, those built on primary drives, may also favor copying if high and hinder it if low. Appetites for particular foods make excellent examples of secondary drive. Hunger is characteristic of all societies, but a secondary drive or appetite for acorns characterized the Indians of California, for the meat of the bison the Indians of the Great Plains, for salmon the dwellers of the northwest coast of America, etc. If the buffalo be exterminated as a food object, as was the case, the Plains tribes would be expected to be in the market, first, for another and similar meat food, and, secondarily, for any kind of food at all. This type of secondary drive would set a preferential demand for an intrusive food trait, e.g., beef-eating. Some secondary drives, such as those for prestige, sociability, and conformity, are probably characteristic of all societies. Others, such as the desire for money in American society, are peculiar to particular groups. In any case, the contention is that strong but unmet secondary drives can be operating conditions for the spread of social habit. The drive for money in American society may, for instance, lead a businessman to cultivate Latin patterns of etiquette in order the better to carry on commercial transactions with South Americans. It is contended that, other things equal, high drive favors diffusion and low drive tends to inhibit it.

If a receiving culture already has an efficient habit which reduces a particular drive, there will be less net effective motive to learn a new habit. This principle apparently accounts for frequent cases of failure of diffusion. Wissler (1923, p. 127), for instance, notes that a current adjustment "need not be the best adjustment of its kind" to persist, especially if it offers immediate and certain returns and is articulated with other elements of the culture. Dixon (1928, p. 145) has referred to the slow spread of papermaking in Europe, as compared with China. In Europe the trait of papermaking had to compete with the existing use of parchment, which was "harder to displace than the far inferior bamboo strips, silk or papyrus" which were used by the Chinese. The drive to learn the difficult papermaking was correspondingly low. Similarly, Dixon (1928, p. 111) states that "to a people already possessed of the bag-bellows, the pump-bellows might have no particular appeal, since its efficiency is not greater than the implement to which they are accustomed." Sayce (1933, p. 182) comments that the practice of tobacco-chewing "did not spread from the Amazon country into the Andes, because the use of coca was already established there, and the need for tobacco did not arise." Many similar examples could be given, showing that the existence of a competing and relatively satisfactory habit reduces the drive which might otherwise favor the adoption of a new and similar habit.

Favoring the diffusion of a particular trait will be the presence in the receiving society of sub-responses which are necessary to the learning of the incoming trait; units of response which are functionally equivalent to any of those in the incoming pattern will likewise increase the probability of diffusion. The presence of such responses makes learning the new trait easier, since they shorten learning time and thereby increase reinforcement. It is easier, obviously, to introduce a new card game into a culture where the people already play cards than into one where they do not. Likewise, but conversely, the absence of sub-responses or equivalents lengthens the time of learning of a new trait or prevents its intrusion. This state of affairs is clearly present in the case of societies with a markedly inferior technology who try to borrow from societies superior in this sphere. Aborigines the world over have had notorious difficulty in mastering European technology. The amount of learning required to perfect all of the sub-responses in our technological processes is so great for them as to be forbidding. Sayce notes (1933, p. 181) that the "Bushmen borrowed little from the Europeans in South Africa; their whole mode of life was too dissimilar." Dixon (1928, p. 109) gives a parallel reason for the failure of the Mayan calendar to diffuse to the simpler peoples to the southward. A learning process would have been involved which, if carried out, would have radically reorganized the cultures of these peoples.

Incompatible habits in a society may also block the spread of an offered trait. Thus Linton (1940, p. 475) observes that the presence of ancestor worship in a society may lead the holders of power, who depend on it in part for their authority, to resist the spread of Christianity, despite gifts and medical aid offered by the missionary. He illustrates the same point (1940, p. 492) in remarking that Europeans cling to their prestigeful, uncomfortable clothing in the tropics despite the superior comfort to be derived from dressing in native style. The transfer of the trait of native dress is blocked by the high status evaluations placed on the sub-arctic clothing of the conquerors. Thus, incompatible habits, like efficient competing habits, may block the spread of a trait.

Some of the sub-responses which favor diffusion have to do with the technique of copying itself, and, in turn, some of these sub-units are general and cross-cultural in frequency while others are limited to particular cultures. Thus, individuals in every society have a means of recognizing that they are standing when others are standing, know how to look where others look, to judge distance by the size of an object, to grasp, run, walk, and move hands to right or left as others do. They have, therefore, elementary techniques of matching with other persons which are extremely useful in the diffusion of habits from one culture to another. Such learning of matching units is apparently a part of the socialization of most children in most societies. Appreciation of the importance of such units can be achieved by considering how relatively easy it is to teach an American Indian to drive an automobile. He has the primary units in terms of which matching can take place. He can be told to grasp the wheel with his hands, to put his foot down on the brake, to pass to the right rather than to the left, and the like. These generalized units of matching are often overlooked in cultural transmission, but their absence would be energetically appreciated by any teacher.

Other sub-units which aid in the copying necessary to diffusion may be present in one culture but not in another. When present, they are an aid to diffusion and when absent, a block. It is, for instance, easier for English-speaking people to learn to read German than Chinese. German has a general grammatical structure, vocabulary, and alphabet similar to English. Chinese, on the contrary, has a different grammar and different mode of writing. The units favoring diffusion of German to an English-speaking society are therefore present, and learning is facilitated; the reading of Chinese by English-speaking people is much more difficult in the absence of just these matching units.

Where such similar sub-units in the matching process are not present, the learning individual must go into trial-and-error behavior which, although guided, is much more difficult than the rapid production of already learned matched units.

The unit responses in the receiving society need not be absolutely matched with those of the skill required by the incoming trait. If they are functionally equivalent, it seems to suffice. Such a unit, for example, is the presence of the travois (a kind of drag frame) among American Indians. Wissler (1923, p. 121) thinks that the American Indians first used the horse by inserting it in place of the dog in the travois and only later did they learn to ride the horse. Similarly (Sayce, 1933, p. 189), the Eskimos adapted the whaling boat from

European and American whalers but, not having the timber to sheath the boat, covered it with skins in their traditional manner. The habit of covering boats with skins which the Eskimos already had constituted a functional equivalent for the planking and caulking of the European boat. Europeans, likewise, took over maize (Wissler, 1923, p. 124) from the American Indians but sowed it broadcast rather than hillwise as was the Indian custom. "Instructions for use" did not come to Europe with the maize, and the Europeans substituted their usual (and functionally equivalent) habit of sowing grain broadcast.

There is another drive, an acquired one, whose presence in a society makes diffusion more likely. It is the acquired drive to copy. Individuals within a society can be more or less likely to respond to a novel situation with copying tendencies. It seems possible that the same state of affairs is true between societies as well. Such copying tendencies have been noticed by ethnographers among primitive peoples. Sayce (1933, p. 174), for instance, notes that "borrowing starts from what an individual notices and responds to in any new environment." Linton (1940, p. 495) observes the lively interest that "most natives take in everything that the visitors have and do." Such an interest, we infer, is due to an acquired drive to copy and is not to be taken for granted as "natural curiosity," for, as will be contended, such an interest in the novel is not a stable biological characteristic of mankind.

The first stage in copying is, indeed, noticing that the solution of another to some familiar problem is *different* from one's own. A second stage is the observation that the solution is *better or worse* than one's own. Wissler (1923, p. 208) stresses this fact when he observes that copying begins when "man sees his fellowmen performing the same acts as himself, but using a different method." It is not essential to copying that exactly the same responses should be made as are made by the model, but it is essential that the goal to be reached be apprehended by the copier. In case this understanding of the goal is not present, copying cannot take place. Sometimes the understanding of the function of a novelty is swift and immediate, as in the case of the spread of the lucifer match, and, at other times, it is slow. In the latter case, learning the use of the object must precede the attempt to copy.

When the stimulus to learn a new habit is induced by the perception of "something different and something better," we are speaking of the presence of an acquired copying drive. The mode of acquisition of this drive seems obvious on the basis of the material outlined in Chapter X. Individuals have been rewarded in many cases for noticing that others behaved differently and have been rewarded. The success of the other person sets up an anticipatory goal response in the copier, provided that he has been rewarded for the same or a similar response. Part of the cue to initiate copying activity is the success of the other person, exactly as in the case of the "testing" example cited in Chapter IX. The cue of the other's success is part of the stimulus which whips up the copying drive. If, in any given case, the copier then matches responses with the model and is rewarded himself, the perceptions of difference and success become further strengthened as a cue to copying. This process has presumably gone on for a lifetime in the primitives who exhibit the "lively interest" above mentioned.

If the conditions of learning are not propitious, as above outlined, one would not expect the copying drive to develop. This is probably the case with the "conservative" societies often mentioned in the literature on diffusion. Individuals in such societies have evidently been trained not to copy outgroup models. The manner of acquiring such training is easily conceived. If copying has been punished in the course of the individual life history, the perception of difference then stimulates non-copying, even though success of the other be observed. Training to copy is undoubtedly characteristic of every society in certain restricted fields of behavior. One need only think of the constant injunctions to children to do as their parents do. In this case, perception of sameness produces relaxation responses, and perception of difference produces anxiety which drives the subject to the conventional response. Only intensive study of particular societies can reveal under just what circumstances the one or the other of these drives may be developed as characteristic.

We will suppose, however, that the copying drive has been aroused. The story is not yet finished. It is at this point that the activity of the model and the critic comes into play. The model demonstrates the appropriate responses. The critic instructs and scores success or failure. All possible sub-units or functional equivalents in the copier are elicited. The critic uses verbal aids where possible to produce the appropriate response (put your hands like this, watch the pointer on the dial, move the knife away from you, and so forth). Where appropriate sub-responses cannot be elicited, the copier must resort to trial and error, with the critic functioning to limit the range of such responses. It is precisely this process which is often referred to as "inculcation," and it is this very process which shortens the time of learning for the copier and makes copying expedient.

The matter is not yet ended when the correct response, fixed to the right cues, has been elicited in the copier. It is not yet certain that the new act will be rewarded for him. Reward is a real variable. It may or may not be present in the case of any specific copier. Although it is possible to have drive present as a variable without reward ensuing, it is not possible to have reward occur without drive being present. An American may, for instance, learn perfectly to speak a Chinese poem, but may be punished for so doing by his unappreciative countrymen for whom Chinese habits do not have high prestige. Boys in America, again, may learn to knit, but soon find that the habit is not rewarded by their age-mates.

The importance of reward has been noticed by many workers. Kroeber (1923, p. 228), in speaking of the superiority of bronze over stone tools, says that "no people that had once learned the art would be likely to give it up." Sayce (1933, p. 191) remarks on the great rapidity with which the banana and the domestic fowl spread over the greater part of South America in the sixteenth century. One can safely infer that the adoption of these new foods was rapidly and decisively rewarded. Wissler notes (1923, pp. 208–209) that, in the case of a new trait, adoption takes place "if the results are satisfactory." The greater the reward it brings, the more firmly should the new trait be fixed in the receiving culture.

If reward is lacking, it would be expected that the innovation would meet a different fate. In this case, after perhaps a brief trial, the trait should cease diffusing into the particular society and disappear. That such occurs has been noted. Kroeber (1923, p. 329) comments that culture traits die out "from inanition, from sterility of social soil, through supplanting by more vigorous descendants." We take his statement to be a paraphrased reference to the process of extinction. Linton (1940, p. 474) describes how, at the time of early contact with the whites, the Comanche were eager to get muskets. After a time, the usefulness of the muskets began to be compared with that of the bow which the musket had replaced. Though the muskets had greater range, they also had "a much slower rate of fire, were difficult to load on horseback, and required ammunition which was hard to get. As a result, the tribe began to revert to the bow. . . ." It is clear here that the habit of using muskets was not rewarded and was on its way to extinction. Linton has brought out distinctly the comparison of utility which ultimately determines reward.

In the presence of new traits, old traits often lose their reward value and are gradually extruded from the receiving culture. Linton (1940, p. 469) has likewise noted this fact in stating that "when the iron axe comes in the stone axe goes out, the techniques for making it are forgotten . . . and the returns in prestige and profit which went to stone axe makers are eliminated."

Social Conditions Affecting Copying

The most obvious of the social conditions affecting copying have to do with degrees of contact. Contact may be of the face-to-face type or it may be mediated by writing or other forms of remote communication. In the face-to-face type of contact, the different response is exhibited, and the reward attaching to it is demonstrated. Conditions of isolation conceal both from the would-be copier. In face-to-face contact, the model may demonstrate the response to be innovated, and the critic can carry out his functions of eliciting the response units and scoring success or failure. The more nearly the copier and the model share their social habits, the more easy is the copying transaction. For example, a shared language makes it possible for the critic to indicate more readily the desired units of the new response. Hence it seems likely, other things equal, that copying will be more rapid within a society than between societies. The pocketed peoples of the world, like the Polar Eskimos or the Fuegians, show the effects of their physical isolation in the relative impoverishment of their cultures. They have not had the stimulating presence of the social model and critic which has aided the advance of other peoples.

Length of contact between different societies is undoubtedly a variable which bears on the probability of copying. One may say in general that, if diffusion is to occur, contact must be long enough to get the new response tried out and rewarded. Long contact seems to favor the learning of difficult responses if there are no other barriers. In the case of protracted contact, it is easy to form the habit of copying as well; that is, it is easier for one culture to acquire prestige in the sense of being the donor of rewarded habits. Short or inadequate contact seems likely to favor imperfect transmission of a trait. Sometimes the "mere idea" of a trait is transmitted. This process has been labeled by Kroeber (1940, p. 1) as "stimulus diffusion" and has been exemplified by the invention of porcelain in Europe in the early eighteenth century. The Chinese had been shipping porcelain to Europe for two centuries theretofore and thus provided Europeans with the necessary idea of porcelain articles. The process of making porcelain, however, did not accompany the porcelain objects and had to be invented independently by Europeans.

Although isolation may effectively prevent copying, contact does not of necessity guarantee it. If the responses requisite to transferring a trait are not elicited and rewarded, no length of contact will favor diffusion. Thousands of Italo-Americans cook some of their food in olive oil every day, but this trait apparently does not diffuse to the native American population. Native Americans are not rewarded for trying out Italian traits and as a result never make the response required. Since the response is never made, it can never be rewarded and therefore can never diffuse. A more or less parallel case seems to be that of the failure of the Chinese to adopt the practice of using milk as a food. It is obviously a valuable food, and China has had long contact with the Mongol peoples who already possessed the trait. The Chinese, however, never tried out the use of milk and hence could not be rewarded for adopting it. Apparently, they scorned the practice in common with other traits of their "barbarian" neighbors.

The social attitude toward copying is often a decisive variable in determining whether or not diffusion shall take place. There seem to be cases where the members of whole social groups have been sufficiently rewarded for copying in the past so that they adopt a permissive attitude toward innovation. Under these circumstances, diffusion of traits to such societies may be expected to be rapid. American society, for instance, seems to have had a very hospitable attitude toward innovations and to have encouraged copying, especially from its European neighbors. Americans have been repeatedly rewarded for borrowing from European nations. One need think only of the power loom, the steam engine, and the "germ" theory of disease to emphasize this point. All of these inventions have been useful, and their influence has given rise to a favorable attitude toward other European ideas and processes.

On the other hand, a social taboo on copying or bad experience with former copying will tend to limit copying behavior. Dixon (1928, p. 62) has noted the "wide difference in respect to conservatism between different peoples, some being extraordinarily loath to change from established customs, others ready and curious to try anything new." We have no

doubt that the conservatism in question is a result of former
experience with copying and indicates negative results in
earlier copying. This conservatism may be general or specific
to particular innovations. Sayce observes (1933, p. 185)
that the BaKongo are described as being very suspicious and
conservative. They refused many types of presents and
wished from Europeans nothing except "iron, knives, and
salt." The more particular type of conservatism is illustrated
by Dixon (1928, p. 111) who points to the "religious conservatism of Islam, which prevented its accepting the art of
printing from China" and thereby probably delayed the appearance of this art in Europe for some centuries. Moham-
medan religion decreed that the Koran must be written in
longhand, a response incompatible with printing.

A further variable among those affecting the likelihood of
copying is the prestige of the model or model group. Models
of high prestige tend to be copied, for they incite the copying
drive. A model of high prestige is one whose responses have
been copied heretofore with reward. This anticipatory factor
plays a very great rôle, because without it, elements of great
value to a particular culture may remain uncopied for long
periods of time. Linton (1940, p. 497) has recognized this
fact in stating, "Behind all questions of the utility or apparent compatibility of the culture elements available for borrowing there lies the deeper question of whether the borrow-
ers want to be like the donors or not." This "wanting to be
like" is an acknowledgment of the prestige of the donor
culture.

Societies may have prestige for particular elements of
their cultures and be copied in these. In this connection Sayce
(1933, p. 175) notes that the Japanese went to the Germans
for military advice and instruction and to the British for
naval techniques. Once prestige in a particular branch of culture has been achieved, however, it may be generalized (according to the principles developed in Chapter XI) to other
elements of the culture. This case has been well exemplified
by the Japanese, among whom Western clothes and even
some democratic institutions followed the introduction of

Western machines and technologies. Sayce (1933, pp. 178–179) observes the same tendency among primitive peoples. Much of the white man's prestige has been due to his material equipment—his rifles, tools, matches, ships, and so forth. "Once prestige has been acquired in respect to one aspect of culture borrowings connected with other aspects may follow." Even maladaptive borrowings may follow, as when "European clothing is often adopted by peoples living in regions where the climate and mode of life make it unsuitable." Such generalization of copying responses to other than the rewarded aspects of an alien culture is undoubtedly a powerful factor in spreading culture traits, and has unquestionably been in operation since earliest times. The agents of the particular social types who happen to bear prestige need not be considered here. They have included, first and most important of all, traders. Members of technically successful cultures have uniformly had prestige. Conquerors acquire prestige through their capacity to instill fear; migrants and even captives sometimes acquire a degree of status which incites imitation.

Within a society the same factors operate to determine copying as are effective between societies; but there are some differences. The shared language and culture facilitate copying. If a person of high prestige introduces a trait into a society, its diffusion will be favored as compared with the introduction of the same trait by a person of low status. If large numbers of people take up a new habit, the number of models and critics who can teach others is increased. There is further a certain reassurance effect in what "numbers" of persons do. Many people feel comfortable in following the crowd. In the early career of an innovation in a society, however, numbers may tend to inhibit copying. The great mass of people are comfortable when they are following the older behavior pattern. Not until a large number of the daring have taken up the new trait does the reassurance value of numbers intrude to facilitate the process for the remainder.

If it is true that high prestige of the model tends to favor copying, so, conversely, models of low prestige tend not to be

copied, or may even stimulate the witness to do the opposite.
It is not possible to state in every case why a particular
group has little prestige for the members of another group,
but it seems certain that where copying has been attempted
and not rewarded, or punished, the model group has low
prestige. A special case of this fact would seem to be the one
where the model group is viewed with hostility. The conqueror group of superior social technicians may impose its
rule on a subject group, block the traditional habit systems
of this group, and hold it without hope of successful revolt.
Linton (1940, p. 499) has noticed cases of this kind and
writes:

Under such circumstances the hostility expresses itself in
terms of passive resistance and uncooperativeness. . . . Examples of such attitudes are to be found in some of the Mexican
and Central American Indian communities which have succeeded in remaining un-Europeanized after centuries of White
domination. Such communities will often develop elaborate techniques for preventing the introduction of new things, going to
the extent of formally disciplining any of their members who
try to introduce innovations.

In such a situation, the model society (the conqueror) persistently excites punishment expectations in the subject
group with resulting aggression against the conqueror. Copying in such cases has often led to increased exploitation of the
conquered and thus to punishment and extinction of copying
tendencies.

Inexactness of Copying

It has been widely noticed by ethnographers that copying
is rarely exact. Both small and large differences can be dis-
cerned between a trait or artifact as exhibited in the donor
society and in all the copies of it which have wended their way
by diffusion into the culture systems of neighboring tribes.
Sayce (1933, p. 76) reports in this connection, "If a collec-
tion of objects such as spears, clubs, shields, or tobacco pipes,
be examined, it will be found that there are many small dif-

ferences between them, and that there may rarely be two pipes or two spears exactly alike." It is probably only in scientific repetition of the procedures of others that this difference between model and copy is held to a minimum. Scientific description of procedure is indeed a near-perfect recipe for copying. These operational and experimental definitions specify exactly what is to be done with what resources in order to make a desired observation.

The reasons for the inexactness of cultural copying are manifold. In the first place, there is the band of tolerance allowed by the critic in determining what is a reproduction of copy. The important thing is that the copier is rarely trained to an exact reproduction. The critic secures a certain approximation of the behavior desired and then lets the matter drop. Again, copying depends to some degree on the pre-existing habit outfit of the copier. Apparently, some of the units in the copier's habits can never be effectively rooted out and replaced by those most desirable, from the standpoint of the copied trait. Many people find it next to impossible to master all the intricate phonemes of a foreign speech and to eliminate their tendencies to substitute the more or less equivalent units from their own language; hence develops the characteristic and different coloring with which English is spoken by, say, French, Germans, and Japanese.

Again, the copying process may be stopped before it has reached the pitch of correct reproduction. The copier may bring matching only to the point where decisive reward appears, but not to perfection. An American learning to speak French, for instance, will learn well until he can order food, make a date, send out laundry, and the like. Once these skills have been achieved, however, the further learning of French is not rewarded in proportion to the effort expended. Fatigue pressure steps in to cut short copying. If, on the other hand, the reward is withheld, learning of French may continue long beyond this first stage. If the reward should be, for instance, the applause of a group of French scholars, the activity of matching French words will be likely to continue for some years and a much superior technique achieved.

It is frequently true also that an imperfect copy may be just as much or even more rewarded than a perfect copy. This will be especially the case where environmental conditions force a change in the copied trait. While American Indians, for example, took over practically all the elements of the Spanish horse complex, they did not take over the shoeing of horses. This laborious process, while adaptive on cobbled streets and hard roads, was not needed to protect the horse on the American plains. An imperfect copy was therefore as much rewarded as a more perfect one would have been, and the difficulties of mastering the horseshoeing part of the technique were avoided.

Similarly, Kroeber (1923, p. 272) notes that the Greeks, in taking over the Semitic alphabet, did not do so exactly. They did not need the signs for all the consonants which were present in Semitic speech. They did, however, need vowel signs which were not present in the original alphabet. These signs they improvised by changing the values of some of the signs for unneeded consonants. In the same connection, Sayce (1933, pp. 188–189) reports that some of the South American Indians "have rejected the crown of the European hat, but have accepted the brim, which they have copied and wear as an eye-shade." Presumably the labor of making the whole hat is reduced, but the value of the useful eye-shade is retained.

Differing environmental conditions may force a change in the copied habit. The most evident of such conditions would be the absence of the raw material necessary for the fabrication of a new implement. Absence of proper raw materials may stop the spread of a valued trait or force a modification in its form. Dixon (1928, pp. 109–110) describes the fact that the birchbark canoe of the eastern Algonkians became the elm- or spruce-bark canoe among the neighboring Iroquois; birch was a much rarer wood in the forests available to the latter group.

Climatic conditions further limit the feasibility of the spread of traits. Wissler (1923, pp. 134–135) remarks that "the maize of the American Indian, though artificially adapted to dry as well as to moderately humid areas, could not be raised where early frosts were the rule." Such a circumstance may alter or stop the spread of an otherwise desired trait. A pertinent example of the alteration of a trait by the absence of both technique and raw material is reported by Kroeber (1923, pp. 213–214). The English settlers who had become established on the Atlantic coast introduced a tomahawk pipe for trade purposes. "This was a metal hatchet with the butt of the blade hollowed out into a bowl which connected with a bore running through the handle. One end of the blade served to chop, the other to smoke. The hatchet handle was also the pipe stem." These pipes were traded also to the Plains Indians and were apparently much coveted. At any rate, the pipe was copied. But it was impossible for the aborigines to reproduce the metal blade. Instead they copied the pipe in stone, a material which they knew how to work. Such stone "tomahawk pipes" are familiar to all American ethnologists. They serve to illustrate how a trait may be changed by the absence of appropriate raw material.

Perhaps most important of all the pressures that are brought to bear upon a traveling trait are those exerted by the institutionalized habit system of the receiving culture. Malinowski (G. E. Smith, *et al.*, 1927, pp. 41–42) has presented this point most emphatically:

Whenever one culture "borrows" from another, it always transforms and readapts the object or custom borrowed. The idea, institution, or contrivance has to be placed within a new cultural milieu, fitted into it, and assimilated to the receiving civilization. In this process of readaptation the form and function, often the very nature, of the object or idea is deeply modified—it has to be, in short, reinvented.

Linton (1940, pp. 475–476) likewise recognizes this fact and writes:

The native artist who borrows a European design will alter it in subtle ways to make it "look right" or the arrangement of borrowed music will be changed to conform to the preëxisting musical patterns. For example, the ways in which Tahitians have transformed Protestant hymns into lively dance tunes is somewhat startling to the Europeans, while the way in which our own composers have adapted Indian melodies would surprise Indians.

Sayce (1933, p. 199) observes the same process of transforming traits and exemplifies it in the case of tobacco. The use of tobacco among American Indians, who originated it, seems to have been closely associated with ceremonial practices. Europeans, in taking over the trait, completely changed its status and smoked for pleasure, although they seem to have believed, in addition, that it had medicinal properties. Sayce notes (1933, p. 206) that the Chinese of Fu-kien "believed tobacco to be a cure for colds, dropsy, cholera, indigestion, bad circulation of the blood, poor appetite, etc." The trait of smoking tobacco has therefore been altered among the various peoples to which it has spread. Even today women are only slowly coming into the ranks of permitted public smokers.

Traits may not only be changed by diffusion but may actually deteriorate if, as Sayce (1933, pp. 125–126) points out, "an object spreads farther or more rapidly than the complete understanding of it. M. Junod mentions that the natives of Madagascar, when they obtained rifles, knocked off the sights because they got in the way of aiming." The inventive side of borrowing as stressed by Malinowski must be fully taken into account. Where the trait does not fit local needs, the trial-and-error behavior mechanism enters to fill the gaps in borrowing. It is apparently only under these conditions that the trait can be rewarded in the receiving culture. In short, the copying mechanism is no guaranty that the trait will be perfectly transmitted in the first place or that it will maintain the form or function which it had in the donor society.

To summarize briefly: Diffusion takes place by means of the copying mechanism. Copying is expedient because it produces the to-be-rewarded response rapidly as compared with trial-and-error learning. Copying, like all learning, takes place under the pressure of drive. The presence of relevant sub-responses in the copying society is a great convenience in diffusion. The absence of such responses lengthens or prevents learning. Copying can become an acquired drive, providing copying behavior has been rewarded. Conditions of social contact offer the best opportunity for rapid copying, since they bring the learner into contact with the model and critic who can rapidly elicit the correct response. The prestige of the model is the crucial matter in mobilizing the copying drive and setting in motion the attempt to match responses. Copying is rarely exact, owing to various circumstances, chief among them the pressure put on the incoming habit by the preëxisting matrix of the receiving culture.

APPENDIX 1

REVISION OF HOLT'S THEORY OF IMITATION

HOLT has formulated (1931, pp. 37–40) an ingenious theory to account for repetitive and imitative cooing and babbling in the small child. His theory has been so widely noticed and utilized by social psychologists that it seems worth while to address special attention to it. Since the associationist position leads to different predictions of behavior than does a consistent reinforcement position, it is desirable to make clear the logic behind these predictions.

Holt advocates the reflex-circle hypothesis of iterative behavior. His argument (1931, pp. 37–40), condensed and sometimes paraphrased, runs substantially as follows:

Nervous excitations, seeking some outlet of least resistance, find their way purely fortuitously into the motor neurons of the muscles involved in making a given sound. The sound is made as a random response. But then a response occurs which is *not* random. The sound stimulates the child's ears which send a distinctive excitation along the auditory nerves to the central nervous system. But this excitation arrives only a second or two after the above-mentioned random impulses have found, or while they are still finding, outlet from the central nervous system into the muscles which produce the sound. Therefore by simultaneous association the incoming excitation from the ears will find outlet along the tracts just used by the random impulses, that is, will go back to, and will further contract the exact muscles used in producing the sound. After a few repetitions of this process, the specific impulses which the sound elicits in the ears will acquire a synaptic connection with the motor nerves going out to the same muscles used in producing that sound. A reflex-circle will be established. Hence the infant persistently repeats any sound which he hears himself make. As soon as this process is firmly established, he repeats also those same articulate sounds which other persons utter to him. When the child is stimulating himself, the behavior is called iteration; when a second person provides the stimulus, it is called imitation.

The writers, like so many others, are indebted to Holt for focusing attention on the problem of iteration and for taking the first steps in working out an explanation of it. Holt offers valuable clues in the observation that the child can hear himself talk while talking and the inference that this fact might bear on the problem of imitation. The wide attention which Holt's hypothesis has received indicates the great demand which exists for a basic approach to the problems of imitation, especially in relation to the acquisition of speech. It is particularly necessary to be explicit about this debt to Holt since this appendix will be an exploratory modification and amplification of his hypothesis. The position of the writers is occasionally presented in dramatic contrast to his in order to bring out succinctly the different implications of a simple associationist and a reinforcement position.

Reinforcement theorists agree with associationists that infants do make vocal responses and that these responses in turn stimulate the child. It is likewise agreed that children may respond to speech cues from others by making sounds similar to the stimulus. The query arises on a quite different score. Once a child has begun to repeat his own sounds according to this mechanism, how does he ever stop?[1] Since each response is automatically associated with its own stimulus, and it is assumed that each association strengthens the connection, the iterative behavior should continue indefi-

[1] Holt has recognized that his reflex-circle hypothesis presents a dilemma on the score of stopping the iterative or imitative behavior. He states (1931, p. 45): "I do not know that any completely satisfactory answer has as yet been found." In another part of his book (p. 52), he indicates that the automatic flexion and extension of a tendon will continue "until such time as fatigue of the synapses and other tissues or until impulses from extraneous sources step in to interfere." He does not systematically develop this hypothesis or apply it to the crying behavior of children. This is true also of the many social scientists who have adopted Holt's reflex-circle theory.

nitely. Likewise, when stimulated to imitate by another person in the manner above described, the iterative behavior should then continue without ceasing. This expectation from the Holt theory is not verified in the facts of children's behavior, and some modification of the Holt hypothesis is therefore imperative. Some hypothesis must be found which explains how the child can be induced to stop crying, babbling, or cooing.

The weakness in the Holt theory seems to be that he assumes that the connection between the vocal response and the auditory stimulus will be strengthened by mere temporal contiguity of these two events. This single assumption does not adequately interpret the facts. A temporal relationship is undoubtedly one condition of establishing a connection between a stimulus and a response—a response to a cue must occur before it can be learned—but this does not seem to be the only condition essential to learning. It is urged in this instance, as elsewhere throughout this book, that reward is essential to the strengthening of a connection between response and stimulus, and that, without reward, extinction will occur regardless of temporal contiguity of stimulus and response.

The discussion which follows is an attempt to work out the implications of a reinforcement theory for the iterative and imitative vocal behavior of small children. It is put into the appendix of this book because it is tentative and exploratory. The detailed history of even one child cannot be presented to verify or disprove the reinforcement hypothesis. The baby discussed is, like Holt's, a hypothetical baby; but this application of the reinforcement hypothesis may facilitate further discussion and research. At least such casual observation of infants' behavior as comes to hand seems to support a reinforcement interpretation. Investigations have not indicated that children always vocalize at the sound of similar vocal stimuli from other children.[2] What is maintained here is that

[2] Watson reports that "the crying of one infant in a nursery will . . . (not) set off the rest of the children" (1925, p. 310). From the standpoint of our hypothesis this would not be expected among children of the ages studied by Watson. They would presumably not yet have been frequently enough rewarded for crying to establish the necessary stimulus-response connections.

when they do babble or coo they should do so when rewarded and not by mere association.

The application of a reinforcement theory to the vocal behavior of children will be presented with the aid of several examples. Responses selected for special exploration will be those of babbling and crying. Babbling behavior will be discussed first, and very briefly.

Since the mother talks to the child while administering primary rewards such as food, the sound of the human voice should acquire secondary reward value. Because the child's voice produces sounds similar to that of his mother's, some of this acquired reward value generalizes to it. Thus circular connections of the type described by Holt may be strengthened by the rewarding value of the child hearing himself produce a sound similar to that produced by his mother. Whether the acquired reward value would be strong enough to produce a marked tendency to imitative babbling is in doubt; it is also doubtful that children actually have a strong tendency to imitative babbling. If the same sound is repeated in rapid succession without support from some primary reward, the acquired reward value of this sound is extinguished and the babbling response should be weakened until other responses occur. Thus the child should shift to babbling with a different sound and eventually stop babbling altogether. After the passage of time, both the extinguished response of uttering the given sound and the acquired reward value of hearing that sound may undergo spontaneous recovery so that the child will return to uttering the sound. If the sound is again associated with primary reward, still more of its acquired reward value will be restored. As the child learns a better discrimination between the sounds which he utters and those which he hears others utter, the acquired reward value of his own sounds will be reduced. From this hypothesis it may be deduced that children talked to while being fed and otherwise cared for should exhibit more iterative and imitative babbling than children not talked to while being rewarded. An experiment to test a related deduction is suggested in Chapter V, page 81, footnote 9.

The inferences to be drawn from a reinforcement position will be worked out in more detail in the case of crying behavior. The drives for crying are often strong primary drives; those for cooing and babbling are usually weaker and more obscure. If a child babbles iteratively, so ought he to cry. The focus of the discussion will be an infant crying for his bottle. The following questions will be discussed: (1) Why does the child cry at all? (2) Does he cry harder upon hearing himself cry? (3) When ought he to stop crying, if at all, before he gets his bottle? (4) Should he cry harder upon hearing another child cry?

Why Does the Child Cry at All?

This question is neglected in the associationist account. Holt's baby is vocalizing as a result of "fortuitous nervous excitation." The "reinforcement" baby vocalizes only when the common drives are in operation.[3] In a typical case, the motivation is the hunger drive. It should be noted that this drive is itself a stimulus, and a stimulus with both the properties possible. It has intensity and cue value. It provides a motive power sufficient to get the child into action and can acquire the distinctive function of determining which response will be made. At the very first appearance of the hunger stimulus, a large number of responses will be made. Crying is high in the innate hierarchy of such responses. It is a response very likely to be rewarded because of its efficiency in acting as a stimulus for the adults around the child. As compared with wriggling, for instance, it can attract attention when wriggling will not because the adult does not have to be within sight of the child to respond to crying.

[3] Holt has statements about drive scattered through his book but not, from our standpoint, organized in a theoretically significant manner. He does not seem to regard drive, as we do, as a stimulus which excites a member of the innate hierarchy of responses. He does not presume, as we do, that there are connections of differing strengths between specific drives and specific members of this innate hierarchy. Nor does he assume that it is the reduction of the drive strength which constitutes a reinforcing state of affairs. These considerations make it seem reasonable to contrast a reinforcement position to his reflex-circle hypothesis.

Cries carry around corners. Furthermore, adults cannot close their ears to crying, whereas they may, as when asleep, close their eyes to exclude a visual stimulus. Crying is therefore a very efficient response, from the standpoint of the child, which is likely to bring the mother near and to set her in search of the drive in the child which needs to be reduced. The assumption that a crying child is hungry is general among mothers in our society, so hunger-tension reduction in the child is rapidly effectuated. The result of such reduction is to reinforce the immediately preceding responses and, among them, crying. In this way, the crying response rapidly becomes dominant over other responses to the hunger-drive stimulus. Stated another way, the hunger drive has acquired cue value. It impels a specific response, i.e., crying.

This behavioral sequence of drive—crying—being-fed occurs repeatedly in the early weeks and months of the child's life. If standard feeding routines are followed, there will be at least eight hundred trials in the first six months. If the child is fed whenever he is hungry and cries for food, the mass practice will be even more effective. The result is a powerful reinforcement of vocal behavior in the infant. He learns to cry when the hunger drive, or any other drive, mounts.

It is well known that crying can be wholly or partly extinguished in the small child. If the parents are instructed not to feed the child when he is hungry and cries, the crying response will tend to drop out to the hunger-drive stimulus. Its innate dominance as a response to a strong drive is, however, so high that it may never drop out altogether. The trace of a cry may remain in spite of repeated extinction practice, especially when the drive stimulus rises to great intensity.

The associationist theory—at least not without elaboration —apparently cannot predict with certainty when the child will start crying (since the stimulus is fortuitous), when he will continue crying (since there is no fixation of response by reward), nor when he will stop crying (since there is no weakening of bond between stimulus and response by unrewarded trials).

Does the Child Cry Harder upon Hearing Himself Cry?

To this the associationist would answer, "Yes," according to the reflex-circle theory outlined above. The reinforcement theorist would answer, "It depends." The question then becomes: On what does it depend? Certainly not on the reflex-circle theory, because children are still hearing themselves cry just before they start to taper off their crying, and this excitation should tend to perpetuate or increase crying. The inferences which must be made from a reinforcement theory seem more valid.

The first time the child cries to the hunger-drive stimulus there is no reason to expect a difference in the strength of the crying response at any place along the continuum of crying responses. The second time he cries, however, there should be a difference. In the first trial, the crying responses to stimuli at the end of the series have been more strongly reinforced than to ones earlier in the series, according to the principle of the gradient of reinforcement. As practice continues, the child should then cry yet harder at the end of the series than at the beginning. Another variable is present, however, to complicate the situation. When the child cries, he stimulates himself in two ways: First, the response of tensing the larynx gives off characteristic stimuli, and, second, the vocal response sets up an auditory stimulus, as Holt has observed. These stimuli are very much alike along the whole continuum of crying responses, presuming that the child cries for a few minutes before being fed. The child stimulates himself in very much the same way at the *beginning* of the sequence as at the end when these responses are much *stronger*. When he begins, say, the twentieth trial of crying to get a bottle, a new variable has appeared. The child cries to the stimuli of hunger drive, room, light, and so forth, *and also* to the stimuli given off by his first cry. The earlier stimuli, therefore (by the principle of generalization), tend to evoke the response characteristic of the latter part of the series, i.e., the stronger crying response. One would expect, for this reason, that after the first cry, on the twentieth trial, the child would tend to emit the stronger cries characteristic of the end of the sequence; that is, the end response would become anticipatory in the time sequence and become attached to the earlier proprioceptive and auditory stimuli. In this way, the child would cry harder when he hears himself cry after practice than he had done on the first or second trial of the sequence.[4]

If the anticipatory strengthening of the crying response is reinforced by earlier reward, the child will tend to cry harder on succeeding trials when he hears himself cry. Strong crying is, in fact, often rewarded. If, however, the stronger cries earlier in the sequence are not reinforced, one would not expect this type of strengthening. In the latter case, the vehemence of the whole series of cries would be expected to be reduced, although the characteristic curve should be maintained.

When Ought He To Stop Crying, if at All, before He Gets His Bottle?

Holt's hypothesis can scarcely be adapted to answer this question because, as has been pointed out, he offers no mechanism by which the child can stop responding. According to the hypothesis offered here, the child ought to learn finally to stop crying before actually getting the bottle. This would be expected to occur in the following way: In the feeding example under discussion, the child cries vehemently up to the point of reinforcement. During the crying sequence, a fatigue drive has been mounting. Each cry produces its own tension in the throat muscles. The longer the crying persists, the stronger will this new drive be. Two rewards occur at the point of feeding: first, the child gets the bottle and reduces his hunger drive; second, the child stops crying and reduces

---

[4] It is reported by a casual observer that this sequence actually occurs with deaf children who cannot hear themselves cry. On the basis of the proprioceptive stimuli given off by crying, they learn to build up a powerful crying sequence in an exactly analogous manner. The most intense proprioceptive stimuli are given off by the strongly reinforced responses at the end of the series. These proprioceptive stimuli evidently are sufficiently similar to those given off by cries in the early part of the sequence so that the more strongly reinforced end responses can move forward in the sequence.

muscle tension in his throat (the fatigue drive). It is the first response, that of sucking, which actually stops crying in this case because sucking on a bottle is incompatible with crying and is more strongly rewarded. The fatigue drive, however, is simultaneously reduced, as just pointed out, and therefore the last crying response is doubly reinforced.

The last crying response in the series will be examined from the standpoint of the stimuli which it evokes. These stimuli are of three types. First, proprioceptive, that is, feeling himself cry; second, auditory, that is, hearing himself cry; and finally environmental, that is, seeing mother and bottle and hearing her voice or her footstep. Feeling himself cry and hearing himself cry have been present during the entire crying sequence and the end stimuli are apparently very much like earlier stimuli in the series. This fact suggests that the goal responses or fractions of them will become anticipatory and move forward in the sequence. This is probably what occurs. The two responses in question are swallowing and stopping crying. Swallowing is not likely to move forward into the series of crying responses because it is not an efficient response in an anticipatory position, e.g., it does not shorten the time of bearing drive but may actually lengthen it.

The case is otherwise with stopping crying. This response may also become anticipatory and move forward from the point of reinforcement. If crying can be stopped before reinforcement occurs without delaying or reducing it, stopping will tend to occur as a response before the point of reinforcement. The hunger reward is not delayed, but the fatigue drive is reduced more quickly.

How far forward may the stopping response move? Suppose the relaxing response has generalized forward until it occurs at the time point when the drive stimulus passes threshold, a point where the crying response would normally be evoked. In this case, the child does not cry, the mother does not come, and hunger drive continues to mount. Net reinforcement over time is reduced.[5] The relaxation response at

─────

[5] The *net reinforcement* for performing a response is a function of two things: the amount of reward (or reduction of drive) and the immediacy of

this point is not rewarded and is therefore extinguished. Consequently, the response next in dominance occurs, and, eventually, crying.

Since there is a gradient of generalization of extinction, as of reward, the relaxing response will not be tried out on the very next stimulus unit to the drive stimulus. It will move forward along the series toward the point of reinforcement and will be tried out at, say, some distinctive stimulus such as the fifth (of an imaginary twenty) in the series. If it is extinguished here, it will move still farther toward the point of reinforcement and be tried out as the tenth or twelfth response. Eventually, it will be stabilized in the series where net reinforcement is greatest. "Net reinforcement" will be greatest where hunger drive is strongest and most quickly reduced, and the least possible fatigue drive is generated.

Crying will therefore be fitted into the sequence at some point where the cues are sufficiently distinctive and where it does not threaten the crucial reward of hunger-tension reduction. In terms of the actual situation, probably the new stimuli which are present near the end of the sequence serve as the discriminable cues for the relaxing response. Before the baby is fed, the mother's footstep is heard in the hall, the

reward (on a gradient of reinforcement). This may be pictured in a pseudo-formula as follows:

Reward ÷ Units of time between response and reward

Where there is not only a reinforcement for performing an act, but a reinforcement by escape from fatigue for stopping the act, this formula must be modified by taking account of the strength of the fatigue drive. Since the fatigue drive continues mounting as long as the response is performed, its final strength is a function of the length of time that the response has been performed. The stronger the fatigue drive the greater the reinforcement when the fatigue-producing response is stopped. This may be expressed in the following pseudo-formula:

Net reinforce- ment for stopping	=	Increment of fatigue per response	×	Number of responses

Combining these two formulae, the *net reinforcement for performing a response* is:

Reward	÷	Units of time between response and reward	−	Increment of fatigue per response	×	Number of responses

door clicks, the light is turned on, the mother appears with bottle, and the like. The presence of these stimuli, in addition to feeling and hearing himself cry, cue the benign relaxation responses. Feeling and hearing himself cry without the presence of these external stimuli excites further and louder crying; feeling and hearing himself cry *with* these additional stimuli becomes the cue for inducing relaxing responses, i.e., non-crying.

The answer to the question posed above is, then, that non-crying may be introduced into the sequence when it does not imperil the reduction of the hunger drive, i.e., when reward is in sight.

Should the Child Cry Harder on Hearing Another Child Cry?

Although Holt does not discuss this specific question, it seems from his reflex-circle hypothesis that he would have to answer, "Yes." The answer of the reinforcement theorist would be again, "It depends." The writers assume, as does Holt, that generalization occurs from the child's own cry to that of another child. If the other child's cry intervenes in that portion of the crying sequence where the proprioceptive and auditory stimuli of his own crying further intensify crying, the other child's cry should stimulate intensified crying behavior; if the other child's crying intervenes in a portion of the sequence where these stimuli plus environmental stimuli (mother with bottle) cue relaxation responses, the other child's cry should be the cue to increase relaxation responses. The heard cry will have at any portion of the sequence exactly the value which it gains by generalization from the own cry as a stimulus. In other words, the child will iterate his own cry if he has been rewarded for so doing. Likewise, he will imitate, i.e., generalize his crying responses to the cry of another child, if this behavior has been rewarded.

Other Considerations

The reinforcement hypothesis indicates that if the drive which forces and cues crying autonomously is almost at threshold, the crying of another child might evoke crying behavior. In this part of the sequence, the crying responses have been rewarded in the past and the stimuli given off by them acquire a potential to induce crying. The other child's similar cry at this point in the sequence is thereby invested with a potential to induce crying. The drive stimulus will, in many cases, be close enough to threshold so that just the stimulus value of hearing the cry will induce crying in the subject child. This state of affairs might be perceived by an onlooker as imitative crying.

Children are probably not long unable to distinguish between their own cries and those of other children. There is an excellent basis for learning discrimination between the two types of cries. When the child hears himself cry, he feels the stimuli given off by this cry. When he hears another child's cry, even though this be identical as a sound stimulus, the child does not feel himself crying. Probably, the two stimulus patterns are sufficiently distinct so that the child would early discriminate between the two types of cries and learn that he is under stronger stimulation when he himself is crying than when he hears another child cry. His own proprioceptive stimulation is added to the auditory stimulation, even though the auditory stimulus may sound identical to a third person. Actually, the own cry is probably never an identical stimulus to the heard cry of another since the own cry is "heard" partly by bone conduction. The discrimination is based on the familiar principle that the child is much more regularly rewarded for responding to his own cry stimuli than he is for responding to the cry of another child.

Without detailed research no statement can be made as to the various time periods when the above behavioral sequences are learned. Facts are not available as to the number of weeks of practice necessary, for instance, to make relaxation responses become anticipatory in the crying sequence, granted that the child is fed in hunger situations shortly after he begins to cry. Nor can it be stated approximately when the child will learn to discriminate between his own cry and that of another child and will be less likely to make imitative crying responses. But from very rough observation it appears that these learnings actually occur.[6]

Exact Defect in the Reflex-Circle Hypothesis

The major objection to the reflex-circle hypothesis comes to a point in the contention that it is vague about answering the question: How does crying behavior in children stop? According to this hypothesis, crying behavior once started might continue indefinitely. The case analyzed above, while convincing in certain respects, is defective in that it does not bring out clearly just how crying stops. In the feeding situation, crying has to stop either according to the association theory or the writers', because an incompatible response, i.e., suckling, supervenes. One cannot swallow and cry at the same time. A case will be considered (but much more summarily) in which no incompatible response is present at the point of reinforcement.

The point of an open safety pin has become lodged in the child's thigh. Random responses begin, including crying. Crying is a response of high dominance to a pain stimulus and will continue over a period of time. It continues vehemently up to the point of actual withdrawal of the safety pin. A number of trials in the same situation occur. When, then, does the child stop crying, and what are the mechanisms by which stopping crying would be anticipated?

Attention must be directed to the actual point of reinforcement (pin withdrawal) in the early trials of the sequence. At this point, crying has just been strongly reinforced and would be expected, therefore, to continue. On the other hand, the drive stimulus has just dropped out, due to the withdrawal of the pin, so that a part of the stimulus to cry has been removed. Without a quantification of the strengths of these two opposing effects, it is not possible to predict what would happen under the circumstances; i.e., whether crying would stop at once because the stimulus to cry had been reduced, or whether it would continue for some

[6] The data in the chapter on "Imitation" in Lewis are at least not incompatible with this position (1936, pp. 70–102).

time, because crying responses had just been reinforced. Observation of children leads to the supposition that the crying response tends to lag or continue beyond the point of actual pain reduction in some cases.

The fatigue-drive hypothesis is essential in explaining these cases of lag. Fatigue drive, a response-produced drive, has been mounting during the entire crying sequence and continues to mount with each crying response after reinforcement takes place. Eventually, it will mount to the point where responses to it are dominant over the crying responses just reinforced. At this point, a not-crying response will be tried out. This not-crying response is reinforced by escape from the strong fatigue drive which has been built up through the crying sequence.

The last stimulus before the not-crying or relaxation response is the important one from a theoretical standpoint. Two responses are attached to this stimulus. One is the response of crying, and the other that of relaxing. The response of crying is not reinforced as much as the response of relaxing.

The argument runs parallel to the one already presented with regard to the crying-suckling sequence. The stimulus given off by the ultimate crying response in the sequence is much like that of the penultimate, antepenultimate, and so forth. This stimulus has already been defined as having two components, that of hearing oneself cry and that of feeling oneself cry. The relaxing response to this stimulus has just been strongly reinforced, while the crying response has been less reinforced. The relaxing response will therefore generalize backward in the sequence to the point of reinforcement (i.e., pain drop) and will be tried out there. Again it will be rewarded, since it does not lessen net reinforcement from pain-drive reduction and is strongly reinforced by reduction of the fatigue drive. It will be tried out, likewise, just before pain reduction occurs. The relaxation response has now become the last response before reinforcement. It is doubly reinforced at this point because it is followed by reduction of pin pain *and* reduction of throat ache (the fatigue drive). It will tend to become even more anticipatory in the series and will be cut and fitted exactly as was the relaxation response in the hunger example given above. If it moves forward too far in the series it will reduce net reinforcement, i.e., will require the child to bear pin pain longer. It will extinguish at this point and move again toward the point of reinforcement. Eventually, it will be tied to a discriminable stimulus in the series at that point where net reinforcement is greatest. In ordinary language, crying will be abandoned under the pressure of the fatigue drive when it is no longer functional in reducing pain stimulation over time.

Undoubtedly, here also the appearance of the mother (footstep, voice, and so forth) will serve as an auxiliary cue to determine the point at which crying may safely be abandoned. To get a practical picture of this situation, one need only remember how, in many situations, infants will stop or lessen crying when the mother's footstep is heard or her face appears.

What is hammered home by this example is the fact that the reflex-circle hypothesis does not clearly explain how crying stops, if indeed it explains how crying starts at all. Apparently crying responses are joined to proprioceptive, vocal, and environmental stimuli under pressure of reinforcement and not by simple contiguity. Children do not keep on crying long after the pin is withdrawn, although by the reflex-circle hypothesis the excitation of responses and stimuli keeps echoing in the same center of the brain. The connection between response and stimulus is apparently established only when it serves to increase net reinforcement.

APPENDIX 2

A. THEORIES BEARING ON THE NATURE OF IMITATIVE BEHAVIOR

A HISTORY of the imitative concept could take the form of an annotated bibliography. This bibliography, in turn, could be arranged alphabetically or chronologically. Such an attempt would, however, only repeat a type of organization of the materials which is already familiar. It seems better to make an attempt at scientific analysis of theories of the imitative mechanism and to group them in large, rough categories. This device is capable of putting the main streams of thought about imitation into functional groupings, but it has defects peculiar to itself. Some writers are difficult to place in any one of the four main groups because, for instance, a writer's general approach to the problem may often be denied in one or two sentences of his work. Again, problems which are of the greatest interest to us may have been only of the most incidental interest to another author and hence have not been treated by him in sufficient detail to provide a basis for classification. The advantages of a set of functional categories seem nevertheless to be great enough to warrant the risk of oversimplification of placement in some cases.

The most general statement that can be made about theories of imitation is that they follow the psychology current at the time in which they are propounded. When the psychological frame of reference seemed to point to instinct as a concept of great importance in the analysis of social behavior, the imitation theories were instinctivist. Through the investigations of anthropologists and sociologists, a proper appreciation of social factors has increased, and imitation theories have been more affected by the cultural variable. As associationistic theories of learning have tended to become dominant, the views on imitation have changed in this direction. It is plain that the theory presented in this monograph is no exception to this general principle. The history of imitation, then, becomes in part the history of the psychological movements in which imitation theories have been immersed. The theories will be considered under four main groupings.[1]

I

The individuals whose theories are discussed in this group have, in general, stressed imitative tendencies as innate. In some of the cases, especially the early members of the group, a nativistic theory of the source of imitativeness is specifically propounded. In others, it is an inference from the general position, although no such word as "instinct" may be used by the writers. Many valuable suggestions about the imitation problem have been made by these writers who postulate innate imitative tendencies.

A paragraph has been taken to explain the classification in Group I because the words "instinctivist" or "nativistic" are not intended as epithets. Imitative behavior certainly appears early in life and is a strongly marked characteristic of human behavior. It is not surprising that many have thought imitation to be instinctive. If most of the writers in this section had taken it as a "given" at some early age in the development of each child and had avoided completely the dilemma as to whether it was innate or acquired, the development of a useful theory would have been facilitated. The most general objection to their positions is exactly that by imputing an innate character to imitation they have tended to stop scientific inquiry.

Walter Bagehot

Walter Bagehot was concerned with the problem of societal evolution, with the question, How are customs fixed and broken down? He pointed out effectively the tremendous dominance of the preëxisting cultural heritage in determin-

[1] We wish especially to acknowledge the aid of F. B. Karpf's *American Social Psychology* (1932) in organizing thought about the history of imitation. His discriminating references were a great help in tracking down the essentials of the position taken by various social theorists on imitation.

ing behavior. In order to show how custom came to have the power of perpetuating itself, he had recourse to a doctrine of imitation. He seemed to feel that imitativeness was an innate part of man's nature. He said, for instance, "The truth is that the propensity of man to imitate what is before him is one of the strongest parts of his nature" (1873, p. 92). He subscribed also to the probable fallacy that the tendency of imitation is stronger in savages than in civilized man. As for children, they are "born mimics" (1873, p. 101). Such statements seem to place Bagehot on the side of the innate theorists.

It is hard to overdo emphasis on the liveliness with which Bagehot understood and expounded the importance of the traditional social heritage in determining the behavior of any one generation. He wrote: "What is most evident is not the difficulty of getting a fixed law; not of cementing . . . a cake of custom, but of breaking the cake of custom . . ." (1873, p. 53). He was aware that the "cake of custom" itself is fixed by social proscription and reward developed in the struggle for group survival. He seemed to understand also that individuals in the group are relatively rewarded and punished depending on their adherence to the common habits of the group. If he could have taken another step, he would have seen that matched behavior as between individuals need not depend upon an innate tendency to imitate, but upon exactly the same proscription and reward which determines the other behavior of adults. He did not, however, take this step and did not work through his theory of group adaptation into the individual sphere.

Particularly interesting in Bagehot is the important obstructive rôle which he assigned to the old habits which must be rooted out before new habits can be established. He has thrown a bright light on the slowness with which total groups change their modes of adaptation and has, by inference, put emphasis on the importance of crisis situations (i.e., situations involving strong drives) in altering group modes of life. His theory can be very effectively translated into a reinforcement theory of learning. Old habits operate as a hindrance because when they are present new habits cannot be tried out and therefore cannot be rewarded and gain such strength as to supersede the old. Although Bagehot adopted the instinctivist emphasis of his period, he went beyond it in many particulars; the internal evidence seems to show that he would have found useful the principles of social learning as they are now understood.

C. L. Morgan

C. L. Morgan operated quite decisively with an instinct theory of the imitative mechanism. He wrote, "The tendency to imitate is based upon an innate constitutional bias to . . . gain satisfaction by reproducing what others are producing" (1896, p. 173). Once the imitative mechanism is set up there are conditions under which imitative action is satisfying. If matched behavior is rewarded, or non-matched behavior is punished, matching will in the one case produce anticipations of reward and non-matching, expectations of punishment. There seems no reason to believe, however, that such satisfaction is "innate or constitutional." Morgan further divided imitation into "instinctive," "intelligent," and "reflective." In the latter category, for instance, the child reflects on the results attained by matching, realizes that they are imitative, and then, later, makes deliberate efforts to imitate (1900, p. 193). All the essential dilemmas seem, however, to be avoided in this discussion. What is reflection and how does the child come to "reflect" on the results attained? How does it know when it has made a correct copy? Under what conditions do efforts to imitate become deliberate? None of these questions is satisfactorily answered. Morgan was not in possession of a statement of the laws of learning nor of the concept that certain social conditions are necessary to produce imitative behavior. Consequently, he had recourse to the instinct hypothesis.

William McDougall

McDougall did not classify imitative tendencies as genuinely instinctive. He found imitative action to be so extremely

varied that he could not posit an innate tendency to copy all
the kinds of behavior which are actually copied by human
beings. He stated, "There is nothing specific in the nature of
the imitative movement and in the nature of the sense-im-
pressions by which the movements are excited or guided . . ."
(1908, p. 102). However, the instinct theory of imitation reappears decorated with verbal false whiskers. A tendency to
simple imitation is observed in the early life of the child and
is called a "pseudo-instinct." There is "a very simple per-
ceptual disposition having this specific motor tendency"
(1908, p. 106) evidenced, McDougall thought, by the fact
that a child of four months could be induced to put out his
tongue when a person in the environment did likewise. It
seems likely that McDougall was overready to accept such an
example as indicating an innate tendency to imitate. If the
event occurred only once, it might have occurred by chance.
If more than once, it might have been reinforced under conditions not noted by McDougall.

R. S. Woodworth

With some hesitation, we add the name of R. S. Woodworth to the innate theorists of imitation. While Woodworth
feels that there are no reflex mechanisms which guarantee
correct imitation, the child shows, nevertheless, "a natural
tendency to *try* to imitate, along with the ability to perceive
the act imitated with sufficient precision to serve as a check
on the correctness of his attempts at imitation" (1922, p.
185).[2] We cannot find evidence for such innate abilities. One
element in Woodworth's theory is valuable despite the emphasis on innateness. Woodworth uses the innate tendency
toward imitation only to get an imitative act tried out; thereafter he is quite clear that some kind of learning mechanism
functions. If the act so tried out were not successful, presumably it would be abandoned.

Woodworth also puts a useful, though uncertain, emphasis

[2] Reprinted from Woodworth, *Dynamic Psychology*, by permission of Columbia University Press.

on the social conditions of learning and stresses the liking of
the individual "for agreement with his fellows in belief, emotion, purpose, and action" (1922, p. 191). He does not show
clearly, however, just why the individual "likes" this conformity. To do this, he would have to go over to a thorough-
going law-of-effect position. Woodworth considers himself a
dissenter from the pure instinct school of theorists of imitation. He may, indeed, be so, but he retains the nuclear defect
of this position in making instinctive the factor which evokes
the matched act.

C. A. Ellwood

Ellwood falls into the group of theorists who have presumed imitative behavior to be innate. He states that imitation is an instinct, but "always modifiable and sometimes
vague and indefinite" (1917, p. 61). He can scarcely doubt
"that there is a natural imitative tendency which has much to
do in facilitating coordination and unity in human groups"
(1917, p. 101). Ellwood simply rests his social psychology of
imitation on this hypothesis and does little to discuss it in detail. He is primarily interested in the uniformity of behavior
in the social group and needs some principle to explain this
uniformity. It seems clear that a learning theory of imitative behavior could be introduced into his system which would
explain the facts without having reference to an innate imitative mechanism.

Augustin Cournot

Cournot saw in imitation the source of habit and education
of the individual. He wrote:

In all the phenomena of life there is a manifest tendency to
imitation, to the repetition of similar acts. To this tendency is
apparently related the production of particular varieties (of
plants or animals) in the course of successive generations. . . .
Within the individual the repetition of similar acts engenders
habit, and becomes the principle of education of the senses, of

the regular play of all functions, of the perfection or perversion of the faculties and the instincts [1861, pp. 384–385].

Tarde was apparently much indebted to Cournot for his general emphasis on the importance of imitation as a mechanism. Cournot had no very careful theory as to how the imitative mechanism operated in the social life of the individual.

Gabriel Tarde

Tarde is widely known for his emphasis upon the importance of imitation in social life. He has given a clear picture of the nature of culture as a distinct variable in the determination of human behavior. He is not, however, actually very important as a theorist in regard to the imitative mechanism. He was quite properly willing to leave this problem to the social psychologists (1903, p. 74). When pressed, however, he did state a kind of mechanism for the imitative process. He wrote: "But I have always given it a very precise and characteristic meaning, that of the action at a distance of one mind upon another, and of action which consists of a quasi-photographic reproduction of a cerebral image upon the sensitive plate of another brain" (1903, p. xiv). It seems very likely, therefore, that Tarde's theory depended not upon the state of psychology at the time but on an analogy to the process of photography which had recently been invented. The image transmitted from one brain to another could also be labeled "suggestion." With regard to the nature of suggestion, Tarde took an agnostic position and wrote: "Do we know anything more about the essence of suggestion which passes from one person to another and which constitutes social life? We do not . . ." (1903, p. 76). It would seem from the several statements cited that "suggestion" was viewed by Tarde as some kind of innate process which occurred under social conditions.

A modern theory of imitation could be slipped under the superstructure of Tarde's general sociology without altering it profoundly. Such a theory would not diminish the importance of Tarde's emphasis on culture as the social matrix of life for any individual coming into the group. It would certainly not minimize the importance ascribed by Tarde to imitation in the transmission of culture, whether from one generation to another or from one society to another. Learning theory may yet have something to say about the invention process which Tarde stressed as so important. In view of Tarde's vital and invaluable emphasis on the social variables, it is hard to be compelled to point out that his imitation theory is fundamentally only a substitute for an explicit theory of the innate nature of imitative behavior. The point can be made in the following way: Where Tarde said that "society is imitation" (1903, p. 74), we would say that "society is learning." This change in point of view might have relevance for all those who, like the historical school of American anthropologists, have followed Tarde's clear-cut analysis of the nature and transmission of culture forms. Tarde left the field of study of the imitative mechanism to future workers and apparently did not assign great importance to his own theory of the mechanism. He appears as sensible in this act as in his explicit concept of custom.

E. A. Ross

Following Tarde, Ross makes a great deal of the rôle of imitation in transmission of social patterns. He thinks of suggestion as a "cause" and imitation as an effect. He says, following Baldwin, that suggestions are external stimuli which may be defined as " 'the abrupt entrance from without into consciousness of an idea or image which becomes a part of the stream of thought and tends to produce the muscular and volitional effects which ordinarily follow upon its presence . . .' " (Baldwin, 1891, p. 297). For Tarde, the emphasis was on the social results of invention and imitation. Invention explained social change, and imitation the stability of social pattern. Ross's social theory, like Tarde's, is not incompatible with a learning theory of imitative behavior. In referring to Ross, one cannot omit mention of his remarkable capacity for offering vital illustrations from social life in explanation of his views.

Clark Wissler

Wissler ascribes a great rôle to imitation in the transmission of culture. It functions both as between generations of men in one society and as between different societies. Wissler suggests, in fact, that without the imitative function, it is difficult to imagine how men could have a culture at all, "for it must be perpetuated by the imitation of the older by the younger members of the group" (1923, p. 206). Wissler must be classed with the nativistic theorists as regards the mechanism of imitation. He feels that it is due to the inherent suggestiveness of mankind and "yet imitation may be naïve and natural, as well as deliberate and conscious. . . . The cause lies in the suggestiveness inherent in mankind" (1923, p. 208).

He notes, however, that in the diffusion of a culture trait, "the results" must be "satisfactory" (1923, p. 209) if the new way is to be adopted. As already urged in the discussion of diffusion, it would seem that the facts available are much better interpreted by a learning theory of imitation than by any innate theory. Wissler has correctly observed the prevalence of imitative behavior, but has relied on the instinct school for his social psychology. Indeed, his lucid statement of the nature of cultural transmission would be far more compatible with the proposition that imitative tendencies themselves are acquired.

II

It is probably impossible to explain any human act in the absence of all presuppositions whatever as to the nature of bodily function. One must have some postulates as to physical structure and function. The theorists in this second group all seem to reject any innate tendency to copy the social act of another at the instant of its appearance, and this rejection holds for even the simplest cases of such acts. The problem therefore becomes this: How is the first matched act elicited? By one means and another, the theorists in this group manage to give a plausible account of this first performance of the matched act. The difficulties arise in accounting for the cessation of imitative behavior, or how it may be that the act of another is followed by a non-matched rather than a matched act. Some of the first writers suggest a specific neurological mechanism for a primary sort of imitation. Others adopt the circular-reaction principle, omitting neurological reference. Still others attempt to bring the phenomena in line with the Pavlovian conditioned response without always understanding the essence of Pavlov's theory.

Pavlov was, indeed, the great parent theorist in this field, but it must be observed that he did not manage to wring the clearest possible statement of variables out of his experiments. If one were using a single word to describe Group II, it would probably have to be "associationist" theorists, but this term would not do justice to the many innovations in viewpoint which have been advanced by them.

J. M. Baldwin

Baldwin's position is difficult to state simply. It seems probable that he had, in the first place, a theory of simple "ideo-motor suggestion" to initiate the process of imitation. He said, for instance, that the process of conscious imitation runs something like this: First there is an "eye-stimulus, then a central process, then a movement of the child's own member, which itself reinstates the same eye-stimulus" (1895, p. 269).[8] In spite of everything, this sounds something like an innate theory of the genesis of imitative reactions. It is evident, once the matched act had occurred, that Baldwin could deal with it, after a fashion, from this point on. This he does by his circular-reaction hypothesis. He wrote:

The essential thing, then, in imitation, over and above simple ideo-motor suggestion, is that *the stimulus starts a motor-process* which tends to reproduce the stimulus and, through it, the motor process again. From the physiological side we have a *circular activity*—sensor, motor; sensor, motor: and from the

----

[8] From Baldwin, *Mental Development in the Child and the Race.* By permission of The Macmillan Company, publishers.

psychological side we have a similar circle—reality, image, movement; reality, image, movement, etc. [1895, p. 133].[4]

This mechanism he exemplified by a child who has "struck the combination" of putting a rubber on the end of a pencil and taking it off again. Baldwin wrote, "H. found endless delight in putting the rubber on a pencil and off again, each act being a new stimulus to the eye" (1895, pp. 132–133).[5] What is not explained here is how the child strikes the right response, and how it is connected to the preceding stimulus. Once the response and the visual stimulus are connected, they tend to run in series. This explanation does not account for the fact that the child in question undoubtedly learned to stop at some time or other the act of putting the rubber on the end of the pencil.

Baldwin further distinguished between *projective*, *subjective*, and *ejective* phases of the self. The subjective phase is attained by imitation (1902, pp. 13–14). This theory is too vague to be capable of translation into a learning theory. Its one obvious virtue is that it stresses the fact that all biological functions, like the circular reaction, take place in a social milieu and are immediately modified by it. Baldwin could not get along entirely without nativistic presumptions, for he wrote, "The child naturally falls to imitating, and when once this has begun he is a veritable copying machine . . ." (1911, pp. 20–21). Evidently, in Baldwin's case the natural tendency to imitate gets the act started, and then the circular reaction enters to keep the imitation function going. Baldwin's thesis of the circular reaction, in one form or another, has exercised a great influence on the minds of recent psychologists writing on imitation.

E. B. Holt

Holt's theory has already been discussed in considerable detail. It has been noted that Holt is able by his reflex-circle

---

[4] From Baldwin, *Mental Development in the Child and the Race.* By permission of The Macmillan Company, publishers.

[5] From Baldwin, *Mental Development in the Child and the Race.* By permission of The Macmillan Company, publishers.

theory to get the imitative act started. He has further called
attention to the fact that once the child can imitate himself,
another person can also provide the stimulus and evoke the
imitative act.

Holt is also aware to some degree of the fact that certain
social conditions are necessary for imitation. He points out,
for instance, that "individuals of all species often do the same
thing at the same time" (1931, p. 112). This fact provides
the occasion for the stimulus which will unleash the iterative
mechanism which Holt describes. He recognizes also, as his
examples show (1931, p. 113) that parents indicate their
pleasure at certain acts of the child and thus provide "the cue
that stimulates the child to repeat whatever it has just done"
(1931, p. 113). In this example, Holt indicates the selective
rôle of the culture in forming children's behavior and exhibits the influence of secondary rewards in fixing such behavior.
Nevertheless, he does not extract the full theoretical import
of the insight which appears in the examples. As already
pointed out, his reflex-circle theory can start the imitative
act going, but there are no principles offered by which it can
stop. In his case, as in so many others, there is a lack of examples from real life analyzed in detail. Good examples are,
in fact, exceedingly hard to find in any of the writers on imitation theory.

F. H. Allport

Allport's position, while similar to that of Holt, has some
interesting deviations. In the field of sound, he repeats Holt's
theory that repetition of own sounds is due to "the use of
previously established connections between auditory and
speech centers. When others speak syllables to the child, they
put into operation the ear-vocal reflexes which the child has
already fixated by hearing himself talk" (1924, p. 240). He
stresses that imitative action must already be due to "the
conditioning of responses by social stimuli similar to the responses themselves" (1924, p. 240). He is also aware that
under the general term of imitation falls a class of acts which
we have called *same* behavior. He writes: "Many acts of al-

leged imitation are due not to the effect of one individual upon another, but to the fact that all are reacting to the same stimulus" (1924, pp. 240–241). This mechanism should not be confused with matched-dependent behavior. In Allport's examples, he stresses the importance of drive and reward. For instance, he writes: "There is no *general instinctive* drive to imitate. Behind each complex activity in which one individual copies another there is some personal and prepotent interest other than the mere desire to imitate" (1924, p. 241). Imitative behavior is for Allport an instrumental act which is learned in the course of goal-seeking activity. If one already has a law-of-effect position on imitation, it is possible to read the hidden implications of Allport's examples as supporting such a position. What stands out theoretically, however, is his use of the circular associative mechanism. His work remains singularly realistic in its contribution to the literature.

Gardner Murphy and L. B. Murphy

The Murphys seem to accept Allport's circular-reflex theory for "imitation of the conditioned response type." This is, of course, an associationist theory. It is a Pavlovian theory based on an associationistic rather than a "law-of-effect" concept of reinforcement. According to this associationistic concept of reinforcement the meat powder which Pavlov used in his classical experiments supports the conditioned responses solely by its capacity to elicit salivation—the additional fact that food reduces the hunger drive being, from the point of view of this theory, completely fortuitous and irrelevant.

The Murphys give a good description of copying and stress the trial-and-error elements in this form of imitation. They are quite clear that imitation is a learned type of behavior, although they have not described the process by which it can be learned. Again, their examples imply a reinforcement theory which is not vigorously delineated. The Murphys write, for instance:

We cannot discuss the matter here except to point out the highly important fact for social psychology that reward and punishment, pleasantness and unpleasantness, do appear to affect learning. Whether this principle can be identified with that of the conditioned response, or whether it is a different psychological principle, is unknown [1931, pp. 184–185].

The authors are thus unclear about the psychological mechanisms of the various types of imitation. They fail also to stress the social conditions under which imitative behavior occurs. It should be said, of course, that they are reviewing existing literature and extracting the best from it rather than attempting to make an independent contribution to imitation theory.

Smith and Guthrie

These authors maintain that practically all imitative behavior is made up of conditioned responses (1927, p. 131). They cite the Holt "circular" theory of language acquisition and seem to put this forward as their main position. Actually, it would be more appropriate to say that Guthrie's own psychological theory has not been rigorously applied to the imitation process. If Guthrie's (1935) ingenious theory turns out to be true, it reduces the present reinforcement hypothesis to more fundamental principles, but still demands that drive stimuli and the rewards terminating them be assigned an important rôle in any rigorous formulation applied to imitative behavior. Such a formulation has not yet been made.

J. K. Folsom

Folsom, in his *Social Psychology* (1931, pp. 319–323), follows the associationist position of Holt and Allport. This leaves him indistinct theoretically as to how the learning of imitation takes place. Again, one can infer a nascent recommendation of reinforcement theory from the concrete examples. Folsom is, of course, positive on the fact that imitation is learned behavior and not to be accounted for by instinct theory.

Ogburn and Nimkoff

These sociologists follow Holt, for they write: "Imitation is thus not an inborn pattern but results from learning. One imitates someone else when one has imitated one's self, so to speak" (1940, p. 166). In any concrete situation, they stress that an imitative response is "either the release or a slight modification, of existing attitudes or habits" (1940, p. 166). In this statement, we have a hint of the fact that imitative responses can be generalized from one stimulus situation to another. These authors call attention to an "unconscious type of imitation" as well as to conscious copying, an emphasis probably derived from Faris. But there is no attempt to work out the mechanisms of these forms of imitation with the aid of a reinforcement theory.

G. A. Lundberg

Lundberg gives a clear statement of the associationist point of view on imitation (1939, pp. 297–298). He shows an awareness of the complexity of imitative action, but is prevented from making a useful analysis by failing to understand the function of reinforcement in fixing a response-stimulus connection.

J. F. Dashiell

Dashiell seems to follow an association theory, but not one which is specifically based on Holt's neurological notions. He stresses, with many others, that imitation is not to be conceived of as innate, but is, on the contrary, learned. He distinguishes between *habitual* imitation, which we term "matched-dependent behavior," and *intentional* imitation (1928, pp. 434–435), which we term "copying," but does not stipulate the conditions under which each will occur.

George Humphrey

Humphrey also has an associationist theory. He notes, for instance, that simple imitation stops when "the reflex has disappeared by 'lack of support' from the primary stimulus"

(1921, p. 4). He does not explain the way the primary stimulus stops supporting the reflex. He takes the position that imitative acts are merely a special case of "ordinary conditioned reflex activity" (1921, p. 9). It would be easier to agree with him if he had said "ordinary conditioned *response* activity." But, even then, he does not seem to have gotten the force of the elements of drive and reward which are present in Pavlovian experiments, especially as modified by the work of Thorndike and Hull.

L. L. Bernard

Bernard considers imitation as a class term for "a great many concrete instances of the conditioning of responses" (1926, p. 269). In understanding this conditioning, however, he seems to follow the associationists' line of thought. His "suggestion imitation" refers to the mechanism that we have described as matched-dependent behavior. He is also aware of "purposive imitation," or copying, which occurs under conditions of trial and error. He has made a most important contribution in stressing the rôle of the "model," who gives cues to the copier, and he is aware of the fact that such cues narrow the range of trial-and-error behavior and therefore hasten the perfection of the copied act. Bernard also stresses that the shifting and recombining of responses necessary to produce the matched act in the imitator may occur internally or "symbolically," and this results in the (apparent) sudden appearance of a matched act. Bernard is acutely aware of the importance of the social milieu in influencing imitative behavior. Lacking a learning theory which adequately stresses reward, he does not focus attention upon just those crucial social conditions which reward imitation. In his examples, like so many others, the traces of a reinforcement doctrine can be detected, but it is not explicit in his formal theory.

Katz and Schanck

These authors are essentially associationists. They reject an instinct position and are clear on the fact that imitative behavior is learned. They do not, however, have a feasible account of the mechanism. One finds the paradoxical statement that imitative habits are fixed through "frequency and reward" (1938, p. 302). Actually, this statement is incompatible with the associationist theory, which receives the major emphasis.

Alexander Bain

Bain was one of the first to take a decisive stand against the instinctive theory of imitation. He noted that very young children do not imitate, that imitative behavior appears very slowly in the life of the child, that it frequently disappears once it has been hit upon (1855, p. 407). He has also made the discerning observation that adults imitate small children much more than small children do adults.[6] This observation was later repeated by Watson.

His theory of the mechanism, however, turns out to be a simple associationist theory based on repetition.

Imitation progresses with the acquired habits. . . . The grand process of trial and error brings on the first coincidence between a movement and the appearance of that movement in another person; while repetition of the coincidence leads to a cohesion sufficient to render the imitation perfectly easy . . . the fixing of the association . . . is the most difficult part of the process [1855, p. 408].

Mere repetition of the connection of coincidental stimuli and response brings about imitative behavior. The mode of fixing the association was unknown to Bain. Why imitative rather than non-imitative acts are selected out of a welter of chance acts for association with matched stimuli is also unclear from this exposition. Just such considerations drive the theorist to take a reinforcement position on learning.

[6] This takes place in the phase before children have learned to imitate adults. Later, children seem to imitate adults much more than adults do children.

J. B. Watson

It is difficult to state exactly the position of J. B. Watson on imitation. He is quite sure that it is not instinctive, and he has given very instructive examples of this fact (1925, p. 324). He is sure that imitative responses are learned and by the technique of conditioning. The question becomes: What is Watson's position on the nature of the conditioning of responses? He seems to take basically an associationist stand. In one paragraph, he seems to approve of Thorndike's law-of-effect position (1919, p. 259), but he does not actually give a consistent statement of his own theory in these terms.

Watson does point out the importance of *reverse imitation*. He writes, ". . . the parents by repeating the sound constantly offer a stimulus for that which the infant's vocal mechanisms are just set to utter" (1919, p. 319). From our standpoint, the influence of the parents in this case would be that of secondary rewarding agents.

Kimball Young

Young is quite clear that imitative behavior is learned behavior. He writes that imitation is to be regarded as "a particular form of conditioning explained by the fact that the response of another becomes the conditioned stimulus for one's own response to the stimulus" (1932, p. 587).[7] He rejects the instinct theory of imitation; but he does not provide a description of a physical mechanism by which the imitative act, or indeed other habits, can be learned. With him, as with so many others, the defect in his position is not specific to imitation theory but rather to his psychology of learning. He has understood *the fact of temporal association in Pavlovian experiments between stimuli and response, but has not noticed that this association must take place under conditions of drive and drive reduction if the connection between the stimulus and response is to be fixed.* Apart from this fact,

[7] From Young, "Imitation." In *The Encyclopaedia of the Social Sciences.* By permission of The Macmillan Company, publishers.

Young provides a very useful general summary of the history of the concept in his *Encyclopaedia* article (1932, p. 587).

III

In this group are put those writers who have stressed that imitative behavior is learned and, moreover, have indicated that this learning takes place as a result of reward and punishment. These workers differ, naturally, in the clarity with which they have expounded this doctrine and also in the detail with which they have applied it to imitative behavior itself. No completely satisfactory statement comes from any one of them, but it is obvious that they have put succeeding workers on the highroad to a solution of the problem.

E. L. Thorndike

Thorndike has played an important rôle in straightening out imitation theory. He sees no evidence for a "potent tendency of mankind to do what it sees done" (1940, p. 331).[8] His experiments on chicks, cats, and dogs have placed a firm barrier against continued thinking in terms of an innate tendency to imitate. In each of these experiments, he has shown that mere observation of a successful solution does not put the observing animal in any better position to make the same solution. Thorndike holds that imitative habits are generated like any other habits, "by the laws of instinct, exercise, and effect" (1911, p. 251).[9] He is, moreover, quite concrete, as many writers are not, on the powerful influence of the family and social structure in setting up the conditions for imitation. He writes, "Behavior will gravitate toward what is approved and away from what is ridiculed or scorned . . ." (1940, p. 333),[10] and this tendency is as characteristic of

[8] From Thorndike, *Human Nature and the Social Order.* By permission of The Macmillan Company, publishers.
[9] From Thorndike, *Animal Intelligence.* By permission of The Macmillan Company, publishers.
[10] From Thorndike, *Human Nature and the Social Order.* By permission of The Macmillan Company, publishers.

imitative behavior as of any other kind of response. He does not, however, go into detail about the societal conditions under which imitation is rewarded or ridiculed.

Thorndike's position on the details of the mechanism of imitation has never been very well worked out and is not especially consistent. He is capable of saying that some imitative acts are undoubtedly instinctive, such as babies smiling, yelling, looking, listening, running, and the like (1913, pp. 120–121). Undoubtedly, all of these responses are in the innate hierarchy of every child, but it is difficult to see how they can be automatically set off by similar responses in another. Other cases of imitation are "mere adjuncts to the ordinary process of habit formation" (1911, p. 252).[11]

The result of training is expressed by Thorndike as follows: The idea of an act may by previous training lead to the act, and then the sight of others doing the act may cause the thought of the act which then leads to the act (1913, p. 175). This explanation, while it seems concrete in principle, is not scientifically very precise. It does not, for instance, stress that "the idea of an act" is itself a response which stands in series with the gross muscular aspects of the act. Apart from linguistic matters, however, the essence of a useful theory seems to be present in Thorndike. The purist will also feel some objection upon reading in Thorndike that "the child also may feel instinctively a satisfaction when his chance sound is like one he hears" (1911, p. 253).[12] It does not seem possible that this satisfaction can be innate. When such satisfaction is experienced, it must be because the "chance sound" has by some means acquired a secondary rewarding value. Thorndike, like many others, has found it difficult to strip his theory completely of all instinctive references and go on to an unconditional position that imitative behavior is learned. He has nevertheless greatly advanced the fundamental analysis of the problem.

11 From Thorndike, *Animal Intelligence*. By permission of The Macmillan Company, publishers.
12 From Thorndike, *Animal Intelligence*. By permission of The Macmillan Company, publishers.

L. T. Hobhouse

Hobhouse is to be classed with those who believe that imitation is learned through reward. He believed that he found evidence in experiments on his pet dog and cat that they had profited by mere observation of another animal or person successfully carrying out the necessary act. His results, however, are to be questioned because of the poor observational and experimental techniques of his day. The animals were not rewarded for merely looking at the correct solution, but only when they themselves hit upon it and carried it through (1915, pp. 184–185). Thorndike's cat experiment would seem to dispose of the contention of Hobhouse. It is impressive, nevertheless, that Hobhouse put the whole problem upon the positive side and attempted to *teach* animals to imitate. He did not conceive the experimental situation quite accurately and so was not very successful. He did not grasp the fact, for instance, that the watching animal must be *performing* the act while the leader animal is performing it and must then be rewarded for its total watching-performing behavior. When these conditions are met, imitative behavior can be taught even to albino rats.

A. T. Jersild

Jersild has presented the familiar statement of disbelief in the instinctive character of imitation; contrariwise, he stresses that children can learn to imitate (1933, p. 181). He further makes the law-of-effect interpretation, in writing that if a child "repeatedly receives satisfying attention when he returns a smile, echoes a sound, or speaks a word similar to the expressions made by his elders, the acts of his elders may eventually without added prompting, become effective stimuli" (1933, p. 181). Jersild does not, of course, give a theory as to how the attention of parents becomes "satisfying" to the child. It is quite certain that he is correct that imitative responses may be fixed by such secondary rewards as parental praise, smiles, and the like. It must be stressed, however, that these secondary reward stimuli have acquired their reassuring value over a long period in the early learning history of the child.

John Dewey

Dewey's position is rather puzzling. He says, on the one hand, "What is called the effect of imitation is mainly the product of conscious instruction and of the selective influence exercised by the unconscious confirmations and ratifications of those with whom one associates" (1930, p. 42).[13] On the other hand, he adds, "Used for a purpose, the imitative instinct may, like any other instinct, become a factor in the development of effective action" (1930, p. 43).[14] We are inclined to believe that the second citation is a careless use of language on Dewey's part rather than any ratification of the instinct theory. The whole sense of his discussion is to stress the social context of imitative behavior and to deny the instinctive presupposition. He stresses the like-mindedness of human beings as a result of the similar circumstances under which they are trained (*same* behavior), and he thinks no imitative assumption is needed to account for this fact. It is obvious, however, that his discussion is useful only in the broadest outlines. He has no detailed description of conditions under which either matched-dependent behavior or copying can be taught.

IV

In this final group we will include theorists with a variety of points of view. Some take no position on the genesis of imitative behavior, but simply assume it to exist at some given point along the life line. Others hold theories which are internally contradictory and in which the elements have about equal weight, so that it is difficult to state any central position. Still others emphasize sociological variables at the expense of the psychological. It is always possible that an in-

[13] From Dewey, *Democracy and Education.* By permission of The Macmillan Company, publishers.

[14] From Dewey, *Democracy and Education.* By permission of The Macmillan Company, publishers.

justice has been done to some one person by classifying him under this eclectic heading.

Aristotle

Aristotle has the distinction of having first ascribed an important rôle to the fact of imitation. He noted that man "is the most imitative of living creatures, and through imitation learns his earliest lessons; and no less universal is the pleasure felt in things imitated" (Butcher, 1922, p. 15). Aristotle also said that the "instinct of imitation is implanted in man from childhood" (1922, p. 15). If taken literally at his word, Aristotle would be classified as an instinct theorist. There is some reason to believe, however, that it is Butcher, the translator, who is the instinct theorist and not Aristotle. A competent student of Greek[15] thinks this to be the case, adding that in Aristotle's time the instinct vs. learning theory dilemma was not conceptualized. Aristotle certainly believed that imitative behavior appeared early and was essential in human learning as well as in artistic representation. If Aristotle was not an instinctivist, neither was he a learning theorist. He took no position on the problem of the source of imitativeness. He apparently observed only that imitation is "in our nature" (1922, p. 15), but he did not attempt to solve the problem as to when or how it gets there.

Joseph Peterson

It is a far jump in time from Aristotle to Peterson, but this is one of the hazards of belonging to an eclectic grouping. Peterson gives a whole series of positions on the imitation dilemma. He believes that it can be innate, learned, socially influenced, a result of trial-and-error behavior, and the like (1922–23, pp. 1–15). No one of these theories apparently becomes dominant in his thought. He notes the rôle of rewards and punishments in some cases of imitation. The effect of such notation is, however, canceled out by other competing statements which he makes. Peterson calls attention to the fact that there is a good deal of confusion concerning the

15 Mr. Geoffrey Gorer of the Institute of Human Relations.

detailed mechanism by which imitative acts are learned or when they are learned. In attempting to summarize the theory of his time on imitation he seems to have succeeded in giving the correct impression of confusion.

Wolfgang Köhler

Köhler takes the position that chimpanzees (and other primates)

will "imitate" with ease as soon as the same conditions as those required in man are present, i.e., if they are already familiar with, and understand the action to be imitated. If, *in such circumstances*, there is any reason to watch the model (animal or man), and if his actions are of interest, then either the animal "takes part" or "tries the same solution." . . . Where there is no trace of understanding

chimpanzees do not imitate (1927, p. 222). He contends that although imitative behavior in chimpanzees, when it occurs, is similar to that of man, this does not at all prove the existence of an "instinct of imitation" (1925, p. 685). The question then becomes this: How does the chimpanzee know that the solution he has tried is the *same* as that tried by the other chimpanzee or man? Or one might ask: How does the act of "doing the same" acquire a reward value? Until it does acquire such value, it is difficult to see why the chimpanzee should "try the same solution." The stimulus given off to the watcher by the animal making the correct solution must have secondary drive-exciting value if it is to produce similar behavior in the beholder. And, granted that chimpanzees will imitate when placed under the same condition as men experience when they imitate, what indeed are these conditions? Köhler does not touch this problem, so we must consider his observation a useful, but isolated, statement of fact.

G. H. Mead

Mead did not devote much attention to a theory of imitation. He felt, for one thing, that social consciousness is the presupposition of imitation. Here he was directing himself especially to the problem of copying, and what he said is, in a sense, true. It does not seem, however, that he had an adequate theory of social consciousness itself, and so the solution of the imitation problem was not much advanced. He felt that "the conception of imitation as it has functioned in social psychology needs to be developed into a theory of social stimulation and response and of the social situations which these stimulations and responses create" (1909, p. 406). With this we can heartily agree and state that we have been attempting to do exactly what is called for. Lurking in Mead's work is the associationist matrix of learning theory in which his thought apparently functioned. Like many other scholars, he did not grasp the fundamental elements of the Pavlovian experiments. In stressing interstimulation and response as characteristic of social interaction, he has pointed to a part of the crucial mechanism; but it appears that he has omitted the essential conditions for such interstimulation, which are, of course, drive and reward. Pavlovian theory without these elements is an eviscerated affair.

Ellsworth Faris

More detailed attention is given to the imitative mechanism by Faris. He distinguishes between immediate and unwitting imitative behavior (1937, p. 75), slow and unwitting imitation (1937, p. 78), and conscious copying. He gives little attention to the actual mechanisms by which imitative acts evolve, although he seems to believe that imitation is learned behavior. In so far as he has a psychological theory, it may be contained in the following sentence: "When however the person is alone this same type of activity tends to go on, following the pattern of associated behavior" (1937, p. 79). Evidently the phrase "pattern of associated behavior" refers to some principle of temporal association of stimuli and responses. The analysis is useful in stressing the importance of general cultural variables; but since Faris does not understand how imitation is learned, he cannot specify the social conditions under which imitative learning is likely to occur.

The data are, for the most part, imaginary examples. Faris contends that no single psychological mechanism can account for all of the processes which are labeled by the lay word "imitation." To this we agree. We do not, however, agree that imitation cannot be brought within the framework of a single general theory.

LaPiere and Farnsworth

These authors have a very stimulating discussion of imitation. They have fixed on the copying process as the important one and have adopted the term "model" from Bernard. They put forth the interesting suggestion that the term "imitation" be abandoned altogether; in place of it, they prefer to speak of "learning by human example." They stress that one of the great advantages of a model is that it limits the range of trial-and-error behavior and thus increases the chance of a successful response (1936, p. 126). They state also that the child must be motivated in the copying process, and they are almost, but not quite, clear that he must be rewarded as well (1936, p. 126). They write, for instance, "The selection of models is determined for the individual by short-time results—getting attention, a piece of candy, a new dress—and may or may not be of life-adjustment value in the long run" (1936, p. 127).

It is very significant that whenever an author attempts to cleave to real examples, he must deal with cases where drive and reward are operating. This has served to confirm us in the faith that reality stands on the side of a reinforcement theory. It has been repeatedly noted that authors may espouse one formal theory of imitation (say an associationist one) and yet, when they get to discussing examples, they must at least give evidence that reinforcement principles are operating. LaPiere and Farnsworth have a particularly valuable discussion of the social induction of a child into community life by means of a "hierarchy of graduated models" (1936, p. 133). Their discussion is an original contribution, surprising in a textbook, both as to the importance of social variables and as to the utility of the copying mechanism.

C. H. Cooley

Cooley's position implies a learning theory but gives no detailed mechanism by which imitative behavior can come about. He wrote, for instance:

It is a doctrine now generally taught by psychologists that the idea of an action is itself a motive to that action, and tends intrinsically to produce it unless something intervenes to prevent. This being the case, it would appear that we must always have some impulse to do what we see done, provided it is something we understand sufficiently to be able to form a definite idea of doing it. I am inclined to the view that it is unnecessary to assume, in man, a special imitative instinct [1902, pp. 26–27].

Cooley performed the useful task of attempting to produce imitation in young children. He noted that it was not present in the baby's repertory at the outset. Referring to his own baby, he wrote:

Until he was more than two years and a half old all that I noticed that was obviously imitative, in the sense of a visible or audible repetition of the acts of others, was the utterance of about six words that he learned to say during the second year [1902, pp. 21–22].

Cooley therefore plainly maintained that imitative behavior is somehow learned and is a result of trial-and-error processes. Occasional isolated, simple manual imitative acts were observed during the first year. It seems likely that if Cooley had understood learning principles, he might have secured from his child, had he desired, a number of imitative actions much earlier than the third year of life. Cooley noted, with an apparent contradiction, that imitative copying came suddenly. He said, "Imitation came all at once . . ." (1902, p. 23). What Cooley probably observed was the end of a long learning process during which the child had acquired a large number of units of social behavior by trial-and-error learning which could then be rapidly and mentally recombined and could issue as imitative trials in a copying situation.

Charles Darwin

Darwin came across the problem of imitation in studying one of his own children. He was one of the first to call attention to the fact of reverse imitation. He wrote: "Another infant used to amuse himself by shaking his head laterally: we praised and imitated him, saying, 'Shake your head'; and when he was seven months old, he would sometimes do so on being told without any other guide" (1877, p. 290). Although Darwin made no theoretical fuss about it, praise apparently functioned in rewarding the imitative behavior in question. The form of the praise is not stated. Darwin recorded that by the time the child in question was eleven and a half months old, he could readily imitate all sorts of actions, such as shaking his head and saying, "Ah," to any dirty object (1877, p. 291). Darwin did not report how these responses were fixed to parental imitative stimuli, but there seems no alternative to a reward theory of the type hinted at in the observation above.

Meyer Fortes

Fortes has a very sensible account of imitative behavior, although one not concerned with theoretical questions as to the origin of imitation. He states that "Tale children do not automatically copy the actions or words of older children or adults with whom they happen to be without rhyme or reason and merely for the sake of 'imitation'" (1938, pp. 44–45). He implies a reinforcement theory in stating that imitative behavior must be adaptive if it is to survive, and adds "in an unfamiliar or difficult situation the best adaptation is to copy the actions and words of any one who understands the situation" (1938, pp. 45–46). This is a statement of what we mean by matched-dependent behavior; an unskilled child imitates when he needs the cues provided by a skilled child to reach reward. Fortes concludes that imitation becomes a generalized response in Tale children between three and six years of age. He writes that such children seem "to develop a habit of mimicking older children in whose activities" they are trying to participate (1938, p. 46). Fortes gives no detailed description of the mechanisms involved in such mimicking and copying, but he is quite explicit about the social circumstances under which imitative learning occurs. It is reassuring to have this observation indicating that a reinforcement theory of imitative learning may have cross-cultural relevance.

Other Theorists

Park and Burgess take a consistent sociological position on imitation. They do not, of course, accept an instinct theory. They provide a very valuable emphasis, which has been followed by many authors, on imitation as conscious copying. They write, "In imitation attention is alert, now on the copy and now on the response" (1924, p. 346). Imitative activity tends to reproduce the copy. They do not attempt to suggest a psychological theory of the principles of imitation nor to outline the social circumstances under which it is learned. Reuter and Hart apparently follow Park and Burgess in their emphasis. They write: "Imitation is the more or less conscious and intentional reproduction of copy. It is the mechanism of the learning process" (1933, p. 271). This is a strange inversion of emphasis. What needs to be explained is how copying is learned before one can consider the question of how one learns by copying—though it is a fact that copying can become an acquired drive and thus impel independent learning. Boring, Langfeld, and Weld hold approximately the same viewpoint as do the foregoing pairs of authors. They write: "Imitation in this case is merely the first stage of learning. Imitation is the conscious or unconscious attempt of an individual to reproduce in his thought or behavior the same pattern of thought or behavior that he has perceived in another individual" (1939, pp. 12–13).[16] They beg the entire question by indicating that imita-

[16] Reprinted by permission, from *Introduction to Psychology* by Boring, Langfeld and Weld, published by John Wiley & Sons, Inc.

tion is "the first stage of learning." They have no account of how imitative behavior is learned and pay no particular attention to the social conditions under which such learning takes place. We agree (see Chapter XII) that it is correct to say that people can learn by imitation, but we think that in order to make this statement significant, one must analyze the circumstances under which the units of copying behavior are themselves learned.

R. M. MacIver distinguishes between imitativeness and imitation, since the former, he believes, is an attitude and the latter a process (1931, p. 47). It would probably be more correct to say that imitativeness is an acquired drive. MacIver is not helpful on our particular problem—the analysis of the process of imitation. He starts out by assuming as existing the very mechanisms which we want to explain.

B. EXPERIMENTAL WORK ON IMITATIVE BEHAVIOR

Many investigators have studied the capacity of animals or children to imitate; no experimenter seems to have set out deliberately to study the capacity of his subjects to *learn* to imitate. Systematic attempts to take account of learning have been directed only toward eliminating it from the experimental situation. The fact that experimenters studying imitation were interested in ruling out *independent* learning during the experiment, as a possible explanation of their results, seems to have prevented them from becoming interested in the possibility that imitation itself could be learned. Some experimenters were interested in proving that animals had no instinctive tendency to imitate; others were interested in demonstrating that animals had an intelligent capacity to imitate. The latter did not attempt to discover how animals found out when to use this capacity.

Experimenters have investigated whether an individual is able, without further training, to imitate at a particular time; but little attention has been paid to the possibility that the effects of previous training in other situations might generalize to the test. Valentine (1930–31, p. 105) concludes: "The psychology of imitation is in a somewhat chaotic state, partly owing to the ambiguity of the term and partly owing to disagreement as to facts."

Experiments on Animals

Very little experimental work has been done on imitation in rats. Berry (1906) reports observations purporting to show that rats can imitate. Watson (1908b) questions Berry's results. Small (1901, p. 213) says that when two rats meet in a maze, one seldom follows the other. Small (1899) also found no evidence for imitation in a simple problem-box experiment on rats. Bruce (1941) found that there was no tendency for thirsty rats to imitate each other in the path which they took across a table top to water. Warden, Jenkins, and Warner (1936) summarize the studies on imitation and conclude that below the primates imitation among mammalia is all but nonexistent.

The popular conception is that monkeys and apes have a natural tendency to imitate. Thorndike (1901) tested monkeys for imitation in problem-box situations and reports that he observed no behavior which seemed due to genuine imitation, either in experimental situations or in the animals' free behavior in their cages. Kinnaman (1902) reports that a female monkey imitated a male monkey in solving a problem-box dilemma.

Watson (1908a) tested one baboon and three monkeys on seven different problems, giving the animals an opportunity sometimes to imitate the experimenter and sometimes to imitate a monkey. He concludes, "I unhesitatingly affirm that there was never the slightest evidence of inferential imitation manifested in the actions of any of these animals" (1908a, p. 172). Haggerty (1909) gave eleven monkeys many tests in a number of different situations. He reports a considerable degree of imitation. A number of writers have criticized him on the ground that he gave the animals so many trials that they may have learned to solve the problem independently, and hence may have been exhibiting *same* behavior rather than imitation. Pfungst (1912), after observing some two hundred monkeys and apes, concludes that these animals seldom imitate each other.

Yerkes (1934, p. 272) reports that chimpanzees can be influenced to chew filter paper if the experimenter puts a strip in his mouth and chews "noisily and with apparent satisfaction."[17] After being tested several times, the animals cease to be influenced by the example of the experimenter. This would seem to be a case of the extinction of an unrewarded tendency to imitate.

In a recent, careful study of imitation, Warden and Jackson (1935) tested fifteen rhesus monkeys, giving them six tests on each of four different tasks. They conclude that monkeys "exhibit at once a strong tendency to imitate their fellows. . . . Moreover, it appears that observational learning is much more economical than ordinary trial-and-error learning for monkeys as for men" (1935, p. 123). They report no test for subsequent behavior without the leader. Warden and Jackson summarize as follows their standards for a good experiment on imitation:

(*a*) The task must be novel and sufficiently complex, (*b*) the response must appear immediately after observing the imitatee, (*c*) practice must be excluded by the experimental conditions, (*d*) the act of the imitator must be substantially identical with that of the imitatee, and (*e*) a sufficient number of instances must occur, under varied conditions, to eliminate the chance factor [1935, pp. 103–104].

Point *c* of these criteria represents the traditional position of most investigators: that of trying to exclude independent learning from the experiments, rather than to investigate learning to imitate.

Spence (1937) presents an excellent critical review of the literature on primate imitation. He points out that the movement of parts of the apparatus by the leader, and the ap-

---

[17] It would be interesting to determine whether animals that had never had experience eating together would exhibit this behavior.

pearance of food when this animal succeeds, may enhance the stimulus value of that part of the apparatus and hence make the imitator more likely to respond to it. Spence believes that none of the reported experiments, not even those of Warden and Jackson, are completely free of this artifact.

It is obvious that different experimenters have secured apparently contradictory results. It is difficult to come to any certain conclusion as to the causes of these apparent contradictions. On the one hand, they may have been due to the fact that different experimenters tested the animals on different tasks in different ways. On the other hand, they may have been produced by uncontrolled factors in the previous history of the animals which had rewarded some animals for imitating and some for non-imitating in situations similar enough to those used in the experiment so that generalization could occur.

One investigator tested two animals differing markedly in their past training, though he did not employ the same tests on these animals. Shepherd (1923) found that a chimpanzee failed to imitate the experimenter in pulling in a piece of banana with a T-rake. Previously, he had tested a chimpanzee that had had a special type of training: it had been a performer on the stage. This animal (Shepherd, 1915) imitated the experimenter in pressing on the stem of a watch correctly several times, but did not press hard enough to open it. The chimpanzee is also reported to have copied a *T* and a *W* made by the experimenter on a tablet with a pencil. Shepherd is in doubt as to whether or not to call these acts imitative, because the animal may have learned them as part of its histrionic training.

Two experiments seem to have a closer bearing than the rest upon the present hypothesis. One of these, by Crawford and Spence (1939), shows that one chimpanzee may derive benefit from watching another chimpanzee solve a discrimination problem. This study is particularly relevant because it demonstrates that the amount of benefit is determined by the way the reward is administered to the observing animal while the other animal is solving the problem. Since no description is given of the details of what the observing animal did before it was rewarded, a more penetrating analysis of these results is impossible.

The animal experiment most clearly relevant to the problems dealt with in this book is one by Crawford (1937). It is an experiment in which animals learned coöperation by trial and error with a certain amount of guidance from the experimenter. First, each animal was trained to pull in, by means of a rope, a sliding platform containing food. During this stage of training, each animal was trained to time his responses by pulling when the experimenter said, "Pull!" After the animals had been trained separately, they were tested in pairs; the force required to pull in the platform was increased, so that one animal could not pull it in alone. Three stages in the development of coöperative behavior are reported: (1) simultaneous responses to the word "pull" as an external cue from the experimenter; (2) watching the other animal's response and timing a pull to coincide with the partner's; (3) soliciting the partner, with gestures and vocalizations, to pull. In the course of the second stage of acquiring coöperative behavior, it is clear that, because only simultaneous responses moved the reward platform, the animals learned by trial and error to time their pulls by watching each other. In this case, the imitation acquired was to time a response which had already been learned. When an animal that had not had preliminary training in pulling was used, there was no learning by the untrained animal nor tuition by the trained one. This experiment seems to parallel some of the social conditions in which human imitation is rewarded.

Some Studies on Children[18]

Valentine's study (1930–31) is fairly typical of the reports on detailed observations of a few children. His observations, made on his own children, clearly demonstrate that they per-

[18] We have demonstrated (*a*) that children can learn to imitate under appropriate conditions, and (*b*) that these conditions are frequently present in our society. The problem of evaluating the detailed data which specialists

form imitative responses, but leave one in doubt as to the origin of these responses. It is sometimes difficult from the material presented in the notes to determine whether the responses really were specifically elicited by the model's response, or were merely responses frequently occurring to almost any cue.

In one of the few observations reported quantitatively, Valentine (1930–31, p. 108) tabulates the number of croons emitted by a thirty-two-day-old child during minutes when the experimenter was and was not crooning. He reports more croons from the child while the experimenter was crooning than while the experimenter was not crooning. The present authors have calculated the statistical reliability of this difference, applying Student's method suitable for small samples (Yule and Kendall, 1937). There are only two chances in one hundred that this difference would have been produced by chance. The experimenter's voice apparently did have some effect on the child. It is not definitely proved, however, that this effect was a specific connection between the specific cue, crooning, and the response of crooning in the child. Crooning seems to be more characteristic of the relaxed than of the fretful child. It may be that the sound of the experimenter's voice served merely to pacify and relax the fretful, hungry child,[19] thereby putting it into a state in which "spontaneous" crooning was much more likely to occur. The sound of the voice could have acquired such reward value through association with feeding. As a control, it would be interesting to note what effect some other stimulus, such as the child's bottle, might have had upon the child's rate of crooning.

Valentine's results suggest that not all responses which a

on child behavior have collected and of determining whether or not learning can account for *all* types of imitative behavior which have been observed lies outside of our particular fields, and is left to those whose greater experience with children gives them better bases for judgment. The following studies are mentioned as samples of the types of data available.

[19] Apparently, this test was given while the child was hungry. In one of Valentine's notes (1930–31, p. 108), he reports, "B. began to cry for food, so test stopped."

child is capable of performing can be elicited imitatively, that not all people are imitated equally, and that the child will respond imitatively at some times and not at others. Such observations would be consistent with learning theory.

An observation which Valentine mentions in passing (1930–31, p. 114) shows that one imitative act can be learned. Concerning a 388-day-old child, he reports:

To my amazement I was told that the nurse had taught Y. to wink. I was sceptical. Y. was brought and at E.'s command and example winked definitely with the left eye several times: and so later, in response to my winks, without any command. Sometimes the right eye-lid also moved: but several times I have to-day seen a distinct closing of the left eye without movement of the right eye-lid.

Valentine gives no systematic treatment to the problem of learning, save to notice that learned coördinations are involved in some acts which may be elicited imitatively. In his conclusions (1930–31, p. 131), he lists as relevant to imitation a number of different factors, making statements such as:

5. Primary, involuntary, or purposeless imitation seems to be due to the monopolization of attention for a moment by some fascinating impression.
6. Some imitations seem to serve the purpose of helping the subject to realize or enter into the experience of the imitatee more vividly.
7. Some imitations are of a reflex type, if the term reflex can be applied where sight provides the only stimulus.

He does not consider learning important enough to be listed with these factors in his conclusions.

A number of investigators have given standardized tests for imitation to children of different ages. Reliable norms of behavior have been established in connection with more general projects of constructing tests for studying mental development. These studies give relatively clear evidence on what responses children are able to make imitatively at different ages; they do not analyze the factors responsible for the appearance of these imitative responses.

Shirley's (1933) tests seem to indicate an upward trend through the ages of fifty-four to seventy-four weeks in the amount of imitative behavior observed. She notes, however, that it was extremely difficult to determine whether or not the behavior was clearly imitative, because the copy was so inexact.

At slightly more advanced ages, evidence collected with various mental tests clearly demonstrates that as children grow older, their ability to reproduce a model which they are told to copy improves. In a chapter on adaptive behavior, Thompson (Gesell, *et al.*, 1940) gives norms for a number of tasks involving copying. At eighteen months, the child is able to build a tower of two-to-four blocks after seeing the adult do it; at two years, he is able to build a tower of seven blocks. After a demonstration of paperfolding, the two-year-old child may turn over the edge but not crease the paper; the four-year-old child will copy horizontal, vertical, and diagonal folds. Sentence repetition improves from three-to-four syllables at two years to twelve-to-thirteen syllables at six years.

Tests with block-building seem to indicate that it is easier to copy a model structure if the child can watch it being built than if he has only the finished project as a model. At three years, the child is able to copy a bridge of blocks after a demonstration; at four years, he is able to succeed from the model alone. At four years, he is able to copy a gate of blocks after demonstration; at five years, he succeeds with only a model present.

In the revised Stanford-Binet, Terman and Merrill (1937) report norms on sixteen items involving copying between the years two and seven, inclusive. It is clear that the child's ability to copy is greater at higher mental ages. Similarly, Bühler (1935) lists eight tests, ranging from mimicking the friendly or angry expression of an adult at the sixth month[20] to copying diagrammatic drawings at the fifth year.

The data from tests of the type which have been mentioned indicate what children do, but not how they become able to do it. In some activities, such as block-building, a comparison of the child's behavior in the copying situation with his behavior when playing alone seems to indicate that he acquires the criteria of sameness and difference (so that he can try to copy) about as rapidly as he acquires the motor skills which enable him to balance one block on another. In other instances, such as the copying of letters, it is clear that the children are able to perform the coördinations involved in making the letter *E* before they have acquired responses to sameness and difference which enable them to discriminate that an *E* that is turned on its side or upside down is incorrect.

The types of imitation and copying employed in mental tests seem to involve situations such as block-building, drawing, repeating words, and so on, in which the child has had ample social opportunity for learning to imitate.

[20] The origin of this early imitative act is not clear. It would be interesting to observe the reactions of children who were consistently glowered at while being fed and smiled at while frightened.

Kwint (1934) has demonstrated that the ability to mimic facial expressions improves with age. Six hundred and seventy-six subjects, ranging from four through sixteen years of age, were tested in this experiment.

REFERENCES

ADRIAN, E. D. (1928.) The basis of sensation. New York, W. W. Norton.

ALLPORT, F. H. (1924.) Social psychology. Cambridge, Mass., Houghton Mifflin, The Riverside Press.

ALLPORT, G. W. (1937.) Personality. New York, Henry Holt.

BAGEHOT, W. (1873.) Physics and politics. New York, D. Appleton.

BAIN, A. (1855.) The senses and the intellect. (First edition.) London, John W. Parker.

BAKKE, E. W. (1940.) The unemployed worker. New Haven, Yale University Press.

BALDWIN, J. M. (1895.) Mental development in the child and the race. New York, Macmillan.

—— (1891.) Handbook of psychology. New York, Henry Holt.

—— (1902.) Social and ethical interpretations in mental development. (Third edition.) New York, Macmillan.

—— (1911.) The individual and society. Boston, Richard G. Badger, The Gorham Press.

BARD, P. (1934.) Emotion I. The neuro-humoral basis of emotional reactions. In MURCHISON, C. (ed.), Handbook of general experimental psychology, pp. 264–311. Worcester, Mass., Clark University Press.

BEKHTEREV, V. M. (1932.) General principles of human reflexology. New York, International.

BERNARD, L. L. (1926.) An introduction to social psychology. New York, Henry Holt.

—— (1931.) Crowd. In SELIGMAN, E. R. A. (ed.), Encyclopaedia of the social sciences, pp. 612–613. New York, Macmillan.

BERRY, C. S. (1906.) The imitative tendency of white rats. Journal of Comparative Neurology, 16, 333–361.

BIRGE, J. S. (1941.) The rôle of verbal responses in transfer. Ph.D. dissertation, Yale University. Deposited in the Yale University Library.

BORING, E. G., LANGFELD, H. S., and WELD, H. P. (1939.) Introduction to psychology. New York, John Wiley.

BRUCE, R. H. (1941.) An experimental analysis of social factors affecting the performance of white rats. I. Performance in learning a simple field situation. *Journal of Comparative Psychology, 31,* 363–377.

Bühler, C. (1935.) From birth to maturity. London, Kegan Paul, Trench, Trubner.

Butcher, S. H. (1922.) The poetics of Aristotle. (Fourth edition.) London, Macmillan.

Cannon, W. B. (1929.) Bodily changes in pain, hunger, fear and rage. (Second edition.) New York, Appleton.

Cantril, H. (1940.) The invasion from Mars. Princeton, N. J., Princeton University Press.

Carlson, A. J. (1919.) The control of hunger in health and disease. Chicago, University of Chicago Press.

Cooley, C. H. (1902.) Human nature and the social order. New York, Scribner's.

Cournot, A. (1861.) L'Enchaînement des idées fondamentales dans les sciences et dans l'histoire, vol. I. Paris, L. Hachette.

Cowgill, G. R., *et al.* (1926.) Studies in the physiology of vitamins. IV. Vitamin B in relation to gastric motility. *American Journal of Physiology, 77,* 389–401.

Crawford, M. P. (1937–38.) The cooperative solving of problems by young chimpanzees. *Comparative Psychology Monographs, 14,* No. 68, 88 pp.

—— and Spence, K. W. (1939.) Observational learning of discrimination problems by chimpanzees. *Journal of Comparative Psychology, 27,* 133–147.

Darwin, C. (1877.) A biographical sketch of an infant. *Mind, 7,* 285–294.

Dashiell, J. F. (1928.) Fundamentals of objective psychology. Boston, Houghton Mifflin.

Davis, A., and Dollard, J. (1940.) Children of bondage. Washington, D. C., American Council on Education.

Davis, A., Gardner, B. B., and Gardner, M. R. (1941.) Deep south. Chicago, University of Chicago Press.

Dewey, J. (1930.) Democracy and education. New York, Macmillan.

Dixon, R. B. (1928.) The building of cultures. New York, Scribner's.

Dollard, J., *et al.* (1939.) Frustration and aggression. New Haven, Yale University Press.

EINSTEIN, A., and INFELD, L. (1938.) The evolution of physics. New York, Simon and Schuster.

ELLWOOD, C. A. (1917.) An introduction to social psychology. New York, D. Appleton.

FARIS, E. (1937.) The nature of human nature. New York, McGraw-Hill.

FOLSOM, J. K. (1931.) Social psychology. New York, Harper.

FORD, C. S. (1937.) A sample comparative analysis of material culture. *In* MURDOCK, G. P. (ed.), *Studies in the science of society*, pp. 225–246. New Haven, Yale University Press.

—— (1939.) Society, culture, and the human organism. *Journal of General Psychology, 20*, 135–179.

FORTES, M. (1938.) Social and psychological aspects of education in Taleland. *International Institute of African Languages and Cultures, Memorandum XVII*. London, Oxford University Press. (Pamphlet.)

GESELL, A., *et al.* (1940.) The first five years of life. New York, Harper.

GOLDENWEISER, A. A. (1922.) Early civilization. New York, Alfred A. Knopf.

GUTHRIE, E. R. (1935.) The psychology of learning. New York, Harper.

—— (1940.) Association and the law of effect. *Psychological Review, 47*, 127–148.

HAGGERTY, M. E. (1909.) Imitation in monkeys. *Journal of Comparative Neurology and Psychology, 19*, 337–455.

HILGARD, E. R., and MARQUIS, D. G. (1940.) Conditioning and learning. New York, D. Appleton-Century.

HOBHOUSE, L. T. (1915.) Mind in evolution. London, Macmillan.

HOLT, E. B. (1931.) Animal drive. London, Williams and Norgate.

HULL, C. L. (1920.) Quantitative aspects of the evolution of concepts. *Psychological Monographs, 28*, 85 pp.

—— (1929.) A functional interpretation of the conditioned reflex. *Psychological Review, 36*, 498–511.

—— (1930a.) Simple trial-and-error learning: a study in psychological theory. *Psychological Review, 37*, 241–256.

—— (1930b.) Knowledge and purpose as habit mechanisms. *Psychological Review, 37*, 511–525.

—— (1931.) Goal attraction and directing ideas conceived as habit phenomena. *Psychological Review, 38,* 487–506.

—— (1932.) The goal gradient hypothesis and maze learning. *Psychological Review, 39,* 25–43.

—— (1933.) Hypnosis and suggestibility. New York, D. Appleton-Century.

—— (1934a.) Learning: II. The factor of the conditioned reflex. *In* MURCHISON, C. (ed.), *Handbook of general experimental psychology,* pp. 382–455. Worcester, Mass., Clark University Press.

—— (1934b.) The concept of the habit-family hierarchy and maze learning. *Psychological Review, 41,* Part I, 33–52; Part II, 134–152.

—— (1934c.) The rat's speed-of-locomotion gradient in the approach to food. *Journal of Comparative Psychology, 17,* 393–422.

—— (1935.) The mechanism of the assembly of behavior segments in novel combinations suitable for problem solution. *Psychological Review, 42,* 219–245.

—— (1939a.) Simple trial-and-error learning—an empirical investigation. *Journal of Comparative Psychology, 27,* 233–258.

—— (1939b.) The problem of stimulus equivalence in behavior theory. *Psychological Review, 46,* 9–30.

—— (1941*.) Principles of behavior.

HUMPHREY, G. (1921.) Imitation and the conditioned reflex. *Pedagogical Seminary, 28,* 1–21.

JERSILD, A. T. (1933.) Child psychology. New York, Prentice-Hall.

KARPF, F. B. (1932.) American social psychology. New York, McGraw-Hill.

KATZ, D., and SCHANCK, R. L. (1938.) Social psychology. New York, John Wiley.

KINNAMAN, A. J. (1902.) Mental life of two *Macacus Rhesus* monkeys in captivity. *American Journal of Psychology, 13,* 98–148, 173–218.

KÖHLER, W. (1925.) Intelligence of apes. *Pedagogical Seminary, 32,* 674–690.

—— (1927.) The mentality of apes. (Second edition.) New York, Harcourt, Brace.

* An asterisk indicates the manuscript is in preparation for publication.

KROEBER, A. L. (1923.) Anthropology. New York, Harcourt, Brace.
—— (1940.) Stimulus diffusion. *American Anthropologist, 42,* 1–20.
KWINT, L. (1934.) Ontogeny of motility of the face. *Child Development, 5,* 1–12.

LAPIERE, R. T., and FARNSWORTH, P. R. (1936.) Social psychology. New York, McGraw-Hill.
LASHLEY, K. S. (1941*.) An examination of the "continuity theory" as applied to discriminative learning. *Journal of Genetic Psychology.*
LEEPER, R. (1935.) The rôle of motivation in learning: a study of the phenomenon of differential motivational control of the utilization of habits. *Journal of Genetic Psychology, 46,* 3–40.
LEWIS, M. M. (1936.) Infant speech. New York, Harcourt, Brace.
LINTON, R. (1936.) The study of man. New York, D. Appleton-Century.
—— (1940.) Acculturation in seven American Indian tribes. New York, D. Appleton-Century.
LIPPMANN, W. (1930.) Public opinion. New York, Macmillan.
LUNDBERG, G. A. (1939.) Foundations of sociology. New York, Macmillan.

McCARTHY, D. (1933.) Language development. *In* MURCHISON, C. (ed.), *Handbook of child psychology,* pp. 329–373. Worcester, Mass., Clark University Press.
McDOUGALL, W. (1908.) An introduction to social psychology. London, Methuen.
MACIVER, R. M. (1931.) Society, its structure and changes. New York, Ray Long & Richard R. Smith.
MEAD, G. H. (1909.) Social psychology as counterpart to physiological psychology. *Psychological Bulletin, 6,* No. 12, 401–408.
MILLER, N. E. (1934.) The perception of children: a genetic study employing the critical choice delayed reaction. *Journal of Genetic Psychology, 44,* 321–339.
—— (1935.) A reply to "sign-Gestalt or conditioned reflex?" *Psychological Review, 42,* 280–292.
——, and STEVENSON, S. S. (1936.) Agitated behavior of rats during experimental extinction and a curve of spontaneous recovery. *Journal of Comparative Psychology, 21,* 205–231.
—— (1941a.) An experimental investigation of acquired drives. *Psychological Bulletin, 38,* 534–535.

—— *et al.* (1941b.) The frustration-aggression hypothesis. *Psychological Review, 48,* 337–342.

MORGAN, C. L. (1896.) Habit and instinct. London, E. Arnold.

—— (1900.) Animal behavior. London, E. Arnold.

MOWRER, O. H. (1941.) The Freudian theories of anxiety: a reconciliation. Address given before Monday Night Group of the Institute of Human Relations, March 3, 1941. (Mimeographed.)

MURDOCK, G. P. (1934.) Our-primitive contemporaries. New York, Macmillan.

—— (1941*.) Sex regulation and social structure.

MURPHY, G., and MURPHY, L. B. (1931.) Experimental social psychology. New York, Harper.

OGBURN, W. F., and NIMKOFF, M. F. (1940.) Sociology. Cambridge, Mass., Houghton Mifflin, The Riverside Press.

PARK, R. E., and BURGESS, E. W. (1924.) Introduction to the science of sociology. Chicago, University of Chicago Press.

PAVLOV, I. P. (1927.) Conditioned reflexes. London, Humphrey Milford, Oxford University Press.

PETERSON, J. (1922–23.) Imitation and mental adjustment. *Journal of Abnormal and Social Psychology, 17,* 1–15.

PFUNGST, O. (1912.) Zur Psychologie der Affen. *Bericht über Kongress für experimentelle Psychologie, 5,* 200–205.

REUTER, E. B., and HART, C. W. (1933.) Introduction to sociology. New York, McGraw-Hill.

ROSE, W. B., STUCKY, C. J., and COWGILL, G. R. (1929–30.) Studies in the physiology of vitamins. X. Further contributions to the study of gastric motility in vitamin B deficiency. *American Journal of Physiology, 91,* 531–546.

ROSS, E. A. (1912.) Social psychology. New York, Macmillan.

SALTER, J. T. (1935.) Boss rule. New York, McGraw-Hill.

SAYCE, R. U. (1933.) Primitive arts and crafts. Cambridge, England, University Press.

SHEPHERD, W. T. (1915.) Some observations on the intelligence of the chimpanzee. *Journal of Animal Behavior, 5,* 391–396.

—— (1923.) Some observations and experiments on the intelligence of the chimpanzee and ourang. *American Journal of Psychology, 34,* 590–591.

SHIRLEY, M. M. (1933.) The first two years. Intellectual development. vol. 2. Minneapolis, University of Minnesota Press.

SMALL, W. S. (1899.) An experimental study of the mental processes of the rat. *American Journal of Psychology, 11,* 133–165.

—— (1901.) Experimental study of the mental processes of the rat. II. *American Journal of Psychology, 12,* 206–239.

SMITH, G. E., MALINOWSKI, B., SPINDEN, H. J., GOLDENWEISER, A. (1927.) Culture. New York, W. W. Norton.

SMITH, S., and GUTHRIE, E. R. (1927.) General psychology in terms of behavior. New York, D. Appleton.

SPENCE, K. W. (1937.) Experimental studies of learning and the higher mental processes in infra-human primates. *Psychological Bulletin, 34,* 806–850.

STONE, C. P. (1929a.) The age factor in animal learning: I. Rats in the problem box and the maze. *Genetic Psychology Monographs, 5,* 1–130.

—— (1929b.) The age factor in animal learning: II. Rats on a multiple light discrimination box and a difficult maze. *Genetic Psychology Monographs, 6,* 125–202.

SUMNER, W. G., and KELLER, A. G. (1927.) The science of society. (Four vols.) New Haven, Yale University Press.

TARDE, G. (1903.) The laws of imitation. (Trans. by E. C. Parsons.) New York, Henry Holt.

TERMAN, L. M. (1904.) A preliminary study in the psychology and pedagogy of leadership. *Pedagogical Seminary, 11,* 413–451.

——, and MERRILL, M. A. (1937.) Measuring intelligence. New York, Houghton Mifflin.

THORNDIKE, E. L. (1901.) The mental life of the monkeys. *Psychological Monographs, 3,* No. 5, 57 pp.

—— (1911.) Animal intelligence. New York, Macmillan.

—— (1913.) Educational psychology. The original nature of man. vol. 1. New York, Teachers College, Columbia University.

—— (1914.) Educational psychology. New York, Columbia University, Bureau of Publications of Teachers College.

—— (1940.) Human nature and the social order. New York, Macmillan.

THURSTONE, L. L. (1928.) The fundamentals of statistics. New York, Macmillan.

TOLMAN, E. C. (1932.) Purposive behavior in animals and men. New York, D. Appleton-Century.

—— (1933.) Sign-Gestalt or conditioned reflex? *Psychological Review, 40,* 246–255.

ROTTER, W. (1917.) Instincts of the herd in peace and war. New York, Macmillan.

VALENTINE, C. W. (1930–31.) The psychology of imitation with special reference to early childhood. *British Journal of Psychology, 21,* 105–132.

WARDEN, C. J., and JACKSON, T. A. (1935.) Imitative behavior in the Rhesus monkey. *Journal of Genetic Psychology, 46,* 103–125.

WARDEN, C. J., JENKINS, T. N., and WARNER, L. H. (1936.) Comparative psychology, vertebrates. New York, Ronald.

WARNER, W. L. (1941*.) Yankee city. New Haven, Yale University Press.

WATSON, J. B. (1908a.) Imitation in monkeys. *Psychological Bulletin, 5,* 169–178.

—— (1908b.) Recent literature on mammalian behavior. *Psychological Bulletin, 5,* 195–205.

—— (1919.) Psychology from the standpoint of a behaviorist. Chicago, J. B. Lippincott.

—— (1925.) What the nursery has to say about instincts. *Pedagogical Seminary, 32,* 293–326.

WENDT, G. R. (1936.) An interpretation of inhibition of conditioned reflexes as competition between reaction systems. *Psychological Review, 43,* 258–281.

WHITING, J. W. M. (1941.) Becoming a Kwoma. New Haven, Yale University Press.

WISSLER, C. (1923.) Man and culture. New York, Thomas Y. Crowell.

WOODWORTH, R. S. (1922.) Dynamic psychology. New York, Columbia University Press.

YERKES, R. M. (1934.) Suggestibility in chimpanzee. *Journal of Social Psychology, 5,* 271–282.

YOUNG, K. (1927.) Source book for social psychology. New York, Alfred A. Knopf.

—— (1932.) Imitation. *In* SELIGMAN, E. R. A. (ed.), *Encyclopaedia of the social sciences.* New York, Macmillan, 7, 586–587.

YULE, G. U., and KENDALL, M. G. (1937.) An introduction to the theory of statistics. London, Charles Griffin.

INDEX

abstraction, 72–73
adaptation, 35 n.
Adrian, E. D., 35 n.
afferent interaction, 154 n.
age-grade superiors, imitation of, 165, 168, 184–188
aggression, 6, 8, 62–64, 200, 268
  cues for, 245, 248, 250
  displaced, 241, 249
  in crowd, 230, 244, 247
  in lynching, 237, 241, 246, 249
  permission for, 242–244, 246, 248
Allport, F. H., 300–301, 302
Allport, G. W., 39
anonymity, as factor in crowds, 224, 251
anticipatory response, 24, 33, 49–53, 79–80, 133, 135, 136, 148, 156, 282, 285, 288
anxiety, as a cue, 61, 79, 154, 157–158, 160, 201, 224
  See also drive, acquired
appetites. See drive, acquired
Aristotle, 311
association theories, as contrasted with authors', 42 n., 274–288
  survey of, 298–306, 313
associative learning, 27, 313
attention, 71–72, 160, 162, 211–217, 286, 324

Bagehot, W., 290–292
Bain, A., 305
Bakke, E. W., 67 n.
Baldwin, J. M., 296, 298–299
Bard, P., 60 n., 61
Bekhterev, V. M., 45
Bernard, L. L., 153 n., 218, 304, 314
Berry, C. S., 319
Birge, J. S., 77
Boring, E. G., 317
Brennan, K. A., 128
Bruce, R. H., 319
Bühler, C., 325

Burgess, E. W., 157, 317
Butcher, S. H., 311

Cannon, W. B., 60 n., 61
Cantril, H., 222
Carlson, A. J., 57, 57 n.
caste, 191, 193, 197, 236, 238–240
catharsis, 64 n.
circular reaction, in crowd, 227–228, 232, 251
class-typing, 197
  See also social class
clique, 7, 153, 159, 163, 201
concept formation, 72
conditioned inhibitors, 85 n.
conditioning of responses, 26–27, 301–302, 304, 306
  See also response, hierarchy of
connection between stimulus and response, 17, 29, 145, 195, 276, 288, 306
  definition of, 24–25
Cooley, C. H., 315–316
copying, 91, 92, 153–164, 179, 203–205, 251, 260–261, 303, 304, 314
  and independent learning, 203–217
  conscious and unconscious, 164, 185, 254, 303, 313, 317
  definition of, 11, 159–160
  inexact, in diffusion, 268–273
  usefulness of, 255, 259
  See also diffusion and imitation
counting, 73–74
Cournot, A., 294–295
Cowgill, G. R., 57 n.
Crawford, M. P., 321–322
critic, rôle of, in copying, 153, 154, 159–160, 184, 200, 262, 264
crowd behavior, 218–234
  emotionality in, 230–231, 237–238, 245–246, 249, 251
  factors in, 233–234, 248
  uncritical response in, 232, 247, 251
crowd stimulus, 219–221, 237, 246–248, 251